Cinemachismo

Masculinities and Sexuality in Mexican Film

✦ ✦ ✦

Sergio de la Mora

University of Texas Press
Austin

Printed in the United States of America
First edition, 2006

Requests for permission
to reproduce material
from this work should be sent to:
Permissions
University of Texas Press
P.O. Box 7819
Austin, TX 78713-7819
www.utexas.edu/utpress/about/bpermission.html

♾ The paper used in this book
meets the minimum requirements
of ANSI/NISO Z39.48-1992 (R1997)
(Permanence of Paper).

Library of Congress Cataloging-in-Publication Data
Mora, Sergio de la.
Cinemachismo : masculinities and sexuality in Mexican film / Sergio de la Mora.— 1st ed.
        p.   cm.
Includes bibliographical references and index.
ISBN-13: 978-0-292-71296-6 (cloth : alk. paper)
ISBN-10: 0-292-71296-0 (cloth : alk. paper)
ISBN-13: 978-0-292-71297-3 (pbk. : alk. paper)
ISBN-10: 0-292-71297-9 (pbk. : alk. paper)
1. Motion pictures—Mexico.   2. Men in motion pictures.   3. Masculinity
in motion pictures.   I. Title.

PN1993.5.M4M67   2006
791.43'6521—dc22

2005037449

Para mis padres
Victoria y José de la Mora
y para mis hermanas y hermanos,
especialmente Verónica

✣   ✣   ✣

Contents

✛ ✛ ✛

PREFACE
How I Too Came to Love Pedro Infante
viii

Acknowledgments
xv

INTRODUCTION
Macho Nation?
1

ONE
"Midnight Virgin"
Melodramas of Prostitution in Literature and Film
21

TWO
Pedro Infante Unveiled
Masculinities in the Mexican "Buddy Movie"
68

THREE
The Last Dance
(Homo)Sexuality and Representation in Arturo Ripstein's
El lugar sin límites *and the* Fichera *Subgenre*
105

Contents vii

FOUR

Mexico's Third-Wave New Cinema
and the Cultural Politics of Film
135

EPILOGUE

Mexican Cinema Is Dead!
Long Live Mexican Cinema!
163

Notes
180

Works Consulted
197

Index
227

How I Too Came to Love Pedro Infante

✢   ✢   ✢

Inside el Colón you can watch el mero mero, el merito, nuestro querido, Pedro Infante, the world's most handsome man love the world's most beautiful women. . . . He is the man whose child we want to bear. He is the man we wish we could be. Ay, Pedro, most fortunate and unfortunate of men. Dead at age forty. Papi, we miss you still.
DENISE CHÁVEZ, *LOVING PEDRO INFANTE*

J still remember the shock and delight I experienced when I innocently came across a book with the nude photograph of Pedro Infante taking a shower. I was floored! My mind was reeling! I could not believe my eyes! There he was *en cueros*, the Mexican lover of the century, dubbed by his fans and Mexican media as *el ídolo nacional*, all soaped up and caught by surprise in a candid private moment, displaying his athletic and muscular body and his family jewels. Seeing Infante nude was like seeing Jesus Christ without a loincloth! It broke Mexican culture's rigid taboos that strictly limit the visual representation of male nudity. After regaining my composure, all I could think of was, Where could I see more? If before I discovered this image I had resisted Infante's playfulness and charm, due to how much I linked him with heterosexism and male heterosexual privilege, my interest was now perked. The photo was the initiation to a journey of discovery, a mission to explore the archives of classic Mexican cinema, not only for more special glimpses of Infante, but also for other images of same-sex relations that I was hungry to find. Searching through his extensive filmography I was pleased to find that this photo is not the only example, though certainly the most explicit, of the use of Infante and his body as an object of erotic pleasure; more than a handful of his films depict Infante in queer-friendly contexts. At that moment I realized that Infante's cultural legacy was ripe for queer appropriation and rereading through a different interpretive lens. To further titillate me, years later, word came to me that Infante's family jewels were touched up before the photo was first made public. Apparently he was so well endowed that the curators and/or the owner of the copyrights to the photograph felt they needed to tone it down.[1] Truth or myth? It didn't matter: I had been fully won over by this man who seduced spectators throughout the Spanish-speaking Americas.

The origin of this book is twofold. First, it can be traced to my desire to see how male homosexuality and homoeroticism are represented in Mexican film and popular culture specifically and in the philosophy of Mexican national identity (*mexicanidad,* literally "Mexicanness") more broadly. Second, this project is intimately linked to my desire to feel connected to my inherited national patrimony, specifically as a first-generation, working class-born Mexican immigrant in the USA. At the heart of this desire is my obsession with Infante, the most beloved and revered figure of the classic period star system, roughly 1933–1957. This obsession was further driven by the discovery of the Infante nude during one of my research trips to Mexico City while leafing through the exhibition catalogue *Asamblea de ciudades: Años 20s/50s, Ciudad de México* (1992), celebrating popular culture in Mexico City. This discovery changed how I perceived Infante and how I understood the sexual politics of *mexicanidad.* Infante had appeared shirtless in many of his more than fifty feature films and in publicity photos. Before the exhibition at the Palacio de Bellas Artes, Mexico City's most prestigious museum, spectators had not been privy to full frontal (or backside) nudes of the Mexican superstar par excellence (nor, for that matter, was male nudity permitted on screen during his lifetime). The photo rubbed uneasily against my strict Catholic upbringing. The photograph opened up many questions regarding the differences between and within various paradigms of Mexican masculinities, power, national (homo)erotics, the politics of visibility, and pleasure. The photograph opened for me the Pandora's box of the mythology of Infante and Mexican styles of manliness, adding another layer to his cult following.

The controversy that erupted after the nude photograph of Infante was reprinted in *Hijo de tigre . . . pintito. Hablemos de sexualidad* (Rodríguez and Aguilar Gil 1994), a sex education textbook for grammar school teachers published by the Secretaría de Educación Pública (SEP, State Department of Education), further underscored the scandal caused by the unusually revealing photograph.[2] The controversy is clear evidence of how the photographic representation of nude male bodies elicits discomfort and conflict because it unsettles traditional gendered conventions of looking, where man is conferred the active role of seeing and woman is assigned the passive role of being the object of the gaze. Furthermore, male nudes raise the specter of homosexuality, the fear of men looking at men as erotic objects. The controversy underscored the taboo of male nudity and the absence of in-depth critical analysis of the politics of visual representations of the male body, desire, and power, most notably in Mexico.

A headline from the leading Mexico City business paper *El Financiero* dated September 17, 1996, reads: "Pedro Infante Is Put on Trial. The Moralists Wage a War Against Sexual Education."[3] The article begins,

> Pedro Infante not only provokes idolatry. Additionally, there are those whom he also scandalizes and bothers, such as the Unión Iberoamericana de Padres de Familia, an organization that includes groups from 12 countries in the continent, because a nude photograph of the legendary artist appears in the book *Hijo de tigre . . . pintito*, published by the Secretaría de Educación Pública in 1994. (Vizcarra Castillo 1996: 79)

The textbook instructs parents and teachers on how to introduce sexual education to secondary school children. It covers pregnancy, contraceptives, abortion, AIDS prevention, and homosexuality, among other themes. All its illustrations are stills from Mexican films. Infante's photo is reproduced in a chapter on nudity and the primal scene—when children see their parents naked, a moment that condenses much sexuality.

The spokesperson for the Unión Iberoamericana de Padres de Familia (Iberoamerican Parents Union) protested the inclusion of Infante's nude photo in the book published by the SEP, and in an interview broadcast by Radio Red he demanded "the right to supervise the education of our children." He said, "We don't want our children to be exposed to unnatural practices, and in many cases aberrant practices, as if these were viable options for their sexual life." According to the Unión's criteria, the photo of Infante was "proof that concepts contrary to morality are being imposed [on our children]" (Vizcarra Castillo 1996: 79). The newspaper article did not specify if the Unión expressed indignation because the members considered the nude male in general to be immoral or if they were offended specifically by the fact that it was a nude photograph of the most revered figure of the Mexican cinema, the emblem of working-class virility. If the latter is the case, then the nude proves to be doubly transgressive and potentially disrespectful to the memory of some of his most conservative fans.

The photo calls attention to itself because it is the only nude, among the dozens of movie stills and photographs, reproduced in the book and can seem out of place and inappropriate. The photo is a low-angle, full-body shot in black and white and covers an entire page. *El ídolo del pueblo* is displayed in an open space, a humble-looking patio or rooftop with cracked and discolored walls, his entire body all soaped up. He has his arms crossed in a V shape over his chest. His penis is visible although it is somewhat camouflaged with soap foam. Infante's look is fixed at the camera with a facial expression that is serious and guarded but that doesn't convey surprise at being photographed in this private moment.

The book also received praise. María Consuelo Mejía, an anthropologist and director of Catholics for the Right to Decide, argued in Mexico's leading feminist journal, *Debate Feminista*, that one of the most important contributions made by the SEP textbook is precisely the strategic inclusion of the Infante nude.

> Our stars are given sexual attributes, and with that the attitudes with which the camera froze them, reinscribing them with new meaning. It's as if in the core of our national memory, which to a large degree is our cinematic memory, was the sexuality that we had not fully been aware of. In that very private zone, the most hidden place where we store our moral values, we also have the right to ask ourselves about the manifestations of sexuality. (1996: 438–439)

Mejía makes a strong case in support of the public circulation of the photo since it underscores the silence that historically has existed about male sexuality.

The controversy the photograph generated highlights that the representation of the body and of sexuality are highly contested terrains, and it reminds us of the political function of the body, its symbolic power, and emotional investments. Infante's nude photograph opens an important dialogue on how the male body gets inscribed with cultural values that tend to reinforce gendered social institutions, cultural practices, and patriarchal relations. The photo also reminds us that the conventions for the visual representation of the male body are not fixed and stable and that their production, circulation, and reception fluctuate according to historical and cultural contexts. This photograph has multiple functions and interpretations, depending on location and context. Critical reception of the photograph draws attention to what can happen when man occupies the status conventionally reserved for women: that of erotic object of desire and visual spectacle.

This photo pushed me to rethink Mexican masculinities, the concept of *mexicanidad,* and the State's role in the circulation and promotion of gendered identities via cinema. The photograph enabled me to review Infante's cultural legacy and Mexican cinema with new eyes, new ways of seeing facilitated by my intellectual formation in cultural studies, film studies, literature, feminist theory, gay and lesbian scholarship and activism, queer theory, gender studies, and Chicana/o studies.

Infante was an actor who actively participated in displaying his body to the press. His keen interest in physical fitness and the culture surrounding it converted him into an emblem of a healthy, authentic, and natural man. His rugged side is balanced by his portrayal as a romantic *bon vivant,* which softens his manly image: he is accessible and prone to playful *relajo,* fooling around. Infante indulged in physical pleasure and excess, from eating to fucking. Critics and mass media enabled the construction of his legendary sexual appetite. Thus, as I discuss in Chapter Two, Infante possesses a duality: he can easily shift, accentuate, (de)activate his virile qualities as well as his vulnerable and almost childlike playfulness.

Infante's sudden death on the morning of April 15, 1957, contributed to his status as a secular saint. Read as national allegory, his death emphasized the end of the popular sector's aspiration for economic success and social justice, which they experienced vicariously through Infante, unveiling the exploitation and impoverishment of the popular classes and the failure of the Mexican Revolution to break with the unequal distribution of wealth that characterized Porfirio Díaz's regime.

This book is also born of more ordinary origins, however—namely a passion for Mexican movies. Like other Mexican immigrant kids growing up in the 1970s, I was seduced by movies and quickly became an addict, a film junkie. Eventually, cinema took over my life, every moment of my existence. My childhood and early adolescence were singularly shaped by Mexican movies, *telenovelas,* and popular Mexican music from the late 1960s, '70s, and '80s, as well as U.S. popular culture. Every Sunday after mass, I religiously saw with my mother, Victoria, and my two younger sisters, Verónica and Lucila, a double bill of Mexican movies at one of the theaters that once showed Mexican movies in San Francisco's Mission District, where I grew up from age five onward. Most of these theaters (the Tower, Latino, Grand, New Mission) were on Mission Street, dubbed the Mission Miracle Mile because it was the main commercial strip of the once predominantly Latino and working-class area in the heart of San Francisco. In 1991, the Tower was the last of these glorious movie places to close, another casualty of the changing film consumption habits of U.S. Latinos/as, the Mexican film industry's loss of the Spanish-language market in the United States, the rising costs of living in San Francisco, and the gentrification of the Mission. Ironically, the closure of the Tower occurred just as the new Mexican cinema was emerging and on the eve of an explosion of scholarship about Mexican cinema that would profoundly inspire my own research.

Cinema was not all-encompassing, however. Nor did it stand alone and detached from my socialization. Catholicism and patriarchal family values played as important a role as Mexican movies and popular culture in shaping my affective relations with my social surroundings and sentimental education. Mexican movies especially informed my understanding of what and how proper men ought to look, think, feel, express themselves, and behave. I'm still fascinated by representations of Mexican men in the movies and by how Mexican men perform their masculinity in daily life. I'm intrigued by celluloid performances of heterosexual masculinities, since as a gay man and a sissy from childhood, I lived outside it, never having conformed to dominant images of Mexican masculinities, never quite mastering "how to be a proper man." I was both fascinated and put off by the representations of butch Mexican men, by *los machos mexicanos*. In Mexican movies, virility is a metonym for Mexicanness, and this manliness is literally larger than life. I'm interested in how Mexican movie stars embody their gender and their sexuality and in how they perform their gender. So I confess that my investments in Mexican film culture are both libidinal and linked to fantasy. My relationship to cinema is bound up with desire and sexuality. Cinema for me is linked to the forbidden, the outlawed. Cinema can show what should not be seen and articulate what social strictures deem should remain unsaid; it enables us to establish affective affiliations within our communities as well as with other communities with whom we seldom or never come face to face; cinema shows us how to imagine other realities; cinema nurtures that most beautiful and precious quality we all possess, fantasy. I see this project as a vindication of the validity of my childhood (and into adulthood) pleasure in looking and in fantasizing.

This project was thus conceived as an engagement with my scholarly interests in the role cinema plays in the formation of national culture as well as a way for me to understand myself and my sense of belonging. Cinema enabled me to imagine the many possibilities that life has to offer if we allow ourselves to live our fantasies.

Acknowledgments

✛ ✛ ✛

Many people and institutions made this book possible. At the University of California, Santa Cruz, where I did my graduate work, I was fortunate to be mentored by Julianne Burton-Carvajal, Norma Klahn, and José David Saldívar, who enthusiastically supported my research. Julianne's pioneer work on the New Latin American Cinema—which I read as an undergraduate at California State University, San Francisco, in a course taught by John Hess—first inspired me to study Latin American cinema. I thank her for encouraging my research since the very first day I climbed up the hills of Merrill College at UCSC to introduce myself. Both Julianne and Norma were crucial in introducing me to a broad community of scholars and filmmakers whose work continues to nourish and inspire me.

My colleagues in Chicana/o Studies, Richard Berteaux, Angie Chabram-Dernersesian, Miroslava Chávez-García, Adela de la Torre, Yvette Flores Ortíz, Lorena García, Kevin Johnson, Malaquías Montoya, Beatriz Pesquera, Refugio Rochín, and Adaljiza Sosa-Riddell, continue to be tremendously supportive. I owe special gratitude to my mentor and friend Angie Chabram-Dernersesian for believing in me and cheering me on to the finish line and for making me feel at home at UCD since I first interviewed for the job. Ada's enthusiasm and fiery spirit continue to inspire me. Many thanks to the fabulous staff, past and present, at Chicana/o Studies, especially Delfina Redfield, Griselda Castro, Alma Martínez, Kathy S. Hayden, Nitzia Ramírez, and Mark Williams.

Rosa Linda Fregoso and Kent Ono played a crucial role in helping me transform the dissertation into a book. Both were incredibly generous with their time and gave me feedback and support at various stages of the writing. I am very lucky to count both Rosa Linda and Kent as mentors who, despite their demanding professional schedules, took the time to give me sound advice and positive encouragement. Rosa Linda is for me a model scholar and colleague. I am deeply grateful to my *hada madrina* Zuzana M. Pick for her generosity in both her recommendations for revising and her always encouraging support through the very last stages of completing this project. I am very thankful to the anonymous readers whose concrete feedback improved the quality of this book considerably. Gwen Kirkpatrick and Francine Masiello gave me shelter at their lovely homes in Berkeley. The love, advice, and generosity they gave me have made all the difference in the world.

I am profoundly grateful to the University of Texas Press team, led by Jim Burr, who oversaw the project from beginning to end. I thank Lynne Chapman, who guided the project during its final stages, and Tana Silva for her enthusiastic and engaged editorial assistance. Nancy Bryan was responsible for marketing. Finally, I thank Tom Gelsinon for his professional editorial assistance.

I'd like to thank all the people and institutions that have funded my research: Office of Research and Division of Humanities, Arts and Cultural Studies, College of Letters and Science, University of California, Davis; UC Davis Humanities Institute; Chicana Latina Research Center, UC Davis; Humanities Institute at the University of California, Irvine; Chicano/Latino Research Center, UC Santa Cruz; the Literature Department and the Graduate Division, UC Santa Cruz; National Research Council Ford Foundation Dissertation Fellowship.

Many colleagues and friends provided support and/or critical feedback at various stages in the research and writing. First I'd like to thank the Latin American and Latino film scholars who've been a great source of inspiration: Tamara Falicov, Itzia Fernández, Gustavo García, Ramón García, Rita González, John Hess, Randal Johnson, Jesse Lerner, Ana M. López, Carlos Monsiváis, Kathleen Newman, Chon A. Noriega, Vicki Mayer, Paulo Antonio Paranaguá, Charles Ramírez Berg, B. Ruby Rich, Jorge Ruffinelli, Dolores M. Tierney, Carlos Alberto Torrico, Julia Tuñón, Juan Carlos Vargas, Eduardo de la Vega, Margarita de la Vega Hurtado, and especially Gilberto Blasini, Susan Dever, Laura Podalsky, Elissa J. Rashkin, Patricia Torres, and Lucy Virgen. I am indebted to Lucy and Patricia for generously sharing their resources and always making themselves available for feedback.

At UC Davis I thank my colleagues, friends, and folks who've supported my work: JoAnne Cannon, Carolyn de la Peña, Nicole Fleetwood, Joaquín Galvan, Francisca González, Gayatri Gopinath, Inés Hernández-Avila, Tom Holloway, Barbara Horwitz, Robert Irwin, Douglas Kahn, Elizabeth Langland, Neil Larsen, Jay Mechlin, Judy Newton, Lorena Oropeza, Pablo Ortíz, Ana Peluffo, Sara Projanski, David Quijada, Juana María Rodríguez, Kathleen Rosanno, Ron Saufley, Karen Shimakawa, Scott Simmon, Michael Peter Smith, Julie Sze, Patricia Turner, George van den Abbeele, and Clarence Walker.

At UC Santa Cruz I want to thank Julie Brower, Luz Calvo, Debbie Condon, Guillermo Delgado, Michael Doylen, Carla Freccero, Lizbeth Haas, Jon Hunt, Earl Jackson Jr., David Luis-Brown, Tina Luis-Brown, Olga Nájera-Ramírez, Renato Ramírez, Ivelisse Rivera, Phil Rodríguez, Catriona Rueda Esquibel, Ann Scherz, Aureliano de Soto, and Carter Wilson.

Many thanks also to Daniel Balderston, Mary Pat Brady, Jaime Cárdenas, Emma García, Ramón Gutiérrez, Teresa "Osa" Hidalgo de la Riva, Lourdes Portillo, Arturo Ripstein, Dennis St. Peter, Tere Romo, and Rosalía Valencia for their support along the way. A special thank you to two teachers who inspired me to apply for a Ph.D.: John Hess and Donald M. Lowe.

Last but not least, I'd like to thank my students at the University of California at Davis and Santa Cruz who have inspired me in so many ways, especially Santiago Castellanos, Monica de la Torre, Dina Fachin, Angie López, and Hazel Wetherford.

Across the years a number of venues and institutions have nurtured my cinephilia and advanced my research. Staff at IMCINE; Filmoteca UNAM; Cineteca Nacional; Pacific Film Archive; Festival Internacional de Cine en Guadalajara; Festival Internacional de Cine de Morelia; Festival Internacional del Nuevo Cine Latinoamericano, La Habana; and Festival Internacional de Cine de Donostia-San Sebastián have all been very supportive. At IMCINE and the Filmoteca UNAM I'd like to thank Ignacio Durán Loera, Moisés Jiménez, Patricio Luna Huerta, Claudia Tovar, Lina Valdéz, Marina Stavenhagen, and Iván Trujillo.

I am very grateful for the generous assistance of staff at the Centro de Investigación y Enseñanza Cinematográficas (CIEC) at the Universidad de Guadalajara, especially Ignacio Mireles Rangel, Ulises Íñiguez, and Eduardo de la Vega Alfaro, who made available to me the photo collection. I am indebted to Ignacio, my photographer guardian angel and magician, for kindly securing several stills and other photographs. I thank Patricia

Torres for introducing me to Ignacio. Many thanks to Juan Carlos Vargas for making available for me many films and articles. An extra-special thanks to my cinephile colega Lucy Virgen for opening doors for me at the Festival Internacional de Cine en Guadalajara, for sharing her knowledge of all things related to Mexican culture, and for her critical feedback.

I thank the individuals and institutions for granting me permission to reproduce movie stills, photographs, and artwork. Many thanks to Lic. Raúl Padilla López, Lucy Virgen, Jonathán Chait Aurbach, Rafael López Castro, Ismael Rodríguez Vega, Miguel Villalobos, Marina García-Vásquez. I am very grateful to Películas Rodríguez S.A. de C.V. and Cinematográfica Rodríguez for permission to reprint the Pedro Infante photo that appears on the book cover.

Extra-special thanks to my very best friends and colleagues for their endless support, kindness, and inspiration: Ana Patricia Rodríguez, my rock of Gibraltar and soulmate, Michelle Habell-Pallán, Maylei Blackwell, Christine Acham, Ía Carbonell, Christopher A. Shinn, Susana Gil, Jeanne Vaughn, Elena Feder, Felicia Fahey, Martivón Galindo, Adan Griego, and Deborah Vargas. I can't thank them enough for their companionship, advice, and encouragement.

I'd especially like to thank Benjamin Lawrance for giving me food, shelter, love, and endless support during the last and most difficult stages in the completion of this book. He read my manuscript numerous times and gave me feedback on just about every page I wrote. He also shared with me his excellent editorial skills and computer knowledge. I am deeply grateful for his generosity, companionship, and kindness.

As the youngest child in a family of sixteen, I was fortunate to have the opportunity to pursue a higher education. I thank each member of my family, and extended family, for their kindness, support, and for the wealth of love they've given me. Todos ellos fueron los primeros en enseñarme el significado del respeto, el amor, y la generosidad. En primer lugar quiero agradecer especialmente a mi madre Victoria que es la luz de mis ojos y la presencia más fuerte en mi vida. A ella le debo todo. Sin su apoyo incondicional, su amor sin medida, sus consejos, su comida, su fortaleza, sus rezos, su alegría, optimismo, y tantas otras cosas, no hubiera podido terminar este libro. No sé cuantas veces ella y su fe en dios y en San Judas Tadeo me salvaron de mis momentos de desilución. Estoy endeudado con mi padre José por apoyarme en esta difícil carrera que escogí y por permitirme vivir en su casa más allá de los años que se acostumbra vivir con sus padres. Mis hermanas y hermanos me han apoyado muchísimo de una forma u otra pero quiero agradecer especialmente a Alicia, Bertha, Elena, Lucila, Ernesto y Verónica que estuvieron más a cargo de mi y cuyas sonrisas y consejos me alentaron enormemente. I am forever grateful to Verónica, who has been there for me through thick and thin. I want to express to her my deepest gratitude for her amazing kindness, for patiently listening to me and holding my hand when I most needed it, and for her financial help. I can never repay her for everything she's done for me. Mil gracias también a familia en Guadalajara, especialmente a Alicia y Claudia, Rodolfo y Rodolfo Jr., por la hospitalidad y cariño que me brindaron en cada viaje que hice a Guadalajara durante el festival de cine. Me siento muy afortunado por tener tantos sobrinos y sobrinas, cuñados y cuñadas que también me apoyaron muchísimo. Quiero agradecerle especialmente a Claudia por su entusiasmo, sentido de humor, y por conseguirme libros y DVDs en muchas ocaciones; y a Diego por ayudarme cuando me encontraba en aprietos con la computadora.

Sections of individual chapters were previously published in different versions. I thank the publishers for granting me permission to reprint and the editors for their feedback. Brief sections of the preface appeared in "Masculinidad y mexicanidad: Panorama teórico-bibliográfico," in *Horizontes del segundo siglo: Investigación y pedagogía del cine mexicano, latinoamericano, y chicano-latino*, edited by Julianne Burton-Carvajal, Ángel Miquel, and Patricia Torres (Mexico City: Universidad de Guadalajara/ Instituto Mexicano de Cinematografía, 1998): 45–64. Parts of Chapter 2 appeared in "Pedro Infante y el culto al cuate," translated by Frederic Chaume and María Teresa Albero, in *Archivos de la Filmoteca* 31 (February 1999): 88–104. Parts of Chapter 3 appeared as "Fascinating Machismo: Toward an Unmasking of Heterosexual Masculinity in Arturo Ripstein's *El lugar sin límites* (1977)" in *Journal of Film and Video* 44.3/4 (Fall/Winter 1992–1993): 83–104. A shorter version of Chapter 4 appeared as "Packaging Mexico: The Politics of Mexican Film Culture in the NAFTA Era" in *Las Nuevas Fronteras del Siglo XXI/New Frontiers of the 21st Century*, edited by Norma Klahn, Pedro Castillo, Alejandro Álvarez, and Federico Manchón (Mexico City: La Jornada Ediciones/Universidad Nacional Autónoma de México/Universidad Autónoma Metropolitana/Chicano-Latino Research Center, University of California, Santa Cruz, 2000): 39–61.

Introduction

Macho Nation?

✥   ✥   ✥

Cinema is the richest medium of expression ever made available to humanity. . . . All the arts, every skill, history, the world, the cosmos, all bow before it with devotion.
EMILIO FERNÁNDEZ, QUOTED IN FEDER 1997

Cinema teaches us everything. God teaches us through the cinema.
PAZ ALICIA GARCIADIEGO, *EL EVANGELIO DE LAS MARAVILLAS*

Since the end of the nineteenth century, film has furnished a vehicle for the circulation of narratives of Mexican national identity. My interest lies with the various strategies used by cultural producers and consumers to negotiate and contest cinematic representations of national identity that depict highly gendered and sexualized roles for men and women. I am especially interested in revisiting the highly abused and misused terms "macho" and "machismo" in order to offer critical and alternative interpretations of these concepts. I am attracted to the question of how gendered and sexualized narratives of national identity are represented in three traditional genres and a subgenre: the revolutionary melodrama, the *cabaretera* (dance hall) prostitution melodrama, the musical-comedy "buddy movie," and the picaresque *fichera* brothel-cabaret comedy (a variant of the *cabaretera* melodrama).[1] By commenting on the central conventions embedded in these genres I underscore larger ideological questions surrounding the reproduction and resistance of gendered and sexualized national subjectivities. In particular I discuss how Mexican films have circulated a refashioned notion of Mexican identity in the years leading up to and following the signing of the North American Free Trade Agreement (NAFTA). Given the privileged place that the visual media occupy in the formation of social identities and the inordinately important role the Mexican State has historically played in the develop-ment of Mexico's film industry in particular and the visual arts in gen-eral to educate and foster a national consciousness, I hope to show how Mexican cinema continues to be a dynamic and contested area of cultural production. The assumption underpinning this study is that cinema, like other expressions of popular culture, is a crucial site where social and po-litical discussions about the nation's past, present, and future take place.

I was originally going to title this book *Macho Nation?* but decided that *Cinemachismo* was more appropriate.[2] This is why. "Macho nation?" re-fers to the contested male-centered modern national project ushered in by the Mexican Revolution of 1910. The concept is a reference to the cult of a particular form of masculinity—and therefore also femininity and womanliness—that was aggressively promoted by the cultural nationalist post-revolutionary establishment. To be sure, the specificity of Mexican machismo resides in its self-consciousness and its officially decreed status as the distinctive component of Mexican national identity (O'Malley 1986: 7), rivaled only by the nation's deep religiosity manifest in the cult of Our Lady of Guadalupe, Mexico's patron saint. The push to claim Mexico as a virile nation gained momentum in the 1920s as a strategy to counteract the alleged effeminacy of the Contemporáneos group, avant-garde poets, artists, and intellectuals, many of whom held jobs in the civil service and some of whom were homosexual.[3] These full-scale gay-bashings raged from the mid-1920s forward in widely publicized polemics intended to establish a new national literature and to promote the work of "virile" writers such as Mariano Azuela's *Los de abajo* (*The Underdogs,* 1916), his now-canonical novel of the Revolution and disillusionment.[4] Macho is also the quintessential virile image of the post-revolutionary Mexican na-tion, embodied by the *charro* (cattle rancher), an image widely circulated through film, popular music (*rancheras, mariachi*), performance, sports (rodeo, equestrian), the graphic arts (Jesús de la Helguera's famously il-lustrated calendars, for example), and literature.[5]

What I mean by the term *cinemachismo* is to identify the particular self-conscious form of national masculinity and patriarchal ideology articulated via the cinema and also vigorously promoted by the post-revolutionary State as official ideology. Whereas "macho nation?" refers to the contested modalities of gender in Mexican cinema and Mexican society, *cinemachismo* explains the institutional deployment of a masculinized *mexicanidad* through the camera lens. Cinema is the modern technology that enables the invention, reinvention, and circulation of national models of manhood and womanhood.

Cinemachismo points to the indispensable role Mexican cinema plays in reshaping social identities and modern definitions of the nation. Underscoring the links between machismo and nationalism, this study explores key moments in which the cinema contributed to struggles surrounding the redefinition of *mexicanidad*. Underlying this project is this question: How do cultural representations mediate the contradictions of the modern male-centered, post-revolutionary, and post-national State project in Mexico? Reflecting on my approach to this broad concern and the numerous issues it conceals, I analyze the social anxieties and tensions over changing representations of masculinity and manhood as well as femininity and womanhood in terms of how films shape our understanding of gender and sexuality and how films attempt to solve social problems. The films I examine here are particularly emblematic of the national and transnational circulation of images and symbols of *mexicanidad*.

The genres and subgenre I have chosen to focus on have not only proven to be of lasting sociocultural importance but have also been the most popular, both in terms of historical continuity and in their pervasive presence across Mexican popular culture. The revolutionary melodrama, the musical comedy "buddy movie," the prostitution melodrama—notably the sometimes classy, more often pot-boiler *cabaretera* films—and the *fichera* movie all express a desire for national, regional, and/or local community through specific representations of individual and collective trajectories, which in turn are played out in the context of heterosexual, homosexual, and bisexual couplings. Here I trace the circulation and reception of these genres and the representations of their specific but fluctuating conventions. I argue that these genres reproduce and contest gendered and sexual forms of national identification across nearly six decades, from the 1950s until 2004. Close textual interpretations of genre tropes, narrative structure, and visual design ground my analysis of tensions between individuals and society when they confront questions of sexual and gender identities and sexual practices as these issues impinge upon the power relations between the State and its national subjects. I contend that gendered and sexualized national ideologies both accommodate and marginalize "normative" as well as "non-normative" subjectivities. I do this by underscoring the distinct ways in which cinema mediates sociopolitical conflicts and shapes social discourses and consciousness. I illustrate how spatial locations such as brothels, cabarets, dance halls, cantinas, and musical performances (including dance and singing) are crucial sites for understanding the power dynamics involved in the construction of cultural identities.[6] I sustain that theatrical and musical performances and their specific social settings are marked as the sites/sights for the reinscription and contestation of gender and sexual norms.

Considerable research has been conducted on the history and traditions of Mexican cinema, especially in relation to gender, genre, and nationhood. *Cinemachismo* expands upon existing scholarship in a number of ways. Most book-length studies of gender and Mexican film have focused on representations of women and women filmmakers in Mexico.[7] "Gender" is not equivalent to "woman," however, and I believe masculinity merits critical scrutiny, for it can help us denaturalize and defamiliarize the institutions and practices that make gender. In studies on gender and cinematic representation in Mexico, masculinity is, with few notable exceptions, often rendered invisible. Analysis of the complexity of the representations of Mexican masculinities in film has only just begun.

This book builds on arguments put forth in an earlier essay that provides a critical overview of the scholarship about masculinity and the representation of the male body in Mexican film in light of the dearth of analysis on this subject matter.[8] My book provides case studies on renderings of gender, sexuality, and the body in film, literature, and popular culture. Through my interdisciplinary and multimedia focus I strive to link issues related to the social construction of masculinity with questions of representation, self-representation, and power. I examine masculinity in its plural manifestations, encompassing heterosexual, homosexual, and "queer" (an in-between, deliberately indeterminate, umbrella designation for non-heteronormative sexuality) desires and practices.

By foregrounding non-normative forms of social identity and subjectivity, examining often forbidden desires and pleasures, I hope that this book will encourage others to take up avenues of research that I initiate here and thus continue to expand the fields of Mexican film studies, national cinema, gender and masculinity studies, queer studies, Chicana/o studies, and cultural studies.

By focusing on the multiple expressions of national and post-national identities, including new interpretations of the cultural tropes of macho and machismo, *Cinemachismo* expands Charles Ramírez Berg's groundbreaking *Cinema of Solitude: A Critical Study of Mexican Film, 1967–1983*

(1992). Through my interpretations of Pedro Infante's buddy movies, I identify and celebrate the rich queer legacy in Mexican film and popular culture, focusing on the multiple and often conflicting readings made possible by adopting queer reading practices. I also address how cinematic representations of Mexican masculinities depart from how "white" masculinities in Hollywood and European films have been theorized in Euro-American film theory. My analysis of Ripstein's *El lugar sin límites* and the popular *fichera* movies of the 1970s and '80s moves beyond the positive-negative analysis of stereotypes, arguing that gay characters, imaged as queeny *jotos* (Mexican colloquialism for male homosexual) function as minstrel figures and are a site of pleasure and celebration of sexual difference while at the same time registering homophobic and misogynist anxieties about heterosexual masculinity. Although *joto* is a derogatory term, I appropriate it here as a form of what Michel Foucault calls "reverse" discourse that challenges the oppressive effects of homophobic discourse, emphasizing instead how the category *joto* also enables the production of knowledge about male homosexuality in Mexico. For Foucault, the pathologizing construction of homosexuality in nineteenth-century medical discourse signals the moment when "homosexuality began to speak in its own behalf, to demand that its legitimacy or 'naturality' be acknowledged, often in the same vocabulary, using the same categories by which it was medically disqualified" (1980: 101). My appropriation of *joto* is ironic and playful while at the same time affirming the cultures of "deviant" subjects that first appear in national discourse in 1901, a result of the famous police raid of a private party in Mexico City when forty-one men, half in female drag, were arrested.[9]

I contend that machismo needs the *joto* to define and affirm itself as much as it needs a clingy woman, a fact that is continuously acted out not only in cinema and popular culture but also in everyday life.[10] Unlike Ramírez Berg's important study of the macho-*maricón* dyad, I argue that there is a space for homosexuality in Mexican culture but that that space is fraught with tensions and contradictions. Like Rosa Linda Fregoso's pioneer analysis of cinematic renditions of Chicano masculinities in *The Bronze Screen: Chicana and Chicano Film Culture* (1993), I also underscore the complex history and meanings of Mexican machismo and its imbrication with colonialist practices as well as the central role it played in the Mexican Revolution's national decolonization project. Discourse about the Revolution foregrounds that for men the Revolution involved recovering their manhood, which in turn reflects back on the hypermasculinized nation-state.

Close textual analysis and interdisciplinary research makes it possible to identify the shifting social practices and institutional discourses shaping representations of Mexican manhood as they specifically relate to the nation's macho national image. I place masculinities as the central subject of this study because historically the concept of machismo (whose meanings encompass a broad range of interpretations, some of which will be discussed in Chapters Two, Three, and Four) is an integral component of Mexican nationalism. Machismo is intimately linked to State power and to the highly contested gendered social contract extended to Mexican citizens in the post-revolutionary period. Indeed, the machismo attributed to Mexican men (the *charro*, popularized through *mariachi* music and the *comedia ranchera* film genre, or combatants who fought in the Revolution) is among Mexico's most internationally recognized symbols. Mexican film historians and cultural critics have argued that the Mexican cinema's first international superstar was Francisco "Pancho" Villa, the popular revolutionary leader from northern Mexico. To date, he is still the epitome of the Mexican macho, as I will discuss later in this introduction.[11]

Mexican cinema actively partook in the construction of post-revolutionary Mexican national culture. The discourse of *mexicanidad* that circulated through popular culture was instrumental in consolidating the post-revolutionary Mexican State, its institutions, and the ruling classes. Since the late 1930s, cinema helped to forge a hegemonic political system. As a pedagogical and socializing technology, cinema assists in engendering subjectivities and various forms of identification. Interpreted thus, gender is not a transparent, self-evident biological fact of nature; gender is not anatomy. Gender achieves its material and social reality through ideological means. For film theorist Teresa de Lauretis, gender is "the product and the process of both representation and self-representation" (1987: 9). Cinema is a meaning-making technology and as such plays a crucial role in constructing gender. However, in order to not ascribe a totalizing function to cinema and in order to not assume that spectators are passive and uncritical, it is important to emphasize that cinema can also enable us to re-imagine ourselves differently, to conceive of other possible worlds, other possible realities. As conceptualized by de Lauretis,

> the construction of gender goes on today through the various technologies of gender (e.g., cinema) and institutional discourses (e.g., theory) with power to control the field of social meaning and thus produce, promote, and "implant" representations of gender. But the

terms of a different construction of gender also exist, in the margins of hegemonic discourses, posed from outside the heterosexual social contract, and inscribed in micro-political practices, these terms can also have a part in the construction of gender, and their effects are rather at the "local" level of resistance, in subjectivity and self-representation. (1987: 18)

I consider aspects of film production and consumption as social practices that enable particular forms of subjectivity and national identification. I introduce new analytical lenses by discussing the queer and homoerotic grounding of spectatorship in order to re-view sacred icons of Mexican cultural nationalism. Through my queer appropriation of Pedro Infante, for example, I hope to add nuance and complexity to the largely unexplored areas of audience reception and spectatorship in the available scholarship on Mexican cinema.[12]

My project proposes a transformation in Mexican film studies by recasting masculinity as a visible and highly contested system of power—the "macho nation?" of which I spoke earlier—that is operative in all social institutions and practices, focusing on the pervasive presence of machismo in cinema, what I call *cinemachismo*. My understanding of machismo is that it is an ideology of heterosexual male supremacy that in Mexico gets wedded to the institutionalized post-revolutionary State apparatus, of which cinema is a crucial component. Unlike previous studies of gender in Mexican cinema, I argue that sexuality is an indispensable category of analysis that helps to unlock the politics of power and social relations.

Cinema was instrumental in the invention of the Mexican macho: virile, brave, proud, sexually potent, and physically aggressive. Masculinity is rendered into a visual spectacle on the battlegrounds of the Mexican Revolution, becoming the focus of the camera lens and receiving unprecedented international cinematic and photographic coverage, by far surpassing the Greek-Turkish War of 1897, the Spanish-American War of 1898, and the South African War of 1899–1902. Documentary filmmaking flourished during the Mexican Revolution to a great extent to satisfy the demands of audiences in Mexico and in the United States of America. Film spectators in these neighboring nations avidly followed the latest news of the war. Politicians as well as revolutionary leaders understood the value of film to promote their roles in the war and to circulate the goals of the Revolution.

Film historian Margarita de Orellana argues that revolutionary leaders took great measures to ensure that only positive images be circulated about their social and political agendas. She interprets their deep investment in the power of film to shape historical narratives and social consciousness as a "desire for self-representation" (1991: 17). A case in point is the cinematic trajectory of the complex revolutionary leader Pancho Villa. A master of public relations, Villa famously signed a contract for $25,000 with Frank M. Thayer, the representative for the New York City-based Mutual Film, giving the U.S. firm exclusive rights to film battles Villa and his followers fought. According to Aurelio de los Reyes, the leading historian of silent Mexican film, Mutual "agreed to only exhibit the filmed footage if Villa's troops won; in turn, Villa agreed to simulate battles in case the camera operators weren't able to shoot scenes of violence" (Reyes, 1996: 43).[13]

The charismatic Villa became the emblem of the Mexican macho through the wide circulation of his image in cinema, photography, and print media. Speaking to this issue, Carlos Monsiváis, Mexico's leading cultural critic, notes, "During the armed phase of the Revolution, the limits of behavior were set by Pancho Villa: excess, vindicatory eagerness, and primitivism— attributes which authorize his folkloric metamorphosis by the bourgeoisie in both film and literature" (1997b: 12). But the attributes given to Villa outside of Mexico were as important as those generated within the geographic boundaries of the nation. Indeed, Villa's hypermasculine image was forged in a transnational context, given that he was filmed, photographed, and written about by international narrative and documentary filmmakers, photojournalists, newspaper reporters, novelists, and political figures; these include Mexican documentary filmmakers such as Salvador Toscano (*Memorias de un mexicano* [*Memories of a Mexican*], Carmen Toscano, 1950) and photographers such as Agustín Víctor Casasola. Future Hollywood director Raoul Walsh met General Villa and played Villa in *The Life of General Villa* (1914), a film directed by D. W. Griffith's protégé William Christy Chabanne. U.S. journalist John Reed, founder of the U.S. Communist Party, wrote *Insurgent Mexico* (1914) based on his experiences in Mexico following Villa's troops. German camera operator Fritz Arno Wagner covered the war in Mexico for the U.S. branch of Pathé Films. And Mexican novelist Rafael F. Muñoz wrote ¡*Vámonos con Pancho Villa!* (*Let's Go with Pancho Villa!*, 1931), a landmark novel of the Mexican Revolution that was adapted to the screen in 1935 under the direction of Fernando de Fuentes.[14] Indeed, in his discussion of Villa's cinematic career, historian Enrique Krauze refers to him, not without a hint of sarcasm, as "Pancho Villa superstar" (1997: 27).

The meanings attached to Villa as political and cultural figure have fluctuated dramatically across Mexican and U.S. film history, ranging from populist champion of the poor (*The Life of General Villa,* 1914, and *Viva Villa!,* Jack Conway, 1934) to the critical and demythologized representation of Villa as a cold and authoritarian military strategist (*¡Vámonos con Pancho Villa!,* 1935) to the irreverent and parodic depiction of Villa as a buffoonish, primitive-like, and virile sex symbol (*Entre Pancho Villa y una mujer desnuda* [*Between Pancho Villa and a Naked Woman*], Sabina Berman and Isabelle Tardán, 1995) to savvy media and public relations specialist (*And Starring Pancho Villa as Himself,* Bruce Beresford, 2004). The title of Krauze's biography of Villa synthesizes the polarized associations attached to this legendary bandit-hero: *Francisco Villa, entre el ángel y el fierro (Francisco Villa, Between an Angel and the Gun).*[15] Filmmaker Gregorio Rocha deftly shows in his self-reflexive documentary *Los rollos perdidos de Pancho Villa (The Lost Reels of Pancho Villa,* 2003) how U.S. filmmakers were central in transforming the image of Villa from ally to blood-thirsty and impetuous Number One enemy and hence manipulate public opinion to suit the economic and political interests of the United States.

The lasting impact of associating notions of machismo with Mexico that is felt to this day is a sign of how efficiently cinema operated as a vehicle for propaganda and social control. The hold that the stereotype of the Mexican macho exerts does not mean that notions of manhood and manliness are ahistorical, unchanging, monolithic, and uncontested. On the contrary, this study focuses on the changing notions of what it means to be a man in Mexico.

Expanding upon the specific forms of machismo deployed cinematically, it is important to also note that the Mexican State today continues the earlier post-revolutionary tradition of investing in film production and promotion. By examining the cultural politics and institutional practices the State carried out during the presidential administration of Carlos Salinas de Gortari (1988–1994) in the areas of film production, distribution, exhibition, and promotion, I highlight how changes in film policy make this period pivotal in restructuring Mexico's film industry and repositioning the future of its national cinema. I argue that during this regime, Mexican national identity was significantly refashioned in light of NAFTA in order to shift the nation's public alliances closer to U.S. and global economic interests. *Cinemachismo* thus connects specific qualitative shifts to the increasing "Chicanoization" of Mexico through the rethinking of

U.S.-Mexico relations in light of the Mexican State's promotion of globalization through the cinema.

My study raises questions for future research, particularly the relationship between Mexican cinematic developments and the modalities of the "Latinization" of the United States in the late twentieth and early twenty-first centuries. Why the Mexican government has historically played an inordinately important role in the development of Mexico's film industry is a fascinating question. This book highlights the transnational economic and social interests impacting State policies and politics that, in turn, inform the representation of sexuality and gender in classic and contemporary films.

The major thread woven throughout the book's chapters is the role cinema plays in maintaining and contesting the Mexican State's hegemony. This interdisciplinary project combines auto-ethnography with historical analysis of State social and cultural policies, literature, and film history using various theoretical frameworks and approaches, notably feminism, queer theory, close textual readings, auteurism, genre and star studies, national cinema, theories of spectatorship, and image analysis.

Before I outline the content of each book chapter, I first want to survey how masculinity and representations of the male body are theorized in Anglo-U.S. film studies in order to contextualize how Infante cannot be understood through a wholesale adoption of these theories. I find many similarities in the cinematic representations of Mexican masculinities in classic Mexican cinema with the Greek masculinities that film theorist Dimitris Eleftheriotis discusses in his essay "Questioning Totalities: Constructions of Masculinity in the Popular Greek Cinema of the 1960s" (1995). I draw from his essay to outline some of the blind spots in film theory about masculinity as they relate to Infante's star persona.

In the early 1980s, Anglo-U.S. film studies articulated the representation of masculinity and the male body using psychoanalytic terms (spectatorship and identification) and film semiotics (textual analysis). With some notable exceptions (Dyer 1992, 1993a; Mercer and Julien 1988), masculinity in "mainstream cinema" was theorized as monolithic, ahistorical, heterosexual, and racially unmarked, although for the most part the images of men analyzed were those of "white" men.

The terms for the analysis of masculinity in cinema were established by British academics associated with the film journal *Screen*. Steve Neale's "Masculinity as Spectacle: Reflections on Men and Mainstream Cinema" (1993, first published in 1983) is usually the starting point for discussing this subject; Neale's essay, in turn, draws from Laura Mulvey's "Visual Pleasure and Narrative Cinema" (first published in 1975), which theorizes from a feminist and psychoanalytic perspective the cinematic constructions of femininity, masculinity, and the gendered structures of looking in Hollywood films.

In her influential essay Mulvey notes,

> According to the principles of ruling ideology and the physical structures that back it up, the male figure cannot bear the burden of sexual objectification. Man is reluctant to gaze at his exhibitionist like. Hence the split between spectacle and narrative supports the man's role as the active one of forwarding the story, making things happen. The man controls the film fantasy and emerges as the representative of power in a further sense: as the bearer of the look of the spectator, transferring it behind the screen to neutralize the extra-diegetic tendencies represented by woman as spectacle. This is made possible through processes set in motion by structuring the film around a main controlling figure with whom the spectator can identify. As the spectator identifies with the main male protagonist, he projects his look onto that of his like, his screen surrogate, so that the power of the male protagonist as he controls events coincides with the active power of the erotic look, both giving a satisfying sense of omnipotence. A male movie star's glamorous characteristics are thus not those of the erotic object of the gaze, but those of the more perfect, more complete, more powerful ideal ego conceived in the original moment of recognition in front of the mirror. (1989b: 20)

Neale's essay addresses the conflicts that arise when another man is the erotic object of the gaze. Among the limitations Eleftheriotis finds in Neale's psychoanalytic approach is that it privileges a presumed universal heterosexual masculinity that is "characterized by the central position occupied by notions of control, power, aggression, domination, emotional poverty, the preoccupation with order and mastery and a resistance to looks that objectify and eroticize the male body" (235). He expands the discussion of masculinity in the cinema as theorized by Mulvey and Neale and subsequent research by noting that there is no universal masculinity. He questions the relevance of Freudian and Lacanian psychoanalysis to cinemas that are not Hollywood, Canada, Australia, and some European countries (United Kingdom, France, Germany, Spain, Italy) that have been the subject of most English-language film theory and criticism about men in cinema. Eleftheriotis argues that masculinities must be studied in their local contexts, attending to specific cultural, historical, and political processes. "Passing masculinity [*sic*] off as universal and eternal not only naturalizes and essentializes gender difference but also conceals important relations of domination and power" (Eleftheriotis 1995: 237).

There are a number of important parallels between my readings of Infante and Eleftheriotis's analysis of two Greek actors. For example, actor-singer Nicos Xanthopoulos, like Infante, was also known as "the son of the people." For both Greek and Mexican film spectators, a great part of the appeal of these actors resides in their rich emotional expressivity. Unlike Mulvey's and Neale's analysis of masculinity in Hollywood films where men are characterized as silent, stoic, and hell-bent on always being in control, Xanthopoulos and Infante talk, sing, and cry excessively about their joy and sadness (Eleftheriotis: 239–240). Eleftheriotis argues that the enormous empathy and pleasure Greek audiences derived from seeing close-ups of their idol externalizing his emotions requires being sensitive to "the different ways in which emotions are expressed in different cultures" (240). While the well-known adage "Men don't cry" holds in Mexico, the fact is that in classic Mexican melodramas, as in *ranchera* music and in real life, some men do cry, especially when under the influence of alcohol. Indeed, Infante distinguishes himself from his contemporaries by his cathartic sequences where he bursts into authentic, impassioned tears, as I will discuss later in this introduction.

Eleftheriotis's analysis of the comedies of actor Kostas Voutsas focus on how the films reject "the omnipotent masculinity described by Neale as dominant" (Eleftheriotis: 241). Similarly, Infante's films frequently center on struggling working-class men with flawed personalities, compulsive behavioral patterns, and addictive tendencies—such as gambling, alcoholism, and sexual promiscuity—who must come to grips with their weaknesses and tragic fates by adapting to their restricted horizon of possibilities. Infante and Voutsas are revered not because they are omnipotent, perfect, and capable of controlling all; these actors and the characters they played are loved because they are imperfect and resemble real-life men with whom audiences can identify.

Infante is frequently eroticized and can "bear the burden of sexual objectification" (Mulvey 1989b: 20). Unlike the masculinity theorized by Neale and Mulvey, Infante's sexual objectification does not generally create anxieties. This being said, I do not want to discard some of Mulvey's and Neale's insights that are applicable to my project. For example, Infante also portrayed men who functioned as powerful ego ideals for (male) spectators. The association of masculinity with spectacle is also a productive way to examine the performance of Mexican machismo.

In the 1990s, publications about men in film increased considerably, adding greater nuance and complexity to the issues raised by Mulvey and Neale. The contributors to the anthology edited by Steven Cohan and Ina Rae Hark (1993) propose to interrogate the terms that link the "masculinity of the male subject with activity, voyeurism, sadism, fetishism, and story" and the female and femininity with "exhibitionism, masochism, narcissism, and spectacle" (2). The essays as a whole address concerns commonly associated with femininity: "spectacle, masochism, passivity, masquerade, and most of all, the body as it signifies gendered, racial, class, and generational differences" (Cohan and Hark 1993: 3). Cohan and Hark's anthology, along with two additional anthologies also published in 1993—by Constance Penley and Sharon Willis and by Pat Kirkham and Janet Thurman—and more recently two edited volumes—by Peter Lehman (2001) and Phil Powrie, Ann Davies, and Bruce Babington (2004)—have successfully expanded the scope of discussion of masculinities in the cinema. However, these anthologies continue to primarily focus on U.S. and European cinemas. The emergence of the new queer cinema in the early 1990s, accompanied by a complex critical apparatus, as well as research by scholars of color on the interface of race, ethnicity, gender, and sexuality, have greatly enriched the study of men in film.[16] My project, informed by the scholarship of my elders and my contemporaries, aspires to introduce the analysis of masculinities in Latin American cinema and therein expand the conversations begun in Anglo-U.S. film studies.

Chapter One contrasts the literary origins of the didactic prostitution melodrama *Santa* (Saintly Woman, 1903) written by Federico Gamboa with the epistolary erotic travel narrative *Demasiado amor* (Too Much Love, 1990) by Sara Sefchovich, reading the latter novel as a feminist revision of Gamboa's master narrative of the victimized and degraded but also eroticized and idealized Santa, the mother of all subsequent fallen and transgressive prostitutes. The chapter analyzes the figure of the prostitute, along with the nightlife milieu of cabarets and brothels, as allegories for Mexico's modernization project in two films—*Víctimas del pecado* (*Victims of Sin*, 1950) directed by Emilio "el Indio" Fernández, the leading auteur of the classic period and co-creator of the classic Mexican film aesthetic, and María Novaro's internationally successful second feature film,

Danzón (1991), which rewrites the *cabaretera* (dance hall) variant of the prostitution melodrama from a woman-centered perspective. Novaro was the first and, to date, still the most internationally successful Mexican woman filmmaker, both commercially and critically.

Prostitution and the spaces of urban nightlife allow a discussion of the representation of socially sanctioned, transgressive, and "outlawed" sexualities. Through discursive analysis I show how female sexuality, and by extension male sexuality, is a fraught political arena. Sexuality is a critical category of analysis because it shapes gendered forms of national identification. I discuss the social control of sexuality via public health policy, the law, urban planning, and the mass media.

The enduring popularity of the prostitution melodrama and the ubiquity of the brothel-cabaret in Mexican culture have as much to do with Mexico's violent history of colonialism as they do with the nation's deep sense of religiosity and spirituality. Patriarchal control of women's sexuality in Mexico has a complex and contradictory history. The anthropologist Roger Bartra (1987) coined the term "Chingadalupe" to address the dual models of womanhood forged by the key female figures in narratives of national origins: La Malinche—also known as La Chingada, the violated mother of the mixed-race mestizo—and the pure, virginal, and suffering Our Lady of Guadalupe, the brown Virgin Mary, protector of the Mexican nation and Empress of the Americas. The Chingadalupe model of womanhood condenses the attributes promoted by sexist gender ideologies that deny "good women" sexual agency and the right to erotic pleasure and deny "bad women," those who embrace sexual pleasure and/or engage in work linked to sexual commerce, the right to be considered fit as mothers.

Post-colonial feminist theorist Deniz Kandiyoti (1994) discusses the highly politicized nature of the State's investment in gender by examining State-led and religiously based nation-building projects that posit women as "mothers of the nation." Feminist writings on sexual commerce in Mexico—such as the work of historian Katherine Elaine Bliss (2001) and cultural critic Carlos Monsiváis (1980, 1990, 1991, 1997b)—clearly demonstrate that prostitution is a key site for examining the State's investments in creating and maintaining gender differences and relations of power. Extrapolating from Kandiyoti's work on women's roles in national projects, I suggest that sex work can both tell us much about the obvious male fantasies of women's sexuality and illuminate the gender and sexual politics underpinning the State's intervention in regulating prostitution through laws and public health care policy. Listening to the oral testimony of Mexican activist and ex-sex worker Claudia Colimoro (Colimoro and Cabezas, 1998) sheds light on the international sex workers' movement for human rights and workers' rights and their struggle to change the exploitation and oppression associated with sexual commerce. More specifically, Colimoro's testimony shows that Mexican sex workers in the 1990s—like their counterparts in the late 1920s and 1930s (Bliss 2001)—demand respect, in the form of specific legislation to ensure their rights as citizens, from a government that only sees their labor as a "necessary evil" and as a negative aspect of society.

The prostitute and the spaces of the brothel-cabaret have historically functioned as vehicles that safeguard patriarchal privileges, laws, and institutions. They index changing gender roles: women's struggles against patriarchal double standards; shifts in ideas about proper Mexican womanhood and motherhood, as well as proper manhood and womanhood; and shifts in the gendered public-private division of labor. It is also an ambiguous staging ground for male fantasies of domination, subordination, and the victimization of women and other men. It can be a powerful site for representing desire and women's sexual agency. Prostitution and the brothel-cabaret are also sites that contest heteronormativity, standards of female propriety, rigid codes of masculinity, and racialized, gendered, and class-based codes of honor. The prostitute and the brothel-cabaret condense men's fears of and desires for female difference.

Chapter Two shifts the critical lens from figures that represent difference and "otherness" to the singer-performer Pedro Infante, who is still considered the maximum embodiment of Mexican masculinity and the archetype of the working-class heterosexual male. I look at Infante from another angle. This chapter examines the ambiguities and tensions surrounding male relations in erotic triangles where women function as mediators between the men. I focus on four of this superstar's classic buddy movies: Rogelio A. González's *El gavilán pollero* (The Womanizer, 1950) and three of director Ismael Rodríguez's most successful star vehicles, *ATM (A toda máquina)* (Right On, 1951), *¿Qué te ha dado esa mujer?* (What Has That Woman Done to You?, 1951), and *Dos tipos de cuidado* (*Two Serious Guys*, 1952). I situate Infante's work in the post–World War II crises ensnaring the Mexican film industry, signaling the beginning of the end of the classic period, and inaugurating the state of crisis as the national cinema's permanent condition. I read the representations of gender relations in Infante's buddy movies, in particular the homoerotic inflections in the bonds between men and the sexist attitudes toward the female rivals that disrupt the primacy of the male couple, as symptomatic of the increasing masculine anxieties over the shifting role of women. I discuss how *Dos tipos de cuidado* is especially riddled with palpable tensions embedded in how the film self-consciously stages the coexistence of the traditional with the modern. My reading of *ATM* also discusses how the film thematizes U.S.-Mexico relations.

How one reads any given text is indeed determined by the specific historical and sociocultural location of the spectator. In regard to sexual representation in the cinema, this issue is addressed in the documentary film *The Celluloid Closet* (Rob Epstein and Jeffrey Friedman, 1996) based on Vito Russo's pioneer book-length survey on the history of gay and lesbian images in (mostly) Hollywood films. In the film, media critic Richard Dyer makes a cogent argument about sexual representation and cinematic reading practices. He notes that before the emergence of a gay cinema in the United States, film censorship and social restrictions created the conditions for homosexuality to be read between the lines since it was most often represented indirectly. I use insights from queer theory to bear upon my discussion of the homosocial and homoerotic ground of cinematic spectatorship.[17]

Alexander Doty's work (1993, 2000) provides a framework for thinking through the emerging field of queer spectatorship. He argues that queer eroticism is not marginal to mainstream culture but occupies the center, that it both inscribes and resists mainstream heteronormative practices. His insistence on the centrality of queerness in mainstream culture is a productive approach for reading the homoerotic wordplay involved in the culture of the *albur*. The *albur* is a Mexican form of picaresque wordplay linked to the popular classes and is gendered male, especially since it often involves sexual puns, "indecent" jokes, and activities coded as male. Indeed the *albur* is among the most emblematic oral traditions of popular culture. The *albur* is also the quintessential linguistic domain of the Mexican macho. It is remarkable how saturated the culture of the *albur* is with references to homosexuality and phallic chauvinism. In their foundational studies of *mexicanidad,* both Samuel Ramos (1934) and Octavio Paz (1950) devote considerable space to discussing how *albur* contests function to symbolically homosexualize the man who fails to match the *albur* of a rival. The *albur* is relevant to my analysis of spectatorship and identification and to the star image of Pedro Infante because male homoeroticism, homosexuality, and homosociality are central components of Mexican national culture.

"Outing" the queer elements in Infante's classic buddy movies offers a model for constructing a history of queer visibility, most notably in the tensions, ambiguities, and contradictions embedded in filmic representations of male camaraderie and bonding. Infante is so intimately associated with *mexicanidad* that to proffer alternative readings of his films risks being misconstrued as a virtual attack on Mexico's biggest screen idol, the lover of the twentieth century. However, in using a queer lens to reveal the contradictions in Infante's performance of lively and mischievous working-class masculinities, I seek to enrich his cultural legacy by multiplying the range of interpretive possibilities available. In this light, Infante's buddy movies provide the occasion for examining how male homosocial and homoerotic relations fit into the specific constructions of masculinities in Mexican popular culture. They provide ways to understand how masculinist and misogynist agendas underpin the celebratory, and often homoerotically infused, relations between *cuates* (buddies). Infante's buddy movies provide a prime example of the textual and narrative strategies used to stage differing national virilities. I aspire to show that *mexicanidad* is not by any stretch of the imagination a monolithic and uncontested terrain.

These films also open a space for examining the visual and narrative design used in classic Mexican cinema to accommodate homoerotic expressions. Finally, I propose that the representation of male homosociality in Infante's buddy movies, along with other films from the classic period like Matilde Landeta's *La negra Angustias* (Black Angustias, 1949) and some of Cantinflas's early films, provide a foundation for mapping the emergence of queer representations in Mexico's rich and varied film history.[18]

Chapter Three presents a reading of the macho's sexual Other, the *joto*, a key figure in a subgenre of the prostitution melodrama. Through a comparative analysis of the queen gay male stereotype in director Arturo Ripstein's "art" film *El lugar sin límites* (Hell Has No Limits / The Place Without Limits, 1977) and the commercial *fichera* picaresque comedies popular in the 1970s, I argue that homosexuality is a constitutive element in the construction of Mexican heterosexual masculinity. An important critical and commercial success, Ripstein's representation of the dilemmas of homoerotic desire stands as a cult classic, especially because of its sympathetic portrayal of the male transvestite brothel owner, La Manuela. The deadly kiss between La Manuela, decked out in her seductive red flamenco dress, and Pancho, her hypermasculine, muscle-bound suitor, stands as a provocative and ironic comment on Mexico's macho image.

Following the lead of visual media theorist Chon A. Noriega (1992), this chapter emphasizes the importance of recuperating image analysis because of the political stakes stereotypes carry for marginalized groups, notably racial and ethnic groups and women as well as gays and lesbians, all of whom share a history of discrimination.[19] Image analysis underscores how stereotypes affect the perception of underprivileged groups (and/or those that occupy the position of the other) and reproduce narrowly defined and politically conservative ideologies about sociocultural differences. Unlike conventional image analysis, my interest is in moving beyond positive and negative stereotypes and addressing instead the broader discursive spaces opened by stereotypes when read outside a Manichean binary scheme that privileges the "uplifting" of marginalized groups through positive images over sustained critical interpretation.

An analysis of the celluloid gay male stereotype in the politically innocuous yet socioculturally rich *fichera* subgenre offers promising research directions for determining the place that homosexuality occupies in Mexico's cinematic imaginary. Because they provide a yardstick for measuring "real" (read: heterosexual) men, I argue that gay male figures and homosexual tropes are an indispensable component of the *ficheras* since they prove to be the medicine that cures the phallic impotency of the heterosexual male lead. The homosexual flirtations in which the impotent star partakes help restore authentic, virile, heterosexual masculinity while at the same time unveiling the same-sex sexual practices and desires that mark Mexico's sexual subcultures as uniquely queer. A double-edged weapon, the queen gay male stereotype is thus held in nervous tension and ambiguous esteem. The queen is simultaneously both an abject spectacle of homophobic, derisive laughter and subject of collective pleasure displayed to remind male audiences of the transgressive privileges that male heterosexuals enjoy in Mexico. The consistent inclusion of gay stereotypes also acknowledges and celebrates sexual and gender differences. Homosexuality is thus the other side of the coin shaping and complementing the social construction of Mexican male heterosexuality, the other side without which, I argue, Mexican masculinities would lose their cultural distinctiveness.

The *fichera* film frolics in gender and sexual transgressions within the "safe space" of comedic discourse in order to resolve the crisis of masculinity this subgenre plays out. Ripstein's film was made in the era when these brothel-cabaret comedies attained widespread popularity, and on the eve of the homosexual liberation movement. This landmark film, however, shares none of the frivolity of the *ficheras*. Ripstein's cinematic adaptation of José Donoso's novella *El lugar sin límites* (1965) continues his obsession with marginalized loners and social outcasts. Through La Manuela, the borders between heterosexuality and homosexuality are crossed in giddy sadomasochistic cycles while also being strictly policed with deadly effect. Ripstein's arresting indictment of homophobia is directly linked to authoritarian patriarchal control of an entire range of psychic, sociocultural, political, and geographic spaces.

In both Chapter One and Chapter Three, I foreground ways that female prostitutes and gay males in Mexico share a history of subjection to human rights violations and sexual violence. Carlos Monsiváis incisively notes,

> Dozens of prostitutes—just like homosexuals, the other minority group that is persecuted—are murdered throughout the country in cheap hotels; they are found strangled or stabbed often after being sadistically tortured by having cigarette stubs put out on their flesh, and showing signs of genital mutilation. Few pay attention or give much importance to these murders because in the last instance we find ourselves before the disappearance of non-entities, non-citizens since society views people who choose "vice" and the road to "perdition" as having relinquished all rights. (1980: 104)

Chapter Four examines changes in the revolutionary melodrama genre, most notably its demasculinization in favor of a feminization, and the broader implications for the symbolic meanings of *mexicanidad* in the 1990s. I study these changes in relation to transformations in State involvement in cinema during the early NAFTA era, taking the international box office success *Como agua para chocolate* (*Like Water for Chocolate*, Alfonso Arau, 1991) as a principal case study. I argue that the reduced emphasis on the 1910 Revolution during the 1988–1994 presidential period signals a revised nationalism in accord with the State's neoliberal agenda. Close textual analysis of the movie's re-elaboration of the rhetoric of the Revolution in the context of free trade signals how the gutting of the social justice tenets central to post-1910 Mexico are symbolically represented in one of the few State-funded feature films set during the Revolution that was produced during Salinas de Gortari's presidency. The chapter takes film policy as its focus because during this period the Mexican film indus-try was radically restructured, inexorably affecting the future of Mexican cinema.

This case study on changes in film policy carried out by the State-funded Mexican Film Institute (Instituto Mexicano de Cinematografía, IMCINE) outlines how the orchestrated "renaissance" in Mexican cinema during the early part of the 1990s was a central component of Salinas de Gortari's cultural diplomacy and political legitimation. Mexican films of the 1990s experienced an unprecedented surge in popularity at an interna-tional level in great part due to the *Como agua para chocolate* phenomenon both in the form of Laura Esquivel's novel, published in Mexico in 1989, and later in director Alfonso Arau's screen adaptation. While the leader-ship role taken by IMCINE during the Salinas de Gortari administration facilitated a greater exposure of Mexican cinema in Mexico and abroad, radical changes in State protectionist measures toward the film industry, such as the sale of the State-owned theater chain and the elimination of limits to movie ticket prices at the box office, also made Mexico's film market and film exhibition in particular more vulnerable to Hollywood films. Were it not for new generations of Mexican spectators who want to watch Mexican films that reflect their culture and social realties, Hol-lywood films would completely dominate all the multiplex cinemas.

In the Epilogue I survey the career of actor Gael García Bernal, symbol of a transnational, post-national, and diasporic new Mexican cinema, in light of the international impact of films in which he played leading roles: *Amores perros* (*Love's a Bitch,* Alejandro González Iñárritu, 2000), *Y tu mamá también* (And Your Mama Too, Alfonso Cuarón, 2001), *El crimen del padre Amaro* (*The Crime of Father Amaro,* Carlos Carrera, 2002), *La mala educación* (*Bad Education,* Pedro Almodóvar, 2004), and *Los diarios de motocicleta* (*The Motorcycle Diaries,* Walter Salles, 2004). In these and other films, García Bernal circulates both as a poster boy for the new Mex-ican cinema and as a symbolic cultural ambassador of an emerging trans-national *latinidad*. García Bernal's on-screen performances of both hard and "sensitive" young men, coupled with his off-screen persona as "genu-ine," "down-to-earth," "natural," politically progressive, and cosmopolitan, parallel but also depart from the "new" models of post-revolutionary masculinities proffered by Pedro Infante in the 1940s and 1950s.

"Midnight Virgin"

Melodramas of Prostitution in Literature and Film

✢ ✢ ✢

Virgen de media noche,
virgen, eso eres tú,
para adorarte toda
rasga tu manto azul.
Señora del pecado,
luna de mi canción,
mírame arrodillado,
junto a tu corazón.

Midnight virgin,
that's what you are.
Sweep aside your blue cloak,
so that I may adore all of you.
Mistress of sin,
moon of my song,
see me kneeling before you,
close to your heart.

PEDRO GALINDO GARZA

*W*ith no pretense of objectivity, I surmise that film junkies like myself would be hard pressed to find a more unusual take on the world's oldest profession than the moody, film noir–laced musical *cabaretera* melodramas that were all the rage in Mexico in the 1940s and '50s. Few actresses playing "fallen women" have been as infused with tragedy as Andrea Palma's melancholic look in *La mujer del puerto* (Woman of the Port, Arcady Boytler, 1933) or *Distinto amanecer* (New Dawn, Julio Bracho, 1943); few have shown as much pleasure in unmasking middle-class hypocrisy as Ninón Sevilla in *Aventurera* (Adventuress, Alberto Gout, 1949) and *Sensualidad* (Sensuality, Alberto Gout, 1950); few have expressed the levels of ecstatic joy to be had in performing an Afro-Caribbean dance that the likes of María Antonieta Pons did in *Konga Roja* (Alejandro Galindo, 1943) or Sevilla in *Señora tentación* (Mrs. Temptation, José Díaz Morales, 1947); few have shown as much conviction and piety at earning a living in "the hard life" to pay the costs of a younger sibling's school tuition as

Marga López in *Salón México* (Emilio Fernández, 1948) or to pay for the room and board and education of her illegitimate child than Dolores del Río in *Las abandonadas* (Abandoned Women, Emilio Fernández, 1944); and surely no woman has fought as passionately for the right to raise her child with dignity as Sevilla in *Víctimas del pecado*. Indeed, speaking as if her career were in prostitution, Sevilla triumphantly mused:

> Look at the contrasts in my life. I went from wanting to be a missionary nun and doctor, a profession that my family approved, to becoming an entertainer, which my family did not approve. But I proved to them that some of us do have morals, a sense of decency, and that we know how to have a proper career in spite of being a woman.[1]

These roles underscore the apparent double burden of being both woman and actress, as well as the stigma linked to women whose careers in the performing arts are viewed by conservative Mexican society as leading a life of improper conduct.

Beginning with the foundational narrative of La Malinche, consort and translator to Hernán Cortés and mother of the nation, stigmatized as a traitor and a whore for assisting the Spanish in the conquest and defeat of the Aztec empire, the transgressive woman figured as a prostitute holds a privileged status in the Mexican cultural imaginary.[2] Elite and popular culture, literature, film, music, painting, history, and mythology all place the prostitute, along with spaces linked with urban nightlife, brothels, and cabarets, as one of the most ubiquitous Mexican motifs. Seductive, often tragic and victimized, frequently brave and defiant, the figure of the prostitute—whether cast as a *cabaretera*, a *rumbera*, an *exótica*, or a *fichera*, depending on variants in the immensely popular genre—has shaped the erotic fantasies of readers and audiences for more than a century, not only in Mexico but across the Americas.[3] In a country that until the late 1950s did not permit explicit representations of sexuality or nudes in film, the prostitute stood in for sexuality and the pleasures and dangers incurred by modernity.

The moralistic Catholic dimensions and the indispensable role of popular music and dance in Mexican cinematic melodramas of prostitution differentiate this genre from its counterparts in non-Spanish-language national cinemas. In Mexican popular culture, Marian imagery is frequently used to describe the prostitute as the repository of "romantic"

Ninón Sevilla and musicians in *Aventurera*. Courtesy Filmoteca UNAM.

male fantasies about women's sexuality, a Janus-faced figure who is both virgin and whore. The fantasy of woman as prostitute is a contradictory and unattainable revered object of erotic desire who is paradoxically both pure and corrupt, sacred and secular, as is evident in Pedro Galindo Garza's lyrics for his classic *bolero* (ballad) of the early 1940s, "Virgen de media noche."[4] The same idealized and abstract fantasy of the "fallen woman" is synthesized in Galindo Garza's *bolero*.[5]

The religious dimensions in the Mexican prostitution melodrama have as much to do with Mexico's colonial history and the Catholic Church's role in this process as they do with the conflictive transition into modernity that the nation was undergoing from the early 1900s to the 1940s and '50s, at the height of the genre's popularity in film. The other component that differentiates this Mexican film genre from other national counterparts is the extensive use of music and dance from across the Americas (*bolero, danzón, son,* rumba, samba) and other parts of the world (Middle East, Southeast Asia, and Polynesia). Musical and dance performances frame and are frequently used to interrupt or propel the narrative and to punctuate the primary thematic motifs used by the genre (pleasure, sin, redemption). The cinematic prostitution melodrama depends as much on the theatricalization of "vices"—sexuality and other forms of tainted pleasures—as it does on the romantic ballad and the sensuous Afro-Cuban *danzón*.[6] Historically the prostitute has been a key figure in Mexico's master narratives of national origins, spanning from the foundational colonial period to the tumultuous post-revolutionary years to the uncertain contemporary post-national era. The focus of this chapter is to provide a sociocultural history of prostitution in Mexico through a discussion of the links between discourses and representations of women's sexuality, sex work, and motherhood to national identity, modernity, and urban spaces, as well as the growth of leisure activities and the mass media.[7] I argue that prostitution is a privileged trope that is central for understanding changes in the construction of gender and sexuality in Mexican culture and society.

The cover art chosen for cultural anthropologist Roger Bartra's collection of critical essays on Mexican cultural nationalism, *Oficio mexicano* (Mexican Vocation, 1993), is an index of just how central the figure of the prostitute is in Mexican intellectual and popular culture. The cover features a wax model by José Neira Obcejo titled "Ave sin alas" (Bird Without Wings); the cover art quotes Graciela Iturbide's well-known photograph of an aging prostitute, "Mujer de cera" (Wax Woman, 1972). Seated at a small round table on which sits a shot glass, the haggard middle-aged woman in a tight-fitted floral-print dress rests her arms on the table while in one hand she holds a cigarette. Her facial expression attempts a smile but achieves a somewhat grotesque and melancholic grimace as her eyes gaze at some indefinite point in space.[8] Neira Obcejo's wax model of Iturbide's photograph is accompanied by a reproduction of Iturbide's famous photograph, displayed on an easel next to the table where the prostitute is seated. In Iturbide's photograph, instead of the red curtains used as the backdrop in the wax museum exhibition space, the prostitute is seated in front of a mural of a large skull. One eye socket depicts a hospital ward for women, while the other contains an image of an empty hotel bed and a portrait of the Virgin Mary hanging over it. In the skull's nasal cavity, a tombstone engraved with "R.I.P." can be discerned. The meanings of these images link female sexual commerce with disease and death. Death seems to hover over the sad-looking prostitute. These images invoke the fate of the syphilitic prostitute by the name of Santa, the tragic heroine in Federico Gamboa's *Santa* (1903), the foundational novel of modern Mexico's rich corpus of prostitution melodramas surveyed by Sergio González Rodríguez (1990, 1993) and Debra A. Castillo (1998).

The image of the aged and haggard prostitute functions in the context of Bartra's collection of essays as an allegorical figure for the exploitation of the Mexican nation. In the title essay, "Oficio mexicano: Miserias y esplendores de la cultura" (Mexican Vocation: Miseries And Splendors Of Culture), Bartra critiques the use of art and national culture in the 1990 exhibition "Mexico: Splendors of Thirty Centuries" featured at New York's Metropolitan Museum of Art and the Los Angeles County Museum of Art as a prelude to the signing of NAFTA. Bartra argues that cultural artifacts, as mediators of politics, are used by the State to reproduce the political legitimacy of the reigning party, Partido Revolucionario Institucional (Institutional Revolutionary Party, or PRI) and to promote globalization.[9] Bartra maintains that Mexico, its people, culture, and resources have been exploited since the late 1920s by the ruling PRI government, the self-proclaimed heir to the 1910 Revolution and the guardian of the nation's historical memory and "collective" imagining. Through the figure of the prostitute, Bartra makes clear his view that the PRI has pimped the nation and its cultural patrimony to the business interests of local and transnational capital.

My aim in this chapter is to survey representations of Mexican womanhood through the figure of the prostitute, both across foundational and antifoundational literary and cinematic texts produced between 1903 and 1991. The significations attributed to the figure of the prostitute in cultural and symbolic terms are multiple and contradictory. Discourses of prostitution help unlock the complicated nexus of social relations that have historically shaped the private and public regulation of women's work, their sexual agency, and their assigned role as mothers of the nation. The figure of the prostitute is the emblematic social agent who embodies the anxieties, desires, and contradictions generated by the transition from tradition to (post)modernity. Female prostitution also functions to define class-specific normative and transgressive models of Mexican womanhood and manhood, a marker of the socially acceptable limits of sexuality and morality. The prostitute is the social Other necessary for the construction of the new cult of female domesticity promoted during the Porfirian period (1876–1911) and the moral standards espoused by the post-revolutionary government in the 1930s and '40s.[10] Prostitution is therefore an important phenomenon for the study of the regulation of "proper" models of female and male sexuality. The prostitute's body is simultaneously a site/sight of resistance and collusion with patriarchy. The brothel and cabaret also facilitate the representation of "deviant" sexual practices and identities, including male and female homosexuality.

Early-twentieth-century social purity and antivice moral campaigns, centered on sex work and women who worked in cabarets, register the politicization of sexuality, work, leisure, and disease. Discourses of gender, family, nation, citizenship, criminality, and public health also enable the construction of "dangerous sexualities," assist in the normalization of heterosexuality, and reproduce the patriarchal structures that sustain it while at the same time opening a space for debate and resistance. Contemporary feminist debates, inside and outside the academy, as well as activism around sex work and human rights demonstrate that sexuality is a highly contested terrain where struggles occur along intersections involving gender, class, nation, race, ethnicity, and religion.[11]

In the first part of this chapter, I survey the social and material conditions as well as the discursive fields (history, medicine, law, religion) that inform the literary representation of female prostitution. Two key texts are the focus: Gamboa's classic naturalist novel *Santa* and Sara Sefchovich's *Demasiado amor,* a woman-centered, postmodernist hybrid genre novel.[12] Gamboa's novel is a resoundingly moralizing product of the Porfirian Age.[13] The novel *Santa,* written for a male audience, forms part of a social and moral hygiene campaign implemented by government agencies and promoted by the Catholic Church. *Santa,* Gamboa's now-legendary novel, establishes the paradigm of the simultaneously sacred and abject prostitute who is absolved of her "sinful vices" through her path to Calvary and martyrdom involving expulsion from her family home, sex work, alcoholism, disease, suffering, and eventual death.

Demasiado amor, a best-seller in Mexico written for middle-class female readers, is equal parts epistolary novel and travel diary; it recounts the affective geography of Mexico's varied landscapes and national monuments and the diverse traditional cultural forms and practices that make up the nation's cultural patrimony. I read this novel as a feminist text of resistance that seeks to redefine the meaning of the terms "prostitute" and "prostitution" as well as to explore the limits of emotional and sexual excess. Sefchovich underscores how sexuality is experienced by the narrator, Beatriz, and how sexual activity, desire, and pleasure shape her everyday life and her identity. *Demasiado amor* affirms the radical possibilities offered by nonreproductive sexual practices, female pleasure, and desire. Sefchovich's novel revalorizes women's sexuality exercised outside the restrictions of the traditional family and monogamous relationships. From a woman-centered perspective, Sefchovich rewrites the tropes of prostitution popularized by *Santa*. Sefchovich recuperates progressive ways of understanding sexual practices. She foregrounds the figure of the prostitute as a powerful erotic teacher and self-determining social agent rather than merely a victim, a degraded erotic object, and a safety valve necessary for the gendered division of labor and the reproduction of patriarchal relations of power. At the same time, Sefchovich also critiques consumerism and tourism. *Santa* and *Demasiado amor* form part of an extensive body of work that constructs and positions the figure of the prostitute, the social phenomenon of prostitution, and its accompanying urban nightlife as key tropes in the mythology of *mexicanidad*.

Nowhere in Mexican culture have images and narratives of the prostitute and of brothel culture been more pervasive than in its national cinema. I discuss paradigmatic cinematic representations of female prostitution in mid- to late-twentieth-century Mexico by focusing on two well-known works from representative film auteurs: Emilio Fernández's *Víctimas del pecado* (*Victims of Sin*, 1950), from the classic period, and María Novaro's *Danzón* (1991), from the contemporary new wave of Mexican cinema. Read jointly, these films and novels show how the prostitute is constructed as the Other of the desired model of proper Mexican womanhood. The trope of prostitution also functions as an allegory for the colonization of Mexico. I look to prostitution to see how it comments on the links between the process of industrialization and nation building, the commodification of the female body, the feminization of the labor force, and the exploitation of natural resources.

I. MOTHERHOOD, PROSTITUTION, AND NATIONAL ORIGINS

The two master narratives that condense Mexican models of womanhood are La Malinche and the Virgin of Guadalupe. Structured by the ideology of Catholicism, both models of national origins have counterparts in the biblical figures of Eve, the Virgin Mary, and Mary Magdalene, who in turn are shaped by the violent history of the Spanish colonization of the Americas.

Mexican nationalism is deeply embedded in Catholicism. There is no icon more unifying of national sentiments than the Virgin of Guadalupe. The 1531 apparition of the mother of Jesus Christ on Tepeyac Hill in what is now Mexico City is also the site where the indigenous earth mother Tonantzin-Cihuacóatl was honored. Pope Pius XII declared the Virgin of Guadalupe, Mexico's patron saint, Empress of the Americas in 1945. During Mexico's wars of independence (1808–1821) and the Mexican Revolution, led in the southern part of the country by agrarian reformer Emiliano Zapata, the Virgin of Guadalupe was used as a banner and call to arms. The phenomenon of *guadalupismo* and the use of the mestizo incarnation of the mother of the Christian God as the mediator for secular conflicts across the breadth of Mexican history, beginning with the Spanish colonization of the Americas, is the most powerful component in the various forms that Mexican national consciousness has taken.[14]

Film critics and theorists, cultural critics, and historians Roger Bartra (1987), Susan Dever (2003), Joanne Hershfield (1996), Ana M. López (1991, 1993), Carlos Monsiváis and Carlos Bonfil (1994), Charles Ramírez Berg (1992), and Julia Tuñón (1987, 1998) have all discussed the historic, mythic, and sociocultural dimensions of the virgin-whore duality in the context of Mexican nationalism. The archetypes for Mexican womanhood and motherhood are the already-named Virgin of Guadalupe-Tonantzin-Cihuacóatl and the equally polysemic Malintzin Tenepal—Doña Marina (alias La Malinche, La Chingada, the fucked or violated woman). La Malinche is the Mexican Eve, symbolic mother of the mestizo race, and is by extension also considered a "bad woman," equivalent to a whore, for "betraying" Mexico's indigenous communities by "selling out" the Indians to the Spanish conquerors when acting as translator for Hernán Cortés. Since the 1980s, Chicana feminist scholarship has reinterpreted the figure of La Malinche as a powerful and misunderstood figure linked to the power of language.[15] Hershfield argues that the attributes given to these archetypes "have been continually transformed in an attempt to account for the conflicted and changing positions of woman in Mexican psychic and social structures" (1996: 15). The paradoxical qualities of the virgin/whore binary structure that have historically shaped Mexican womanhood embody multiple positive and negative connotations, ranging from submissive and suffering mother and wife figure who exerts a powerful role within the family structure to the more ambiguous overprotective, controlling, and manipulative mother who threatens the well-being of others, mostly her children.

The Marxist anthropologist Roger Bartra synthesizes the patriarchal virgin and whore archetypes into a duality that he calls "Chingadalupe": "It is the Chingadalupe, an ideal image that the Mexican macho should form about their partner, who should fornicate with uninhibited enjoyment, and, at the same time, be virginal and consoling" (1987: 222). He argues that both Guadalupe and Malinche are two versions of a single myth of national origins related to the cult of the Virgin Mary. The virgin-whore duality, Bartra argues, obeys a pious need to deny the powerful sexual and erotic dimensions of the Virgin Mary in Catholic culture (206).

Along these lines, literary critic Debra A. Castillo identifies the peculiar link between the obsession with prostitution and the tendency to "eroticize weakness and victimization" as one of the most salient characteristics of Mexican male attitudes toward women. Summarizing the insights of her Mexican colleague Salvador Elizondo, Castillo writes, "prostitutes reaffirm a masculinity placed into doubt by the monumentally powerful passivity of the self-sacrificing mother-saint; the loose woman, then, serves as a defensive counter site or as a socially-approved outlet for surplus repression" (1994/1995: 176). Castillo goes on to quote critic José Joaquín Blanco: "'Mexican men tend to eroticize weakness and victimization, intimating that at some level a mother's presumed abnegation and a prostitute's imagined sexual ferment are equivalent, or, at least parallel, erotic structures. . . . These erotic structures are perpetuated through literary and cultural markets that find them valuable aesthetic currency for maintaining social hierarchies'" (176).

What art historian Lynda Nead notes with respect to Victorian Britain can productively be used to interpret the social history of gender in Mexico. Nead argues that the definition of nineteenth-century bourgeois sexual norms and morals was integral to the creation of a hegemonic class and the promotion of a national consciousness. The private conduct of women, particularly mothers, was assigned a central role in the formation of public morals, given that the institution of motherhood was used by patriarchy to transmit and reproduce the dominant ideology. "The moral condition of the nation . . . was believed to derive from the moral standards of woman" (1988: 92). It is well known that in the Hispanic cultural tradition, family honor resides in the chastity and virtue of women. For both the Mexican and the British contexts, private conduct has ample repercussions in the public sphere. The obsessive attention that moral reformers and Positivist social scientists such as Luis Lara y Pardo (1908) gave to the regulation of female prostitution at the turn of the century marks a displacement of class conflict and exploitation into an excessive concern with the sexual practices of the working classes, who were thought to be easily corrupted by "vice." Historian William E. French argues that the prostitute during the Porfirian Age was a symbol of "Mexico's dangerous classes" (1992: 530). Historian Donna J. Guy (1990) makes a similar argument in her study of prostitution in Buenos Aires.

The sexual ideology of the virtues of proper womanhood, whose temporal and spatial dimensions are widespread, has deep historical roots. Early modern European historian Mary Elizabeth Perry, for example, notes that religious symbols legitimate gender(ed) ideologies that organize societies. Religious symbols, particularly those belonging to Mariology, structure and filter our perception of a gendered social order (1990: 41). Perry argues that the Virgin Mary represents an image of perfection, self-sacrifice, and purity that no woman can attain, while the other biblical Mary, Mary Magdalene, represents the image of the weak sinner, an image that "justifies feminine submission and male domination" (6).

Thus far I have provided a context for my contention that the prostitute is a reigning Mexican motif and that the prostitute embodies the crisis and anxieties of modernity that irrevocably altered gender relations and social identities in the post-revolutionary period. My argument complicates feminist insights about woman-as-mother as the central allegorical figure for nationalism because Mexico's national origin narrative consists of mothers *and* prostitutes as well as prostitutes who are also mothers. Moreover, the prostitute consistently crosses familial, moral, class, and geographic boundaries and thus poses a multiple threat to established hierarchies. Sex workers who are also mothers challenge both the rigid distinction made between prostitutes and mothers and conservative criteria regarding who is fit to be a "good mother."

Deniz Kandiyoti builds on R. W. Connell's groundbreaking analysis of the high political and ideological investments the nation-state has in regulating gender. Connell argues that "each state embodies a definable 'gender regime.'"[16] Kandiyoti expands Connell's insights on the relation of State, gender, and sexual politics by showing just how crucial the regulation of gender relations is to the "articulation of cultural identity and difference" (1994: 388). Through discursive analysis, Kandiyoti unpacks "the contradictions inherent in the gender agenda of some nationalist projects" (378). Kandiyoti agrees with Nira Yuval-Davis and Flora Anthias's influential argument that "the control of women and their sexuality is central to national and ethnic processes" (376). What is aptly called the "Janus-faced quality" of modernizing national movements highlights the contradictory impulses of patriarchal nationalist discourses that on the one hand promise modernizing reforms for women both in terms of equal rights before the law and political enfranchisement while on the other hand simultaneously reinscribing the traditional role of women as mothers of the nation and preservers of cultural identity (378). Kandiyoti highlights the limits of modernist reform projects that link the condition of women to the "backwardness" of a society because they are ultimately meant to regulate "the place and conduct of women" (378). This perspective ties the emancipation of women to "a national regeneration project articulated in the language of moral redemption" (379). As I will show later, the discourse of moral redemption is reminiscent of the moralizing campaigns carried out in Mexico from the 1920s to the 1940s in attempts to implement a new "revolutionary moral" aimed at controlling women and their sexuality. Modernity means different things to men and women. Modernity has enabled some men to "adopt new styles of conduct" while binding women to a new set of constraints that demand them to be " 'modern-yet-modest' " (A. Najmabadi quoted in Kandiyoti: 379). Kandiyoti highlights the pitfalls and the gains made possible by the terms used to describe modern cultural nationalisms as they specifically affect women's rights, contending that "the identification of women as privileged bearers of corporate identities and boundary markers of their communities has had a deleterious effect on their emergence as full-fledged citizens of modern nation-states" (380). Finally, this approach warns us against the wholesale adoption of some Western feminist theory and practice that privilege the private as site of resistance. Gains achieved in the private realm have often left many power structures unchanged, such as racial inequality, ethnocentrism, class oppression, and uneven distribution of wealth and resources.

II. LITERARY REPRESENTATIONS: FROM *SANTA* TO *DEMASIADO AMOR*

Santa, the name of modern Mexico's most famous literary prostitute, condenses a masculinist ideology that historically has bound women's sexuality to the control of religious doctrine. Like Roger Bartra's "Chingadalupe," Santa's name indexes the multiple and contradictory inscriptions of "woman" across history, religion, myth, and culture. Her paradoxical name bears the burden of misogynist double standards. Santa is the emblem for the two-sided masculine construction of Mexican womanhood. Simultaneously the Virgin Mary and Mary Magdalene, she is also Mexicanized as Malinche and as the Virgin of Guadalupe.

Gamboa's novel, more widely reprinted than any in Mexican history,[17] tells the familiar story of a young country girl, Santa, who is seduced and abandoned by a general passing through the region with his troops. Upon learning of her dishonor, Santa's brothers expel her from the rural, mother-centered, pre-industrial paradise of Chimalistac. Through yet another deception, the destitute Santa finds her way to Doña Elvira's brothel in nearby Mexico City. Santa's extraordinary beauty allows her to achieve an unusual level of success among the brothel's clients. Meanwhile, the brothel's blind pianist, Hipólito, tirelessly pines away after her without being able to attain her love until the very end of the novel, when Santa— rejected now by the "dives" as well as the first-class brothels to which she was once accustomed—finds herself on her deathbed prematurely, in agony due to cervical cancer. Gamboa allegedly based his novel on "his own observations of the Porfirian underworld, his discussions with prostitutes, and his interest in the 1897 murder trial of [María Villa, alias] 'La Chiquita'" (Bliss 2001: 41).[18]

A highly ambiguous text, *Santa* is filled with contradictions and deploys the quintessential "morality" of melodrama. Although in *Santa* Gamboa denounces the social, juridical, and economic injustices prostitutes encounter, he also inaugurates a sexually titillating literary discourse about the dangers that female promiscuity and other related "vices" represent for the national body politic. A novel at cross-purposes, it is both a voyeuristic invitation to gaze at what is morally forbidden but socially sanctioned and a precautionary tale with a morally edifying conclusion: Women who transgress the social norms by acting on their sexual agency before marriage will eventually face punishment. The figure of the prostitute is represented as a passive and tragic victim of a cruel, hypocritical, and unmerciful society; what distinguishes Santa from the stereotypical prostitute with a heart of gold is her ultra-Catholic martyrdom. But she also circulates as a powerful and destructive figure, a symbol of degeneration, disease, and contagion. Both images contain strong measures of fear and desire. The first image elicits the sympathy of the reader with the purpose of reintegrating the prostitute into "respectable" social norms and affirming her human rights, while the second is driven by an impulse toward containing and isolating the destructive powers attributed to her as a figure of temptation and as a dangerous transmitter of disease. It is this final image that justifies the tragic and relentless fate assigned by Gamboa to his heroine.

The overlapping of these two images plays out male anxieties about female sexuality. Both images define the prostitute as an aberrant and abnormal figure who must be differentiated from the rest of society. Both images are simultaneously deployed to elicit fear and dread, pity and redemption, desire and pleasure. Prostitution functions as a system to define the two extremes of patriarchal constructions of femininity (virgin/whore) and in this way marks the socially acceptable limits of women's sexuality and subjectivity and condones male promiscuity. The figure of the defiant and decadent prostitute can also provide a space for masochistic pleasure in identification. Santa is both sacred and abject. In Mexican popular culture, the prostitute is muse for the film director, novelist, poet, and composer, solace for the exploited worker, and refuge for the bored bourgeoisie; these dominant images simultaneously overvalue and degrade the object of representation.[19]

The prostitute is the central emblem of Mexico's conflicted modernity. She simultaneously displays and masks the contradictory and uneven processes of industrial developmentalism that are intimately linked to the growth of Mexico City's cosmopolitan nightlife in the late 1920s through the '50s and to the entertainment industry based there. The salacious narrative of the perilous descent of a young and innocent country girl through the urban vices linked to female sexual commerce functions as an allegory for modernity's destruction of the pastoral, pre-industrial past. The prostitute is also an allegory for the exploitation and feminization of the labor force. From an economic perspective, prostitutes as wage laborers pose a threat to men's control of women; they are therefore stigmatized and criminalized for transgressing patriarchal dictates of absolute rule and ownership of the labor of women. Marginalized and disenfranchised, sex workers do not have the same rights as other citizen laborers. Representatives of the State either exploit them or turn a blind eye to their existence.

III. THE GROWTH OF URBAN NIGHTLIFE AND THE EMERGENCE OF CONSUMER CULTURE

Few have provided a more complete survey of Mexico City's brothel culture and legendary nightlife than Carlos Monsiváis (1990), the leading contemporary *cronista* (chronicler) of Mexican popular culture. In "Agustín Lara: The Illusory Harem," Monsiváis explores the mythology of the prostitute, focusing on the work of music composer Agustín Lara (1900–1970). Lara is the icon of the forlorn bohemian who, like Gamboa's blind pianist Hipólito, positioned himself as a pious slave to his unrequited love for fallen women, his constant musical muses. The use of Lara's original songs in Mexican films, beginning with his title song for the first sound version of *Santa* (1931), initiated a prolific use of popular music to augment box office success.[20]

Lara's musical trajectory follows those of prominent nineteenth-century romantic poets (e.g., Manuel Acuña, Juan de Dios Peza) in romanticizing the prostitute as well as defying bourgeois morality. Like many romantic poets, Lara employs a religious discourse that overvalues, yet still punishes, the prone-to-sacrifice prostitute who is redeemed from her sins through the love of the composer-poet. To bestow a place of cultural honor on the "fallen woman" represents something more and something less than social defiance. Certainly, as Monsiváis argues, the valorization of one of the most degraded and marginalized social subjects does indeed represent a defiance of traditional morals. On the one hand, Lara reproduces the moral hypocrisy that idealizes the otherwise stigmatized and persecuted sex workers who serve as a safety valve for the sanctity of the family, thus perpetuating patriarchal privilege. On the other hand, the oppositional edge in Lara's compositions comes through in the blasphemous equation of the sinner-whore with the saintly lover-confidante, a reinscription of the Malinche-Guadalupe archetype. The celebration of nonreproductive sexual practices outside the frame of marriage and the family keeps these sacred spaces clean of the sexual "corruption" that Catholicism abhors (sex is for reproduction, not for pleasure).

Prostitution and urban nightlife in Mexico City achieved a legendary status approximately from 1920 to the early '50s, a period when images of and discourse about the dangers and/or pleasures of sexual transgression circulated widely through government campaigns, literature, popular music, and the mass media, creating what Monsiváis calls "the commercial consolidation of the invention of 'Night Life' as a dangerous territory without risk for the middle classes" (1990: 76). The presence of the prostitute, the cabaret, and the brothel in songs from this period was both sign and symptom of modernization, rapid urban growth, and the capitalist development of consumer culture in a newly cosmopolitan Mexico City. For Monsiváis, Lara's oeuvre is one of the key components in the propagation of the myth about Mexico City's nightlife.

Salvador Novo (1972), Monsiváis's predecessor, argued that the place of privilege the brothel occupied in Mexican culture during the *porfiriato* stemmed from the fact that, for the Porfirian elite, the brothel and its variants (*casa de citas*, etc.) were the center of social life for men with access to this particular kind of leisure and sexual commerce (Novo cited in Monsiváis 1990: 65). In a moralistic society, the brothel-cabaret is the ideal "space without limits" for shoring up traditional values associated with the State, the family, and the church. According to the official statistics of registered prostitutes from the first decade of the twentieth century, Paris (with a population five times greater than that of Mexico City) had 4,000 prostitutes registered with public health authorities, while Mexico City had approximately 11,500, excluding the widespread clandestine sex work practiced by maids, among others, to supplement their incomes (Monsiváis 1990: 66). These statistics underscore the dire conditions of poverty in Mexican society that prompted so many women to enter the sex industry; they provide an index of the extent of the State's networks of power and the lack of will to improve social conditions for the majority of the nation's population, especially women.

IV. PROSTITUTION, PUBLIC HEALTH, AND CIVIC MORALITY CAMPAIGNS

The legal status of sex work in Mexico has historically fluctuated. The first attempt to regulate prostitution (*Proyecto de decreto y reglamento sobre la prostitución*) dates to 1851. After the turn of the nineteenth century, the increasing number of people diagnosed with syphilis prompted the Mexican government to intervene more vigorously in public health regulation by legislating two basic measures. First, the 1851 registration of all sex workers was required to enforce minimum medical control over venereal diseases; this legislation mandated a series of licenses that facilitated police extortion. Second, the State issued a series of ordinances concerning the location of brothels, which Monsiváis describes as equivalent to the implementation of "concentration camp-like universes: the 'red light districts' or 'areas of tolerance'" (1990: 67). This social hygiene campaign exempted from medical and legal surveillance not only the men who frequented prostitutes, but also married and sexually active women who were in danger of contracting sexually transmitted diseases, most notably syphilis and gonorrhea. The law placed the onus for responsible sexual practices on sex workers through regular health inspections. The law implicitly targeted sex workers as the principal transmitters of disease.

Wartime conditions, both during the French occupation of Mexico (1861–1867) and during the Mexican Revolution, contributed to the growth of female sexual commerce and prompted government regulation of prostitution. In 1865 prostitutes were mandated to register with civil authorities; this law was subsequently modified several times. Under the French occupation, the Department of Sanitary Inspection was founded in Mexico City to control public hygiene problems resulting from the interaction between prostitutes and the invading soldiers. A registry of Mexico City prostitutes (data included a photograph, vital statistics, and medical record) was a key component in government control of prostitution.[21]

The law that has received the most comment in the literature was the *Reglamento para el ejercicio de la prostitución en el D.F.* of 1926. The law remained in effect until February 14, 1940, when it was rescinded during a period of moralizing campaigns aimed at controlling the spread of sexually transmitted diseases and protecting Mexicans against "harmful" foreign influences, including different forms of mass media deemed pornographic.[22] Since that period ended in the late 1950s, the legality of prostitution varies across the country. According to an epidemiologist in Mexico who wished to remain anonymous, "There are 2,500 municipal governments in Mexico, and the administration changes every three years." He stated that each city makes a decision to regulate or not to regulate sex work in its jurisdiction. Each municipality sets up its own system.[23]

In her discussion of the effects of the law that officially abolished prostitution, Marta Lamas notes that "although prostitution is not prohibited nor is it persecuted, neither does it have any legal standing. In other words, abolitionism pretends as if prostitution didn't exist" (1993: 110). The regulation of prostitution was intended to control who could legally engage in sexual commerce; the law required that sex workers registered with federal public health officials undergo mandatory medical examinations; and sexual commerce was also restricted to specially designated urban areas called *zonas de tolerancia* (zones of tolerance), essentially redlight districts. Various laws issued to enforce "decency" are often used to harass and intimidate sex workers.

Cultural critic Sergio González Rodríguez argues that censorship of representations of sexually oriented material—from literature to related print culture including photography—have their foundations in the Printed Law of 1917 issued by the Revolutionary government of Venustiano Carranza. He notes:

The 2nd article of said Law stipulates that what constitutes an "attack on morals" are all manifestations by means of words or images that defend, excuse, counsel or "publicly promote vices, faults or delinquencies," or which defend them. Also condemned are public offenses against "modesty, decency, or good customs, or [which] promote prostitution or the practice of licentious or obscene acts, by which is understood all acts which, in the public's point of view, are qualified as being contrary to modesty and shame." Finally, punishment is extended to the distribution, the sale or public display of "writings, pamphlets, graphic art, songs, engravings, books, images, advertisements, cards or other papers, paintings, drawings, or lithographs of obscene nature or which represent lewd acts." (1992b: 37)

The ambiguity of the concept of modesty leaves the public regulation of "good customs" to the arbitrariness of judges who, in the final instance, very likely based their decisions on church doctrine. In the "erotic" text of *Santa,* the strong libidinous charge is neutralized through Gamboa's moralizing and edifying project as well as his knowledge of the pseudo-scientific discourse of criminology. Since 1931, the year of the first sound film adaptation of *Santa,* penal code Number 8, which regulated all crimes related to *la moral pública y las buenas costumbres* (public morals and good customs), was used in all moralizing campaigns.[24]

In nineteenth-century European and Mexican intellectual production, the figure of the prostitute was a central figure in discourses regarding the social division of citizens by class, public health, and urban planning.[25] For example, Charles Bernheimer in *Figures of Ill Repute: Representing Prostitution in Nineteenth Century France* (1989) observes that Alexandre Parent-Duchâtelet, a leading nineteenth-century specialist in public health, after carrying out an extensive investigation of the Parisian sewer system with the explicit purpose of regulating and containing the biological decomposition process of urban wastes, conducted an investigation on prostitution in Paris, *De la prostitution dans la ville de Paris* (1836).

In accordance with the capacities conferred to prostitutes and sewers regarding their inherent tendencies to infiltrate and dissolve myriad social barriers, Parent-Duchâtelet established acceptable boundaries between filth and cleanliness and marked pure and impure bodies (Bernheimer 1989: 10). According to popular beliefs and specialized discourses of the period, the prostitute's body, like Parent-Duchâtelet's sewage system, was believed to be a site of decomposition in need of medical and police regulation in order to ensure the cleanliness and efficiency of its function and use. By using a series of literary images that elicit repulsion, Bernheimer points out that the goal of Parent-Duchâtelet's investigation on "public women" was to "assure the salubrity of the sexual channels used to drain the seminal excess of male desire" (16). Both channels for the disposal of human secretions and waste, Parent-Duchâtelet argued, were necessary for the orderly maintenance of civilized society.

Parent-Duchâtelet proposed rigorous strategies for sealing and isolating the Parisian sewage system and trash dumps. Similar methods were used for the regulation of prostitution in brothels. In *Santa*, Gamboa also makes the analogy between the unsanitary condition of sewage systems and the unavoidable and corrupt bodily and mental condition of Santa:

> In the same way as something rots or becomes moth-eaten, and that, at any given moment, no one can impede or avoid, such was Santa's rapid, devastating, and tremendous descent. . . . Santa moved in the pestilent cellars black with lowly vices in the same manner in which dirty and impure waters of the subterranean sewers gallop furiously through the dark intestines of the streets. (1992: 267–268)

This passage combines the highly aestheticized language of *modernista* poetics with a scientific interest for social hygiene, medicine, and criminology characteristic of naturalist literature. Gamboa uses a series of dualities—city/country, life/death, corrupt/pure, hidden/visible, pestilence/perfume, low/high—in his transposition of the prostitute's body to a cartography of urban, national, and continental landscapes.

The British surgeon William Tait, in his 1840 study *Magdalenism*, was among the most influential proponents in naturalizing the myth about the inevitable progress of a prostitute's descent into physical illness and disease if she was not medically supervised. Tait summed up the effects of prostitution on women's physical, material, and social conditions into the following stages: "1. Deprives them of their Minds and Affections. 2. Deprives them of the enjoyment and sympathies of Society. 3. Involves them in the most abject Poverty and Wretchedness. 4. Subjects them to the most loathsome and painful Diseases. 5. Brings upon them premature Old Age and Early Death" (cited in Nead 1988: 146).

Tait's conclusions and diagnosis, reproduced repeatedly by medical experts, gave rise to the conservative and demonizing mythology about sex work. The ideological burden of this medical discourse legitimated the marginalization and exploitation of sex workers by putting emphasis on their lack of diligence instead of focusing on the social conditions and institutions that forced women into sex work. Most importantly, male clients were absolved of all responsibility in perpetuating the low social status of prostitutes.

The first medical text that disputed Tait's conclusions was not published until seventeen years later. In *Prostitution Considered In Its Moral, Social and Sanitary Aspects* (1857), Doctor William Acton, an internationally recognized authority for his work in the area of venereal diseases, contested the myth that "the career of the woman who once quits the pinnacle of virtue involves the very swift decline and ultimate total loss of health, modesty and temporal posterity" (Nead 1988: 147). Acton argued that the prostitute's life that ends in poverty and disease was most often the exception to the norm. Acton's conclusion seems dubious at best. This purported norm is not applicable in Mexico. For example, historian Julia Tuñón noted that in the Mexican context, "prostitution was frequent and its conditions deplorable. Venereal diseases devastated public women, who were many times still young girls" (1987: 97). In 1926, 20,000 prostitutes were registered with the department of public health; only 2,000 were diagnosed as being in good health.[26]

According to Acton's research, English prostitutes frequently enjoyed better health than "respectable" women (Nead 1988: 148). In the final instance, Acton's work supported state regulation of prostitution and responded, according to Judith Walkowitz, to religious and humanitarian accusations "'against the sacrifice of female victims of male lechery'" (cited in Nead 1988: 147). Acton's text initiated a debate within the medical profession, but the debate reconfirmed the image of the prostitute as a dangerous victim in the process of progressive decay, while his research normalized male sexual conduct. Acton did not propose practical measures to secure better working conditions for sex workers.

Gamboa's novel echoes William Tait's deterministic thesis. At the symbolic level, the victimological model used by Gamboa promoted neither greater tolerance nor a better understanding of the social conditions of prostitution. Before the invention of penicillin, the destruction of the prostitute's body as a result of venereal diseases was inexorable.

Santa's ruin became a descent identical to all falls; rapid, implacable, without anything or anyone to prevent it or provide a remedy. There was only one thing that could walk faster than her ruin, her disease, and those pains, which in the beginning were rare and at present were tremendous, frequent, lacerating, pregnant with funereal omens. Santa attributed them to the evil that terrorizes prostitutes, that sooner or later almost always gets them. (1992: 277–278)

The unnamed evil that takes possession of Santa is later named "cervical cancer," a veiled allusion to venereal disease. Santa embodies anxieties about the dangerous contagion of sexually transmitted diseases.

> Clients were advised not to make deals with her, to flee from her because she was a danger and a threat. Someone proposed denouncing her to the authorities, hoping she would leave and with great care isolate the infallible and eminent contagion. (280)

Gamboa's alarmist tone has a historical basis in the reactionary public outcry and public health proposals targeting the high number of prostitutes and their clients infected with syphilis during this period. These institutional and public responses to the syphilis epidemic afflicting a cross-section of Mexican social classes during the first two decades of the twentieth century involved persecution and concentration camp-like isolation, as well as widespread panic that resonates with the reactions provoked during the early years of the AIDS crisis.[27]

The social spheres involved in prostitution encompass a microcosmos divided by class hierarchies. For example, during the *porfiriato* the following regulations were established for the operation of brothels:

> No brothel will be opened in a residential neighborhood home, nor within fifty meters of establishments for beneficial instruction, nor near churches of any religious denomination. ... In the brothels there will only be women who belong to the same class, it being terminally prohibited to allow the mixing of diverse classes. (Cited in Monsiváis 1980: 102–103)

These classifications underscore the fear of the potential erasure or crossing of social differences and class hierarchies. They also connote the bourgeois fear of the "lower" classes infiltrating and contaminating the "respectable" social body. Additionally, these categories function to differentiate and isolate the high from the low, the pure from the impure, the norm from the deviant, and the respectable from the criminal.

Gamboa's text echoes this hierarchical ideology. Toward the end of the novel, the moribund Santa, now devalued as a sexual commodity, rejected by all of Mexico City's high-end and mid-range brothels, finally finds a low-class brothel that admits her.

> To anchor in such a despicable harbor, Santa traveled through all corners of the city, the mediocre and the dregs which large cities enclose in their breast like a skin rash that produces a visible restlessness and a continuous itching that only the police knows how to scratch and that contaminates well adjusted citizens and luxurious neighborhoods. The police urgently desire to scratch and heal her leprosy, while, at the same time, it awakens the dread that physical contact could spread it to healthy persons and dishonor the entire population. (287)

The image of a disease as contagious and stigmatized as leprosy and in constant need of vigilance and containment to avoid infecting the rest of the body, and by extension society, is explicitly coded in terms of class. In Gamboa's novel, disease and evil are phenomena proceeding from the "lower" classes, which, like a plague, threaten the "upper" classes. A liminal figure par excellence, the prostitute transits between the borders that divide society and urban geography. She represents a figure of contamination because of her potential to cross boundaries with men outside her social class; the prostitute, therefore, jeopardizes carefully policed differences.

In 1908 the Mexican sociologist Luis Lara y Pardo published *La prostitución en México*. Lara y Pardo did not believe that social conditions and patriarchy produced prostitution. He instead emphasized heredity as the most important cause of prostitution:

> Science has been able to prove that prostitution is a state of psychological and social inferiority. . . . What is inherited and congenital is moral and social psychological inferiority, which is the indispensable condition to arrive at all forms of degeneration, one of which is prostitution, most frequently found in women. (Cited in Monsiváis 1980: 105)

Gamboa, like his contemporaries, adheres to pseudo-scientific theories to explain the causes of prostitution. For example, "One could presume that [Santa] carried in her blood the traces of a very old vice from some great-grandfather that resuscitated in her this and other vices" (76). Gamboa follows contemporaneous medical theories and eugenic thinking regarding biological degeneration, as registered in his references to bio-logical determination carried in Santa's blood. Gamboa's conservatism does not promote reform. That Santa cannot remain faithful to the An-dalusian bullfighter El Jarameño, when he takes her to live at his boarding house, works to reconfirm the pseudo-scientific thesis that the propensity toward prostitution was hereditary, based on biology and class, an argu-ment closely resembling Lara y Pardo's spurious medical research.

Gamboa's novel, however, also exposes the consequences of the subhu-man conditions prostitutes worked in. Among the images of denunciation and social protest that most stand out in *Santa* are those that represent prostitution and the brothel as a human slaughterhouse. At the end of the novel, Hipólito, the blind piano player helplessly in love with Santa, meditates on his wretched luck in the third person.

> And now when, after persevering and suffering, he believed to have reached his idol, now scoffed and trampled, now that others . . . af-ter infecting, debasing, and prostituting her would, in mid-street, throw her at him because she was now useless, spent, and no lon-ger desirable. Now that he picked her body off the street, that pack of humans, disgusting and drooling like a howling pack of beasts, would hurl itself onto the healthy meat of whores to satiate their thirst. These whores came, like droves of cattle, from everywhere to supply the houses of prostitution, the insatiable slaughterhouses of the large urban centers. (310)

Gamboa uses the grotesque simile of cattle and meat to underline the de-humanization, commercialization, and consumption of the prostitute's body. It is not by accident that the brothel run by Elvira where Santa first works is located next to a "modern meat-market" (16), a symbol of the cannibalistic exploitation that codes the prostitute's body as an object to be devoured by wealthy male consumers. A disposable object, Santa's "young flesh" (19) is sacrificed on the altar of modernity and bohemian lust.

V. REWRITING FOUNDATIONAL MYTHS

Demasiado amor, Sara Sefchovich's neonationalist novel about the ideal romance and ideal lover, is a combination of various genres: epistle, diary, romance, erotic literature, and travel writing. Written in the first person, the novel, first published in 1990, juxtaposes two distinct narrative levels. The first level (epistolary) narrates the entry of Beatriz, the novel's protagonist, a secretary in contemporary Mexico City, into the informal economy of sexual services. Working outside the organized sphere of sexual commerce, Beatriz turns to sex work to supplement her salary in order to help her sister realize their shared dream of opening a boarding house in Italy. Beatriz turns to sex work by chance since the men she begins to sleep with pay her although she doesn't charge them for sex. Beatriz's sexual activities with men who are not her lover are never named as sex work, nor are they labeled as prostitution, nor, for that matter, does Beatriz think of herself either a prostitute or a sex worker. Through this rhetorical strategy Sefchovich seeks to contrast and redefine the terms "prostitution," and "prostitute" most commonly used in Mexico to describe sex work, as well as the concepts of family and community.

This narrative level details Beatriz's internal development, outlining the psychosexual self-knowledge she gains from her night job as a sex worker. Beatriz's original plan doesn't come to fruition since both her own and her sister's needs and desires change radically. Beatriz's anonymous sister gets married and establishes a traditional family life, while Beatriz, in order to maintain the illusion that reciprocal true love exists, ends up breaking off with the man she thought was the great love of her life in order to lessen the pain and the disillusion of the sudden disintegration of her idealized romance. Beatriz opts to stay in Mexico City, exercising her chosen profession as a sex worker in her own "boarding house," where she reigns like a queen in a paradisiacal space where time is suspended and where the logic that organizes the rest of society is left outside the boarding house/brothel door. Operating in a space of fantasy that is for the most part utopian leaves Beatriz ambiguously suspended between the real and the imaginary. Beatriz's coming into consciousness consists of lifting the veil from the patriarchal romantic concepts she held about her lover and about the tourist travels through Mexico that functioned as a background for her ultimately untenable fantasy romance.

The second narrative level catalogues in increasingly fragmented lists Beatriz's travels throughout Mexico with her anonymous male lover while exploring at the same time the emotional landscapes that accompany the great love of her life. Alternating with Beatriz's letters to her sister, these chapters are both travel writing and (erotic) diary of the narrator's experiences. *Demasiado amor* is one of a few novels authored by a Mexican woman that explores female heterosexual erotic experiences in explicit detail. With this novel, Sefchovich created a literary space that no Mexican woman prose writer had previously dared to explore. The commercial and critical success of the novel was, for the most part, resounding.

As well as being an erotic account, this second narrative level also functions as an allegorical national romance, since Beatriz's love for her lover and travel companion grows along with her love for Mexico: the loved man and the loved nation become equivalent, even interchangeable, terms. The anonymity of her lover parallels the allegory of male lover as nation, foregrounding nationalist discourse as a masculine construction.

The romantic discourse, truly an "erotic rhetoric," to borrow Doris Sommer's phrase (1991: 2), is a mix of neonationalism and Catholic religious discourse. Patriotic love functions as a variation of Beatriz's erotic religious discourse.

> It's your fault that I began to love this country. It's your fault, it's your fault, it's your great fault. Because you took me and brought me, up and down, through footpaths and walkways, through towns and cities. . . . And there I followed you, watching you, drinking you, waiting for you to make love to me after so much running around . . . in this everyday country of ours. (7)

In this opening paragraph, Sefchovich parallels Beatriz's coming into consciousness of Mexico's history, landscapes, customs, and people, to her discovery of love, by employing the first two stanzas from the "Act of Contrition," a prayer said before entering the confessional, and by closing the paragraph with allusions to the language used in the Lord's Prayer. Religious rhetoric thereby foregrounds Catholicism as a master narrative of Mexican cultural nationalism.

Sefchovich's hybrid erotic religious discourse is best illustrated at the end of the novel when Beatriz decides to end her relationship with her lover for fear that her fantasy of the ideal romance, the ideal male lover, and the ideal nation will disintegrate with the banality of everyday life, when the thrill of the new begins to wear thin and when, most importantly, conflicts in the relationship begin to emerge. At this point in the narrative, the romance about the ideal lover in the ideally picturesque nation begins to come apart. Knowledge gained from travel becomes tourist trivia that is decontextualized and dehistoricized for easy consumption.

> This is the last time that I love you, I mean it seriously, now is the time to end it, time put an end to so much love, to leave the most

Holy among Men, the Only One, fire, wind, light, heat, flight, semen. Is there another name but yours? Other eyes like yours where the most immense passions burst? (183)

In this passage, Sefchovich self-reflexively underscores the sacred components of sexuality. She codes Beatriz's religious-like idealization of her lover by transforming him, in an almost sacrilegious act, into God. Sefchovich achieves this through her references to natural elements and to semen. Sefchovich critiques the glorification of the male lover and the blind passion in which Beatriz loses her agency and self-determination.

Demasiado amor breaks with the moralizing discourses deployed in Gamboa's *Santa* that persecute and castigate women who practice sexuality outside the institution of marriage. Sex work is used to introduce a nonexploitative narrative about a woman's subjectivity and sexuality from a female point of view. Sefchovich's use of this woman-centered point of view eliminates the male voyeurism, sexual objectification, and fetishism of the female body that characterizes Gamboa's novel. Unlike *Santa*, Beatriz enters sexual commerce of her own free will, although under some economic pressure. The sex worker is not represented either as a powerless victim without agency or as a degenerate sinner, and sex work is not coded as a social vice or as a biological or psychological degeneration, as in *Santa*. Sex work allows Beatriz to achieve a significant degree of self-fulfillment and economic self-sufficiency.

Demasiado amor is a feminist revalorization of the social phenomenon of prostitution. Sefchovich destigmatizes sex work through the use of a first-person narrator who articulates the joy and pride she takes in the sexual services she renders. Far from simply celebrating sex work, Sefchovich also documents the oppression and the dangers prostitutes face from clients, the social stigma accompanying the world's oldest profession, and the health risks incurred. The revalorization and re-presentation of prostitution also involves a critical perspective on the institution of marriage, family, and love of nation, especially when the latter is confused with excessive consumption.

Sefchovich's text also recuperates the high social status of the *hetaira*, the prostitute-philosopher of ancient Greek society, by gradually positioning Beatriz as love goddess and teacher of eroticism, confessor, and therapist.[28] Sefchovich highlights the practical as well as the sexual-spiritual pleasure and knowledge gained by sex work. Thus, the prostitute has multiple social roles and functions: confessor, therapist, lover, and mother. Beatriz and her brothel / boarding house symbolize a space without limits, free of social, economic, psychological pressures, and structured by the exchange of physical pleasure, companionship, and communication.

Beatriz forms a community with her johns, a community united by sensual interests, emotional, and psychological needs. Notwithstanding the celebratory, even euphoric, tone of the pro-sex discourse used in this neonationalist, romantic fantasy narrative about women's sexual agency and sex work, *Demasiado amor* also forcefully highlights the subordinate place assigned to women in patriarchal national projects and cultural nationalist discourse. The ambiguities and contradictions in the representation of Beatriz's brothel/boarding house as utopian space are evident in the self-affirmation and physical and emotional fulfillment that the johns enjoy in using each part of her body as a source of pleasure, comfort, and relaxation. Unlike the idealized women in films and literature who—the narrator argues—merely accompany men in public spaces where they are displayed like cold, inanimate objects, Beatriz's imperfect body is an authentic source of pleasure and self-expression.

Sefchovich's text is a landmark in Mexican cultural production because representations of women possessing full sexual agency without being stigmatized or punished is extremely uncommon. *Demasiado amor* breaks the sacred patriarchal taboo of female sexual agency and, in this way, opens an important literary space for the self-affirming representation of female desire and sexual pleasure. This new symbolic space is, however, limited and restricted to the space of prostitution, still the privileged place for the representation of male fantasies about women's sexuality as well as middle-class female fantasies of the merits of sexual liberation.

Transformations in the representation of the legendary figure of the prostitute and of urban nightlife respond to necessities of the State, the Catholic Church, and the demands of the urban consumer market. Women's bodies and their subjectivity are the spaces on which the changes introduced by post-modernity are registered. Focused in this way, prostitution provides a critical lens to chart the shifting representation of gender, sexuality, motherhood, family, community, and citizenship.

VI. CELLULOID PROSTITUTION: MYTHS OF SEXUALITY AND FILM HISTORY

The "mother" of modern Mexican industrial film production was a whore. This spurious-sounding statement is, in effect, true since Antonio

Incest between siblings: Domingo Soler, far left, and Andrea Palma as the tragic heroine in *La mujer del puerto*. Courtesy Centro de Investigación y Enseñanza Cinematográficas, Universidad de Guadalajara.

Moreno's 1931 remake of *Santa* was officially the first sound feature film made within the emerging national film industry; it was also the most popular film until Fernando de Fuentes's *Allá en el rancho grande* (1936). *Santa* gave birth to Mexican sound cinema. Since Gamboa's novel was first adapted for the screen in 1918, the prostitution melodrama—along with the *comedia ranchera* and the revolutionary melodrama—has proven to be one of the most resilient genres in Mexican film history. Most of the crew members and stars of the 1931 version of *Santa*, including Lupita Tovar in the title role and director Antonio Moreno, were trained in Hollywood and acted in Hollywood's failed attempt at making films for the Spanish-language market.

Mexican cinema produced powerful discourses and counter-discourses on female prostitution that span the foundational melodramas of the genre: the four adaptations of *Santa* (Luis G. Peredo, 1918; Moreno, 1931; Norman Foster, 1943; Emilio Gómez Muriel, 1968), two films loosely based on Gamboa's novel (*Hipólito el de Santa*, Fernando de Fuentes, 1949; *Latino*

Bar, Paul Leduc, 1991), and three versions of *La mujer del puerto* (Arcady Boytler, 1933; Emilio Gómez Muriel, 1949; Arturo Ripstein, 1991).[29] The sequence in Boytler's film in which actress Andrea Palma as Rosario, a jaded prostitute who, like Santa, was also seduced and abandoned, is shown in a long shot standing languidly under a streetlight draped in a silky black full-length dress and smoking a cigarette, circulates widely as an icon of desire, temptation, and ultimately, sin. After her father's death, Rosario resorts to prostitution and ends up sleeping with a sailor, Alberto (Domingo Soler), who turns out to be her long-lost brother, a tragic denouement that pushes her to commit suicide. Arturo Ripstein's remake of *La mujer del puerto,* with its complex multiple points of view narrative and grotesque and utterly abject representation of prostitution and live sex acts, has an antimelodramatic and antimoralistic tenor and none of the tragic glamour pervasive in the 1933 version.

Emilio Fernández's *Salón México* (1948) is another landmark of the genre. In this urban melodrama, actress Marga López as Mercedes fulfills her patriotic duty by being surrogate mother to her younger sister, Beatriz (Silvia Derbez), whom she sends to an elite all-girls boarding school with the earnings she makes in her secret night job as a *fichera* at the legendary Salón México dance club. Mercedes dies from a gunshot wound after fending off her sadistic pimp, Paco (Rodolfo Acosta). All three prostitutes in these classic films are punished with death. These early celluloid prostitutes are sexualized versions of the archetype of the suffering, self-sacrificing Mexican woman. They are emblems of a conflicted modernity still caught in the moral traps of tradition.

The tragic representation of the prostitute as mere victim is challenged in the *cabaretera* films of the early 1950s, most notably in Alberto Gout's *Aventurera* (1949) and *Sensualidad* (1950), both starring the Cuban-born actress and dancer Ninón Sevilla. In both films, Sevilla exposes the moral hypocrisy of the bourgeoisie with a vengeance never before represented. An important precedent to Sevilla's feisty heroines was *La mancha de sangre* (The Bloodstain, Adolfo Best Maugard, 1937), the legendary *película maldita* (forbidden film) of Mexican cinema because of censorship that kept it from public view until 1994. The prostitutes in this realist, noir feature are represented as enjoying their work, and they do not carry the aura of victimization of their cinematic contemporaries.[30]

An important generic predecessor to the updated modern roles and identities of cinematic women whose livelihoods are tied to the cabaret is Bracho's *Distinto amanecer* (1943), in which Andrea Palma plays Julieta, a "proper" woman working part-time in a cabaret to help raise her younger brother, Juanito.[31] Although Julieta's wage labor outside the home as a cabaret hostess is clearly tinged with shame, the narrative neither implicates her nor denies the possibility of being involved in sexual commerce. An ambiguous figure, Palma as Julieta is imbued with the same aura of mystery, deep melancholy, and tragedy that distinguishes her role as Rosario in *La mujer del puerto,* made a decade earlier. Audiences would likely be aware of the intertextual references to Palma's debut in Boytler's landmark film. Julieta is a conflicted modern woman, torn between her responsibilities as surrogate mother and frustrated wife and her desire to fulfill her aborted romance with Octavio (Pedro Armendáriz). Julieta's voice-over narrative in the film's final sequence makes it very clear that this is not an easy decision to make, for she does not know what to do until the very end. Forced to choose between the two roles, Julieta ultimately decides on sacrificing her desire for self-fulfillment. The cliffhanger decision underscores the personal and social costs of Julieta's choice.

In *Trotacalles* (Streetwalker, 1951), director Matilde Landeta draws compelling and pointed parallels between the institutions of marriage and prostitution, revealing how marriage is also a veiled form of prostitution.[32] Between the tragic and weepy victims of foundational prostitution melodramas of the 1930s and the defiant heroines of the 1950s stand major historical social transformations that significantly alter the roles of women in film.

VII. THE "GOLDEN AGE": *VÍCTIMAS DEL PECADO* (1950)

Melodrama was a notoriously neglected metagenre in film studies until the early 1970s. Its association with popular culture, its overwrought expressivity, and its "feminine" concerns kept melodrama a critically undervalued form until the 1970s, when European and American feminist and Marxist film theorists began to reevaluate the social function of melodrama, focusing on the genre's potential critical components and emphasizing the politics of domestic space, gender construction, gender relations, and the importance given to the role of subjectivity. Influential essays by Thomas Elsaesser (1991, originally published in 1972) and Laura Mulvey (1989a, originally published in 1977) emphasized how narrative and formal excess in melodramas express social conflicts and expose social conventions.

At the same time, in Latin America, defenders of the New Latin American Cinema such as Cubans Enrique Colina and Daniel Díaz Torres (1972) were excoriating melodrama as the antithesis of new cinema values. The New Latin American Cinema's failure to reach a mass audience initiated debates that reexamined the enduring popularity and appeal of melodrama, as in Cuban Reynaldo González's "Lágrimas de celuloide: una nueva lectura para el melodrama cinematográfico" (Celluloid Tears: A New Reading of Latin American Film Melodrama, 1990). Given the limited exhibition spaces opened by the New Latin American Cinema together with the erosion of revolutionary master narratives and the changing tastes of audiences, critics of contemporary Latin American cinema shifted their attention to melodrama and classic Mexican cinema, especially underresearched issues around audience reception, gender, and the politics of pleasure and spectatorship.

Carlos Monsiváis and Ana M. López, who have framed the critical debates around Mexican film melodrama in Mexican and U.S. scholarship, are both indebted to literary critic Peter Brooks, who in an influential book argued that the emergence of this theatrical form during the French Revolution functioned as a way to secularize the laws dictated by the Church and the aristocracy. Brooks defines melodrama as "a fictional system for making sense of experience as a semantic field of force that comes into being in a world where the traditional imperatives of truth and ethics have been violently thrown into question" (1985: 152).

In her groundbreaking essay on Mexican melodrama, López (1991) proposes that the predominance of melodrama in Mexican film is not surprising, given the radical changes introduced by the Revolution. Similarly, Monsiváis argues that the Manichean moral structures of classic film melodrama were a pedagogical tool for teaching Mexicans how to adapt to the social changes introduced by the Revolution and modernity. In his essay on the mythologies propagated by Mexican cinema, Monsiváis, referring to the family melodrama, wrote that "the representation of the prostitute staged the potential of desire and affirmed the degraded institution that protects the family" (1995: 121). López (1993) expanded Monsiváis's insights by arguing that "*cabaretera* films were the first decisive cinematic break with Porfirian mentality" (160). Furthermore, she noted that although the *cabaretera* as the fabulous *rumbera* who through her dance performances shows that her relationship to her body is ecstatic and pleasurable is a "social fantasy," the *rumbera* creates a space for imagining and creating "*other* subjectivities . . . other psychosexual and social identities" (160). The new morality and changes in women's roles introduced by the prostitution melodrama in the 1940s paralleled the nation's major social, economic, and political transformations. It is not coincidental that scholars of Mexican cinema describe the prostitution melodrama as the most characteristic genre of Miguel Alemán's (1946–1952) presidential term.

In *Mexican Cinema/Mexican Woman, 1940–1950*, Joanne Hershfield argues that *cabaretera* films of the 1940s echoed the social conflicts introduced by the new roles available for women, "resulting [in the] difficulty of incorporating these changes into patriarchal discourse about female sexuality" (1996: 77). By 1950 women had been integrated into the modern labor force, which had increased during the World War II period, and thus both gender roles and Catholic moral codes required rethinking. Women's participation in national politics also increased. Women gained the right to vote in municipal elections in 1947. Six years later, in 1953, women would finally have the right to vote in presidential elections.

Miguel Alemán, the nation's first civilian president, continued the industrializing policies promoted by his predecessor, General Ávila Camacho (1940–1946). While Alemán pledged to increase democracy, his actions rarely matched his rhetoric. José Agustín notes in his discussion of Alemán's presidency that Alemán "established the repressive tendencies of the Mexican State, which, during the end of the fifties and throughout the sixties, would become an essential part of the personal governing style of the presidents of the Revolution" (1990: 117).

Along with the rhetoric of national unity, rapid industrialization and economic greed characterized this period. Alemán gave little support to land reform, only resuming the program after major protests by *campesinos* in Mexico City in 1949. Agustín also notes that Alemán's economic base was grounded in low salaries and high inflation rates. Alemán's labor policies were geared toward containing the demands of labor to the benefit of the private sector. Additionally, the government cracked down on labor sectors that still exhibited autonomy, such as railroads and the oil industry.

Wealth was increasingly concentrated. For example, Héctor Aguilar Camín and Lorenzo Meyer note that "the percentage of income available to the poorer half of families in 1950 was 19 percent. ... [In] contrast, the top 20 percent in 1950 received 60 percent of available income" (1993: 164). By 1947 the volume of dollars spent on imported goods led to inflation, a devaluation of the peso, and an increase in popular unrest. As social conditions deteriorated for the majority, cinema shifted its eye to the poor in ghetto films, focusing on the *vecindad* (working-class housing project), the *arrabal* (slums and ghettos), and prostitution. For Monsiváis, the *arrabal* melodrama, which proliferated in the 1940s and 1950s, provided models of social behavior for those migrating to Mexico City and who were assimilating into urban modernity (1995: 125).

During the latter part of Alemán's six-year term, the film industry entered a period of prolonged crisis, the repercussions of which are still felt today. The crisis was caused by the loss of a great chunk of the international film market that Mexico had gained during the World War II period. The United States stopped subsidizing the growth of the Mexican film industry (via economic investment in the construction of modern studio facilities and providing film stock), as it no longer needed Mexican cinema to propagate "the American way of life." Hollywood films again flooded film markets, and a dynamic wave of new national cinemas (including Italian neorealism, the French new wave, new German cinema, Brazilian *cinema novo*, revolutionary Cuban cinema) provided alternative models of filmmaking and challenged the Hollywood studio system style of filmmaking and the star system after which Mexico's Golden Age cinema had been patterned. The closed-door union policies that all but barred the entrance of new directors, the pressures of the exhibition monopoly led by American entrepreneur William Jenkins, who held great influence in the State-administered lending agency (Banco Nacional Cinematográfico), as well as the advent of television led to the production of low-budget and formulaic films. These factors proved detrimental to the expansion of the Mexican film industry.

Produced at the tail end of the classic period, *Víctimas del pecado* (1950) is the third prostitution melodrama—after *Las abandonadas* (1944) and *Salón México* (1948)—made by the team of director Emilio Fernández, cinematographer Gabriel Figueroa, screenwriter Mauricio Magdaleno (the script is based on a story by Magdaleno), and editor Gloria Schoeman. *Víctimas del pecado* directly addresses conflicts between motherhood and sex work but unlike its predecessors does not punish the prostitute with death as in *Salón México* or with continual sacrifice and delayed gratification as in *Las abandonadas*. Emilio García Riera notes in his study of Fernández's extensive filmography that *Víctimas del pecado* received mixed reviews in Mexico, where critics attacked its "negative" representation of the urban poor and its salacious sensuality, while in France the film was hailed as being superior to *Salón México* (1987: 177–178). With time, new generations of Mexican critics have reevaluated *Víctimas del pecado,* highlighting its melodramatic hyper-realism and its exuberant depiction of nightclubs, popular music, and dance of the period, as well as Figueroa's incomparably rich compositions of cityscapes.

Packaged as a vehicle for its star, the "blonde" Cuban dancer-actress Ninón Sevilla, *Víctimas del pecado* remains true to Fernández's didactic nationalism while negotiating the seemingly irreconcilable mother/whore dichotomy. With the rhetoric of revolutionary nationalism as strong as in his films from the '40s, Fernández returns to a genre that addresses the decomposition of the nineteenth-century model of the family (with father as head of household) as a result of transformations introduced by urban modernity, changing gender roles, and the effects of years of a civil war that altered social relations. *Víctimas del pecado* posits solidarity across class lines and advocates for a family model not based on blood ties. The gutsy *rumbera* Violeta (Sevilla), who works as a dancer at the Club Changó, adopts a fellow female worker's child after the biological mother Rosa (Margarita Ceballos) is forced by her pimp and the father of the child, Rodolfo (Rodolfo Acosta), to abandon the newborn Juanito in a garbage can as the only condition under which he will take her back.

The plot focuses on Violeta's struggle to be both mother and cabaret performer/prostitute while being persecuted by the film's villain, Rodolfo, whom she turns in to police authorities, identifying him as the one responsible for a robbery and murder. Violeta is thrown out of the Club Changó when she refuses to give up Rosa's child, whom she rescued from a public garbage can minutes after the infant was dumped there by Rosa because Rodolfo commanded her to do so. The club owner does not permit workers to have children.

In a classic masochistic dialogue that suggests the high esteem Fernández places on female obedience, Rosa begs her lover-pimp, "Forgive me, Rodolfo! Do whatever you'd like to me, I deserve it all, but don't abandon me! I can't live without you! Say you'll forgive me! I will work day and night and everything I earn will be yours. I will obey your every command!" In a subsequent sequence, confirming Rosa's conviction that she prefers her man to her child, Violeta confronts Rosa, who is shown smiling but teary-eyed, dancing with a client. Rosa's response is, "Rodolfo has returned to me; he is the only one who matters to me in the world. . . . I would do it again to prove to Rodolfo that he is the most important person to me."

Out of necessity, Violeta turns to prostituting herself on street corners to earn a living and raise Juanito, when she meets Don Santiago (Tito Junco),

Margarita Ceballos must choose between keeping her newborn child or losing her boy-friend/pimp, Rodolfo Acosta, *Víctimas del pecado.* Courtesy Centro de Investigación y Enseñanza Cinematográficas, Universidad de Guadalajara.

who offers her a job at his club, La Máquina Loca. At La Máquina Loca, Violeta reprises her success as the star dancer and raises Juanito under the paternal guidance of Don Santiago. Rescued and redeemed from her life as a prostitute, Violeta and her adopted child, Juanito (Ismael Pérez), with Don Santiago constitute the ideal but fragile and beleaguered family in Fernández's eminently patriotic and didactic universe. Instead of aligning the exploited *rumbera* with the official icon of the law in the figure of the benevolent policeman, as in *Salón México,* the *rumbera* is this time aligned with the figure of Don Santiago, the saintly warrior-cum-businessman.

This new urban family is disrupted with the arrival of Rodolfo, who, after serving his prison sentence, makes his way to La Máquina Loca, where he confronts and kills Don Santiago. Violeta, frustrated by the abuse Juanito receives at the hands of Rodolfo, who tries to involve the child in his heists, kills Rodolfo. While Violeta is incarcerated, Juanito works shining shoes and selling newspapers. The single sequence given to

Ninón Sevilla, with baby in her arms, and Rodolfo Acosta at police station in *Víctimas del pecado*. Courtesy Centro de Investigación y Enseñanza Cinematográficas, Universidad de Guadalajara.

the young boy's livelihood is shot significantly at the Monument to Motherhood in Mexico City, newly inaugurated by President Alemán. Violeta is absolved of her crime when the prison director intervenes on her behalf and contacts the president of the republic, who issues her a pardon for her good behavior and exemplary maternal instincts. The film ends with a rear shot of mother and child walking out of the prison on Mother's Day into a backdrop of industrial fumes and trains. A male voice-over paternalistically encourages them to "go forward together until the light of goodness takes you far away, notwithstanding evil and ambition."

Film critic and historian Julia Tuñón notes that Fernández holds contradictory opinions with regard to prostitutes. To paraphrase his daughter, Adela Fernández, and Fernández's own statements culled from Tuñón, on the one hand he repudiates prostitutes because he believes some are naturally inclined toward sex work, while on the other hand he has a soft spot for prostitutes and tends to embrace them in order to redeem them

Ninón Sevilla shows Tito Junco (Don Santiago) her scarred face, a result of fighting off a sadistic pimp. *Víctimas del pecado.* Courtesy Filmoteca UNAM.

because he sees prostitutes as victims of society (2000: 152–154). This contradiction is played out in *Víctimas del pecado.*

Víctimas del pecado is a fantasy about the paternalistic State's investment in counteracting the disintegration of the traditional family. The rhetoric of the Alemán era promoting national unity and industrialization at all costs is mediated through cross-class alliances. Violeta and her adopted son are taken under the wing of the middle-class businessman Santiago, a good father figure with philanthropic tendencies. His paternalistic instincts are explained by his having lost his own son. A heroic figure, Santiago is aligned with populist ideologies and is marked as an authentically modern Mexican. In all outdoor sequences he is followed by a mariachi playing the song "El tren" (The train). Trains are an important symbol of the Revolution and are featured prominently in photography and films about the Revolution. Santiago is also associated with the working class, since railroad workers frequent his club. His status as protective warrior is underscored by being named after the Spanish military-religious order

The reconstituted and endangered nuclear family—Tito Junco, Ismael Pérez, Ninón Sevilla—celebrating their son's birthday in *Víctimas del pecado.* Courtesy Centro de Investigación y Enseñanza Cinematográficas, Universidad de Guadalajara.

dedicated to the apostle Santiago that was established in 1170 in the Iberian Peninsula to fight against Muslims. Here, Santiago fights against irresponsible father figures, the unproductive, and criminal forces of modern urban society represented by the *pachuco* Rodolfo. The *pachuco* belongs to an urban youth subculture for which the zoot suit is the supreme emblem of cool style.

As a negative yet intriguing model of modern masculinity, Rodolfo Acosta reprises his role from *Salón México* as the cold-hearted and manipulative *pachuco*-pimp. In *Víctimas del pecado*, the *pachuco* is both an attractive and repulsive emblem of the cosmopolitan dandy whose speech is a hybrid mix of Spanish, Caló, English, and French, a linguistic dexterity that marks him as decadent. His hip *pachuco* fashion style and subcultural linguistic and corporeal expressions are caricatured as narcissistic and vulgar and are marked as not Mexican. He is first shown eyeing himself studiously in the mirror while he dolls himself up for the evening.

His extravagant zoot suits make him a spectacular figure and render his style of masculinity as curiously unmanly. Acosta's slick and ruthless (and gum-chewing) brand of *pachuco* masculinity draws as much attention as Ninón Sevilla's star presence. Rodolfo's unmanly sense of style is paralleled by a lack of responsibility as father figure. A classic sequence from this film, mentioned earlier, depicts Rodolfo ruthlessly demanding that his lover Rosa dump their baby into a garbage can, which is strategically placed with the imposing Monument to the Revolution in the background, as the precondition for taking her back. Thus Rodolfo is a foil to the deadly serious, good father, Don Santiago.

Víctimas del pecado follows the conventions of the woman's picture by offering spectators the pleasure of identifying with an active, transgressive female character in the figure of Violeta, a feisty and glamorous performer.[33] As in *Salón México,* motherhood in *Víctimas del pecado* is represented as a willingness to sacrifice oneself for the sake of family and community. Women in Fernández's films, whether as schoolteachers, *soldaderas,* abnegated mothers, or prostitutes, are enlisted in the nation-building project as reproducers of family values. In Fernández's universe, women are heroic warriors in the service of patriarchal ideologies.

The urban setting and the representation of Mexico City's nightlife and sexual commerce underscore the commodification of female sexuality and women's incorporation into the modern urban workforce, laying out a set of tensions around the politics of motherhood and woman's labor. The film locates woman as mother in a grim and conflicted modern industrialized urban context where the train is a recurring musical and visual trope. As noted earlier, the image of the railroad, since the 1910 Revolution, has circulated widely in documentary newsreels, narrative film, photography, and the novel as one of the key icons of industrial modernity. With the Revolution, the railroad becomes the modern machine that links Mexico's citizens and joins the nation's far-flung regions. The sequence in which Violeta first approaches La Máquina Loca shows the cityscape in atmospheric, high-contrast light and shadow cinematography filled with locomotive and industrial fumes.

Víctimas del pecado is a tribute to motherhood and responsible parenting. When Violeta is expelled from the Club Changó because she refuses to give up Rosa's child as the club manager demands, the shrouded figure of Sevilla walking along the Nonoalco Bridge with the child in her arms recalls the iconography of the Virgin Mary caring for those in need of protection. Violeta's lack of success at finding a nanny to nurse her adopted child underscores the urgent need to recover and affirm the traditional values of motherhood. The presidential pardon that Violeta receives suggests that the State will reward the sacrifices of all hard-working citizens. Violeta's release from prison, her final reward for her multiple sacrifices, including domestic abuse, in her quest to raise Juanito absolves the State of all responsibility for not providing economic opportunities to working women who must earn a fair salary to support their family. The fact that in this Fernández film, punishment by death is not issued to a rebellious prostitute who breaks with the established patterns of submission to patriarchal domination boldly acknowledges changes in the social roles of women as heads of households. To a degree, the film honors female sex workers who choose this highly stigmatized labor out of necessity to raise their children and extended families. The State is ultimately represented as the benevolent redeemer of prostitutes, which through its revolutionary social agenda promotes the well-being of families, rather than being marked as complicit with the economic and social exploitation of working mothers and sex workers. The trite conclusion and far-fetched presidential pardon, however, register the persistence of unresolved social conflicts.

VIII. THIRD-WAVE NEW MEXICAN CINEMA: *DANZÓN* (1991)

An international critical and commercial success, María Novaro's *Danzón* is a woman's picture and travel narrative set mostly in Veracruz and steeped in the conventions of classic *cabaretera* melodramas.[34] While *Danzón* is neither a melodrama of prostitution nor strictly a *cabaretera* film, the cabaret-brothel milieu and its denizens are central to the film's narrative. Novaro's second feature film is co-scripted with her sister Beatriz Novaro, with whom she has collaborated on the subsequent films *El Jardín del Edén* (*The Garden of Eden,* 1994) and *Sin dejar huella* (*Without a Trace,* 1999), has the genre markers of the woman's picture as defined by Mary Anne Doane (1987). The Novaro sisters' adoption of the conventions of the woman's picture, however, is neither wholesale nor straightforward. The conventions of this Hollywood genre present in *Danzón* include the use of a female perspective, the focus on the figure of the mother, and the spectatorial address directed at a female audience. The film concerns itself with issues coded as feminine, such as the pursuit of romance, female desire linked to the pursuit of self-fulfillment, exercising agency, and engaging in various forms of pleasure (dance, feeling pretty and desired, attaining sexual and emotional gratification). The similarities end there, however, because, as I will show, while female desire in this film does conflict with the social expectations required of women, the conflict posed by changing gender roles is not insurmountable. Thus, unlike the conventional woman's picture (a Mexican example would be *Distinto amanecer*), *Danzón* does not sacrifice the woman's desire in an effort to plot a patriarchal resolution. Instead, *Danzón* accommodates and promotes female desire and independence, representing changes in gender roles in a positive light while not completely unsettling the status quo as do some *cabaretera* films such as *Aventurera* or Ripstein's scandalous remake of *La mujer del puerto* (1991).

Danzón follows Julia Solórzano (María Rojo), a working-class, middle-aged single mother and switchboard telephone operator from Mexico City who travels to the Gulf Coast of Mexico to the legendary port city of Veracruz in an attempt to locate her dance partner, Carmelo (Daniel Regis), an older gentleman with mulatto features, who has mysteriously disappeared.[35] While in Veracruz—the city that launched the *danzón* (both as dance and musical genre) throughout Mexico and the Americas—Julia is befriended by Susy (Tito Vasconcelos), a gay male drag queen and cabaret performer who, together with his/her friends, helps Julia look for Carmelo and assists in transforming Julia's sense of femininity. Julia's journey is also one of self-discovery and self-fulfillment. As Sergio González Rodríguez (1991) suggests in his review of the film, Julia's external journey to Veracruz in search of her dance partner turns out to be more significant as an internal (psychological) journey into what it means to be an urban, working-class, middle-aged, heterosexual, single mother in late-twentieth-century Mexico.

Since traditionally the man leads the woman in the *danzón,* this carefully scripted dance well illustrates how gendered power relations are inscribed and ritualized through cultural forms and practices. Novaro reverses the gender roles that structure the choreography of the *danzón* through the figure of the gay male drag queen in the sequence in which Julia teaches Susy how to dance the *danzón.* The reversal is staged because Susy, the biological male, refuses to perform the role of the man since s/he feels more comfortable playing the female role. While in Fernández's classic prostitution melodrama *Salón México* musical performance is used to reinscribe dominant gender relations, in *Danzón* musical performance is the vehicle through which to denaturalize and contest normative gender roles and gendered power relations.[36]

Role reversal: María Rojo leads Tito Vasconcelos in a dance lesson in *Danzón*. Courtesy Centro de Investigación y Enseñanza Cinematográficas, Universidad de Guadalajara.

Danzón intervenes by underscoring how relations of domination and subordination are gendered and how these are inscribed and reproduced through cultural forms and practices. For example, Susy teaches Julia that gender roles are not fixed and that gender is not biological but rather is socially constructed. Having learned the "charms" of celluloid femininity from Mexican cinema's famous *rumberas,* Susy teaches Julia how to become more feminine and how gender roles are performed—like the *danzón*—through stylized and theatrical displays of the body, movement, gesture, clothing, and makeup. In an interview with critic Patricia Vega, Novaro notes that "the transvestites are Julia's sentimental educators because they help her dare to live her real femininity" (1991: 28). The filmmaker's statement on gender oscillates between a social constructivist perspective that views femininity as a male social construct and notions of biological gender authenticity in Novaro's references to a "real femininity." The film's gender politics seem to be located in this space of contradiction and tension between discovering an authentic femininity and masquerading as a woman.

Novaro employs conventions from the classic *cabaretera* genre: night-life, Afro-Cuban music and dance performance, the focus on the working-class cultures, the "daily life" of female prostitutes, and, of course, the urban tropical setting. This return to conventions from a key Golden Age genre and to a traditional song and dance form (the *danzón*) resonates on various registers, notably expressing nostalgia for a period when the Mexican economy and film industry were flourishing. By setting most of the film in Veracruz, Novaro establishes intertextual references to *La mujer del puerto*, the foundational melodrama of prostitution that con-cludes with its tragic heroine committing suicide by throwing herself into the sea from one of the wharfs. In the aforementioned interview, Novaro stresses how her film attempts to recuperate values related to Mexicanness and to quality cinema associated with the Golden Age (Vega 1991: 29–30). The film does not, however, necessarily advocate a return to the gender politics of the 1940s *cabaretera* films. The new gender and sexual politics of the recuperated *danzón* and *cabaretera* films can be gauged by the film's incorporation of gay male culture. Veracruz is as famous for its rich legacy of male homosexual culture as is the city of Juchitán in Oaxaca.

Danzón reverses the *fichera* trope of wavering masculinity employed in the immensely popular 1970s prostitution subgenre discussed in Chap-ter Three by instead securing femininity while also calling its naturalness into question. The representation of the gay male drag queen as surrogate mother/caretaker figure and "sentimental educator" operates on vari-ous registers that contest both male and female representations of classic Mexican cinema. As in *fichera* movies, a gay male character is represented as an ally in the central heterosexual character's quest for self-identity.[37] In this case, Julia's quest for romance and "femininity" via the aid of Susy displaces the *fichera* and post-*fichera* subgenre's formula of employing gay male characters as narrative (and visual) vehicles to confirm the viril-ity of the central heterosexual male character. While the central conflict in *fichera* comedies is the sexual impotence that the lead male character suffers, in *Danzón* the narrative focus is not on masculinity in crisis but rather on examining ideologies of womanhood and femininity.

The intervention of Susy and her gay male friends in locating Julia's dance partner moves the narrative forward. The drag queen is also a crucial element in this film since s/he operates as a strategic device in contesting dominant gender and sexual ideologies and hence is key to rewriting the place of heterosexual romance and male-female relationships and motherhood in a woman's picture such as *Danzón*.[38] With Susy's encouragement, Julia has an affair with a young sailor and is able to leave the relationship behind, upon her return to Mexico City, without being stigmatized as an "easy woman," i.e., a whore. The drag queen posits a counter-option to patriarchal versions of heterosexual romance, similar to the manner in which the drag queen La Manuela in Ripstein's *El lugar sin límites* (1977) displaces the narrative and visual focus of the prostitution melodrama from femininity and heterosexuality to masculinity and homosexuality.

The film's conclusion, dramatizing Julia's return to Mexico City, her return to the dance hall, and her reunion with her dance partner, suggests a number of competing interpretations, the first being that only with Julia's return to her "conventional" life as mother and subordinate partner in the symbology of the *danzón* can she reestablish the previous order structuring her life. Upon her return to Mexico City, Julia has given up the gay male-fashioned fantasy of romance proffered and promoted by Susy and embodied by the young sailor to pursue instead her (traditional heterosexual) fantasy of the ideal old-school caballero, embodied by Carmelo and his generation's style of performing masculinity, like a caballero (gentleman).

Pursuing critic González Rodríguez's logic in his review of the film, one might ask to what degree Julia's multilayered journey has made a difference. Reading the film's conclusion against the grain suggests that the lessons learned by Julia on her quest to Veracruz (including that gender roles are not natural and fixed) cannot be contained by her apparently joyous re-embrace of the traditional steps of the *danzón* (with the woman following the man) and the implicit reestablishing of dominant gender roles as suggested by the film's closure. Instead, the destabilization of traditional gender roles initiated in Veracruz via the narrative devices of Julia's alliance with gay men, her contact with women who are both whores and mothers, and her affair with a younger man cannot easily be contained by the film's attempt at closure and the subsequent return to the dominant gender and sexual order. The knowing wink that Julia and Carmelo share during the middle of the closing *danzón* performance, coupled with the loving and somewhat ironic smile proffered by Julia in a moment of self-reflection, acknowledge her complicity in playing the subordinate role ascribed to women. Finally, one of the major differences in Julia's return to traditional gender roles is that throughout this last *danzón* performance, instead of

María Rojo breaks conventions and looks into her dance partner's eyes. Daniel Regis plays Carmelo in *Danzón*. Courtesy Centro de Investigación y Enseñanza Cinematográficas, Universidad de Guadalajara.

looking over Carmelo's shoulder to an indefinite point in space, as scripted by tradition, Julia this time follows Susy's advice and looks straight into Carmelo's eyes. Julia's look thus challenges the gendered gaze of male looking and female to-be-looked-at division, particularly when compared with representations of women in Golden Age *cabaretera* films.

Julia's return to an order regulated by male dominance does not cancel out the woman's point of view that Novaro uses in her film alternately to resist and uphold patriarchal values. Simultaneously, the return to heterosexual male dominance does not render gay males invisible. Following a convention initiated by *fichera* films in the early 1970s, *Danzón* also intervenes in rewriting gay male subculture back into the *cabaretera* genre. One sequence in particular, occurring midway in the film, quotes the dance-musical numbers from one of the dozens of *cabaretera* films produced from the 1930s through the '50s. The difference this time, how-ever, is that Novaro casts a famous gay male actor and activist, Tito Vas-concelos, in the role of the *rumbera* instead of Ninón Sevilla, Tongolele, or another tropical bombshell. The sequence depicting Susy performing "El coquero" in a *rumba* outfit celebrates the *rumbera* as a fabulous and fantastic figure, an icon of pleasure, an object of male desire and fantasy, one who seduces males and females alike, be they gay, straight, bisexual, or otherwise. The sequence self-reflexively denaturalizes the glamorous image of femininity constructed by the Mexican cinema. This sequence highlights the deliberately theatrical and performative aspects of gender through the use of gay male drag performance and the deliberate pans on the artificial breasts sitting on Susy's boudoir, the makeup, and costumes all connoting the psychoanalytic concept of woman as masquerade. In-deed, the film throughout underscores that femininity is a performance. Hence, Julia's return to the traditional order signified by the *danzón* is reintroduced with a level of self-reflection not commonly acknowledged in classic Mexican popular culture.

IX. CONCLUSION

In Mexican society, there is a threefold cult to women, mothers, and prostitutes, often collapsed in films and popular culture into a single ab-stracted figure who represents these three ideals simultaneously. Needless to say, social constructions of Mexican motherhood as a condition and identity that is thoroughly desexualized and based on sacrificing all for the well-being and happiness of children is at odds with reality. For women who are involved in sexual commerce and have children, the idealization of motherhood proves to be a heavier psychological burden.[39] As I have discussed, Mexican films belonging to the classic period play out the ten-sions, social stigma, and shame experienced by sex workers who are also mothers. This conflict remains constant across decades and is repeatedly expressed in social science research about prostitution. Perhaps no event better encapsulates this struggle than the actions taken by Mexico City sex workers in the late 1930s to guard their rights as mothers and workers when their way of making a living was threatened by government efforts to limit the number of women working in cabarets and to dismantle the zones where prostitution was permitted. According to historian Kather-ine Elaine Bliss, "Women who had worked in sexual commerce insisted that their work was temporary and that it was in no way reasonable or just to deny them the right to be mothers and to take care of their children merely because they worked in a 'shameful industry'" (2001: 196). As Bliss argues, authorities did not succeed in eradicating prostitution and effectively controlling the spread of contagious venereal diseases in Mexico City because their reformist measures and the rhetoric of promoting a "revolutionary morality" did not seriously address the sexual habits of men, changing Mexican society's ideas about women's sexuality, nor did the campaign incorporate the concerns of women or prostitutes.

Statistics from an early 1990s report issued by the Mexican government agency involved in investigating AIDS, Conasida, indicate that 80 percent of sex workers have children (Ojeda 1996: 55). A contemporary account by Claudia Colimoro, president of Mujeres por la Salud en Acción contra las Enfermedades de Transmisión Sexual y el Sida (MUSA, Women for Health Fighting Against Sexually Transmitted Diseases and AIDS), explains that the social stigma attached to prostitution pushes working mothers who are involved in the sex industry to lead double lives, hiding their real occupation from family and friends by leading them to believe that they work as maids or nurses (ibid.).

Colimoro argues in favor of legalizing sex work and taxing the wages of sex workers to ensure that they receive social benefits and equal protection before the law and to contribute to changing public opinion to humanize prostitutes. "We need more than health projects; we need social security, low-income housing, medical assistance, tax rights as any other workers, education, as it says in the constitution. We generate a lot of indirect employment, we are a world of people. What we need is legislation similar to labor laws. . . . We must have the opportunity to be treated equally. We are all asking for respect. We need respect, each one of us" (Colimoro and Cabezas 1998: 197). Colimoro says this would be a positive step toward integrating sex workers into the fabric of Mexican society and dispelling the widespread belief that they are a social problem. Carolina, a woman who has worked in the sex industry for twenty-two years, echoes the common desire expressed by sex workers to be seen by Mexican society as human beings: *una también es gente, no sólo aquella puta* (we are also human, not just that anonymous whore; Aranda Luna 1990: 106).[40]

In this chapter I exposed the significance of the relationship between the figure of the prostitute and Mexican cultural nationalist representations of womanhood. Prostitution is an allegory for the nation, and discourse about prostitution reveals the social relations that have historically shaped the private and public regulation of women's sexual agency. Prostitutes are emblematic social agents embodying Mexican modernity's anxieties, desires, and contradictions. My intention is neither to romanticize nor to glorify sex work, but rather I provide some interpretations concerning the unusually important role that prostitutes, prostitution, and the spaces linked to sexual activities and entertainment have in Mexican history, society, and culture.

The prostitute crosses spatial boundaries and transgresses familial, moral, and sexual norms. She is an icon of *mexicanidad* and of the urban experience of modernity. In a similar fashion, Pedro Infante's star image and cultural legacy have complex and multiple interpretations. Just as the prostitute, cast as the quintessential fallen heroine, is the necessary Other for the construction of "proper" Mexican womanhood, Infante is the archetype of the modern Mexican man, the bridge between traditional models of masculinities and the predecessor to the postmodern and post-national Mexican masculinities as embodied by actor Gael García Bernal. The rich textures of Infante's performances of being a man and the prostitute's multivalent embodiment of sexuality and *mexicanidad* are symbols of Mexico's conflicted transition to modernity. The next chapter extends my analysis of cinematic representations of gender and the engendering modalities of nationalism both conceptually and temporally; from the period of the master narratives of national origins we move now into the populism of the 1940s and '50s musical "buddy movies" starring Infante.

2

Pedro Infante Unveiled

Masculinities in the Mexican "Buddy Movie"

✢   ✢   ✢

When I watch Pedro's movies I'm watching the lives of my people, past, present, and future, parade in front of me. Pedro Infante could have been my father, he was my father's age when I was born. He's the man our men want to be. And he's the man we imagine ourselves to be if we are men. The man we want our daughters to love. Pedro's the beautiful part of our dreaming. And his looks still have the power to make my woman's blood heat up like sizzling manteca on an old but faithful sartén. Just watching him on the screen makes my little sopaipilla start throbbing underneath all the folds and tucks of cloth on the old and creaky theater seat, just give me some honey.

DENISE CHÁVEZ, *LOVING PEDRO INFANTE*

𝓘n Mexican popular culture, the sexual and gender transgressions of the archetypal Mexican macho are a constant source of pleasure, fun, and banter. One need only look to the tradition of the *albur* to find sayings such as *macho probado es macho calado* (a real man is he who has been fucked by another man) or the near-universal joke—

> *¿Cuál es la diferencia entre un mexicano homosexual y uno que no lo es?*
>
> *Dos copas.*
>
> [What is the difference between a Mexican homosexual and one who isn't?
>
> Two drinks.][1]

Despite the fact that male homosexuality figures prominently in Mexico's picaresque tradition, it is no less at odds with the country's cult of machismo. Given this uneasy and highly charged context, it is fitting to look for variations regarding what it means to be a man in Mexico and how masculinity and sexuality is experienced and expressed. The films of actor-singer Pedro Infante, the most revered performer of the Golden Age period and an object of desire for both women and men during and after his lifetime, provide an intriguing source for such an investigation. By analyzing the representations of the male bonding rituals in four of his most popular films, I wish to tease out the anxieties around the relationship between gender and style, manhood and national identifications, as these are shaped by the intersections of age, class, ethnic, racial, regional, and sexual differences.

Decades after his death, Pedro Infante (1917–1957) continues to be a source of national pride and an object of unparalleled adoration.[2] Many biographers have dubbed him *el máximo ídolo de México* [Mexico's leading idol]. His cult status is reproduced across generations of film and music audiences for whom Infante—affectionately called Pedrito by his fans—continues to be the most revered national icon for Mexicans both inside and outside the geographic boundaries of the nation. April 15, the anniversary of Infante's untimely death in a piloting accident at age forty, is an unofficial day of commemoration for Mexicans. In the United States, the anniversary of his death is noted in the evening news broadcast by Univisión, the largest Spanish-language television network in the United States, which is partly owned by Televisa, Latin America's most powerful multimedia conglomerate.

Infante embodied the collective hopes and dreams of Mexico's popular sector during the cultural consolidation of the post-revolutionary nation-state. Today, his popularity seems secured in the greater Mexican transnational collective imaginary. The identification of Mexicans and Chicanas/os with Infante is reinforced through frequent television reruns of his films in Mexico and in the United States and through their circulation on video and DVD and other cultural products such as musical recordings, fan magazines, and literature, as is clearly evident in the epigraph from Denise Chávez's novel (2001). Infante's fame is continuously revitalized and reinvented through audiovisual and print media as well as gallery and museum exhibitions.[3] He is among the few to be given the special recognition of being called *el hijo del pueblo* (the people's son).

Throughout his film career Infante often represented the archetypal, post-revolutionary, not-quite-domesticated, working-class migrant from the provinces.[4] He seems forever inscribed as *el muchacho alegre* (the cheerful young man). He portrayed the Mexican common man who is driven by his passions, be they related to the family in general, mother figures in particular, female lovers, musical performance, drinking, and hanging out with his buddies, his *cuates*.[5]

In examining the multiple and sometimes contradictory meanings that Infante's performance of Mexican masculinities has for different spectators, I posit that masculinity is not fixed and monolithic but open to contestation, change, and resignification. My goal is to suggest that we can learn a great deal about Mexican masculinities, society, and culture in the 1940s and 1950s by being attentive to the ambiguities and tensions in Infante's buddy movies. As such, the sexual ambiguities and anxieties surrounding the social institution of *compadrismo*,[6] a close-knit friendship bond and a form of extended family, and the ties between men register a threefold crisis: first, a crisis in Mexico's patriarchal system; second, a crisis in the nation's official "macho" identity; and third, the crisis facing the Mexican film industry once World War II ended, altering the conditions that facilitated the emergence of the Golden Age.[7] In Infante's buddy movies, the representations of the bonds between *cuates* both exceed and uphold compulsory heterosexuality. They actively court homoeroticism only to barely repress and contain it through compulsory heterosexual opposite-sex couplings played out in narratives involving erotic triangulations where women both facilitate and block the physical and affective ties between men.

Through close textual readings I will show how the narrative, visual, and aural codes of the Mexican buddy movie introduce sexual ambiguity and register anxieties about heterosexual masculinity through male homosocial bonds (same-sex social interactions). These tensions are a response to a number of social factors, including the slowdown of the so-called economic miracle Mexico experienced during the World War II period and the changing role of women through their participation in the labor market and electoral politics. Women's increasing visibility and power in the public sphere is hence perceived as a threat to patriarchal privileges and as a potential feminization of Mexican masculinities.[8]

Analyzing four of Infante's most important buddy movies, all musical comedies—*El gavilán pollero* (1950), *ATM (A toda máquina)* (1951), its sequel *¿Qué te ha dado esa mujer?* (1951), and finally *Dos tipos de cuidado*

(1952)—I argue that the representations of the bonds between *cuates* deliberately criss-cross the boundaries between homosociality and homosexuality. Indeed, the association of homosexuality with machismo and nationalism plays a central role in defining post-revolution Mexican (heterosexual) masculinities.

Infante's buddy movies provide the occasion for analyzing the spaces (cabarets and cantinas), the cultural practices and expressions (music, humor, word play), and the codes of honor that make up the glue of male homosocial relations. In these films it is clear that homosocial practices and expressions are central to the construction and stylization of Mexican masculinities. In these films male homosocial bonds are reconfigured and strengthened in cantinas or cabarets through musical performance, functioning as the privileged space and the discursive modality through which singular, bounded, and fixed notions of heterosexual masculinity are simultaneously challenged, modified, and reinscribed. The ideological importance accorded to the nightlife spaces of the cabaret and the cantina provide clues for determining the role male homosexuality plays in structuring male subjectivities and, in particular, for considering how male homosexuality fits into Mexican popular culture. Collectively, the film texts analyzed, in the context of Mexican film history and Mexico's sexual subcultures, reveal how heterosexual concepts of manhood are co-articulated with those of male homosexuality.

Because Infante is so intimately associated with *mexicanidad,* I am aware that to proffer queer readings of his films can be misconstrued as an attempt to defame the reputation of Mexico's most cherished son. Therefore, I want to make it clear that my intention in using a queer lens to unveil the silences and conflicting erotic desires present in his films is to enrich and expand his cultural legacy by multiplying the number of interpretive possibilities available. From this perspective, Infante's buddy movies give us a way to examine how Mexican popular culture accommodates and in fact produces male homosocial and homoerotic expressions, such as the *albur.* They provide ways to understand how homophobic and misogynist agendas underpin the celebratory, and often homoerotically infused, relations between *cuates.*

Additionally, these films open a space for examining the visual and narrative codes used to include, diffuse, and/or contain homoerotic representations in films from the classic period.[9] Finally, I propose that the representation of male homosociality in Infante's buddy movies, along with other films from the classic period, provides a foundation for mapping the emergence of queer representations in Mexico's rich and varied film history. I suggest that the ambiguities in the texts allow spectators to read Infante as a queer icon.[10] Infante's performances also can tell us much about the social construction and symbolic representations of Mexican masculinities in the years during and after World War II. This chapter identifies and celebrates an underresearched queer legacy in Mexican film. Simultaneously, I also suggest how models of Mexican celluloid masculinities depart from how "white" masculinities in Hollywood and European films have been theorized by film scholars in the last three decades.

I. QUESTIONS OF SPECTATORSHIP

As I stated in the introduction, how audiences interpret any given text is determined by the specificities of historical and sociocultural location. Queerness is indeed readily available in texts that are presumably straight and that predominantly concern themselves with heterosexual issues. Moreover, Doty's arguments surveyed earlier regarding the centrality of queerness in mainstream culture serve as a model to read Infante's classic buddy movies and provide a method for locating a history of queer visibility in Mexican cinema.

Doty (2000) revisited and revised his central argument when he wrote that he had to go the extra mile to prove to resistant audiences that he was not reading queerness into the texts in acts of wishful thinking. He objected to the accusations that he co-opted mainstream texts in order to impose a "minority interests" agenda. In academic conferences and lecture presentations my research on Infante's buddy movies has, at times, similarly been dismissed as flat-out wrong and as "reading too much into the text." However, I concur with Doty that queer readings are as valid as straight readings and that queer interpretive practices exist alongside straight or preferred readings.

Doty goes against an inherited critical tradition of "closet reading" that locates queerness in mainstream texts as something subtextual, connotative, secretive, hidden, and masked. He argues instead that "any text is always already potentially queer" (2000: 2). Reframing queer reading practices in this way challenges "dominant representational [and] interpretive regimes that seek to make queerness 'alternative' or 'sub' straight" (2). This theoretical position avoids what he calls "heterocentric traps" and narrow understandings of queerness that assume "that all characters in a film are straight unless labeled, coded, or otherwise obviously proven to be queer" (2–3).

Doty thus seeks to expand the frames of reference that define queerness in stereotypical ways. He argues for more nuanced and complex understandings of queer expressions of sexuality and eroticism in daily life and in representation. He writes,

> In an era when only the most insistently ignorant still think all straights or all gays, lesbians, bisexuals and other queers look and act the same, why do most people still register "queer" only when confronted with visual and aural codes drawn from a narrow (and often pejoratively charged) range? . . . Queerness is frequently expressed in ways other than by nude bodies in contact, kissing, or direct verbal indicators; the reasons for finding different means of expression are many—psychological (fear, repression), cultural (oppression), and institutional (censorship, commerce). Even aside from constraints imposed by these considerations, however, queerness is often (and freely) expressed in subtle ways. (3–5)

Doty challenges readers to think outside of conventional "commonsense" and predetermined labels, categories, and definitions so that we can acknowledge "the complexities of human feeling, understanding, and behavior" (9).

Similarly, Michael DeAngelis's study on gay male fandom and crossover stardom "responds to continuing debates regarding the interrelation of narrative modes, fantasy operations, and the social practices of individual spectators and spectatorial 'communities'" (2001: 235). He argues that queer theory and star studies provide directions for studying "the instability of star/spectator relations across time" (235). His illuminating study examines "the reception strategies that gay men have used to structure their relations with . . . stars" (234). He suggests that gay male appropriations of stars are "fantasies" that "empower disenfranchised subcultures to 'claim' popular cultural icons" (235). Spectators, he writes, "construct their own private versions of public celebrity figures" (236). In this chapter, I advance my claim that the cult of Pedro Infante includes gay and queer fans. It is commonly repeated that women sexually desire Infante and that men want to be like him. What is left out is that some men also sexually desire Infante.

Infante's sexuality is not by any stretch of the imagination tied to a single object of desire or sexual aim; his multiple "romantic" affairs and love

Pedro Infante: muscle man. Courtesy Centro de Investigación y Enseñanza Cinematográficas, Universidad de Guadalajara.

of women underscore an endless quest for pleasure and sexual satisfaction. Infante scattered his "manly seed" across Mexico and the Americas. Several women claim to be the mothers of his children. His films and the manner in which his off-screen "private" life circulated in fan magazines and other media coverage repeatedly sanctioned his polygamy, thereby reinforcing the claim that men are promiscuous by nature. His seemingly polite, fun-loving, charming, and seductive ways with both women and men reinforce the belief that Pedro *era demasiado hombre para una sola mujer* (was too much a man for just one woman). Infante indulged in physical pleasure and other forms of sensual excess, from eating to fornicating. His sexual prowess is legendary, as are stories passed on from generation to generation about the countless number of women he supposedly slept with. According to film critic Gustavo García, author of the most recent biography about the performer, Infante could not say no to sexual proposals because he did not like to disappoint. One of Infante's most notable orgiastic escapades took place during a visit to Havana. According to García, Infante had sexual intercourse with more than forty women in one day—all fans who patiently waited outside his hotel room for their turn.[11] Perhaps it is not too far-fetched to speculate that Infante was a sex addict.

Pedro Infante and Sara Montiel in *El enamorado*. Courtesy Centro de Investigación y Enseñanza Cinematográficas, Universidad de Guadalajara.

Infante was an actor "whose sexual objectification was authorized by the mainstream press" and by his active role in constructing his star persona (DeAngelis 2001: 236). Infante enthusiastically participated in displaying his body through his interest in physical fitness and the culture surrounding it. Press coverage described Infante as an emblem of a disciplined, healthy, athletic, authentic, and natural man of working-class roots. His toned and muscular body was complemented by his *el muchacho alegre* image, a Latin lover, Mexican-style, always ready to party. Infante's on- and off-screen image is coded as honest, unassuming, accessible, and incorrigibly playful; he is synonymous with stereotypically Mexican proclivities to indulge in *relajo* and *vacilar* (playfulness and joking). As I discuss in other sections of this chapter, Infante possessed a duality. He seems to easily downplay or reactivate his virile attributes while at the same time demonstrating sentimentality, vulnerability, an almost childlike playfulness, and a masochistic predisposition to stoically endure sacrifice and humiliation for the sake of maintaining the honor of the family. This malleable image facilitates queer appropriation.

In the next section I discuss how the media, audiences, and critics have constructed the Infante mythology. I address some of the reasons why he continues to be the leading Mexican idol, why so many are compelled to adore him, and why Infante's rendering of Mexican masculinities is still so attractive to his fans.

II. SUPERSTAR CULT: THE MAKING OF
EL ÍDOLO DEL PUEBLO

Infante's rags-to-riches rise to fame was single-handedly shaped by director Ismael Rodríguez, who passed away in 2004. In their collaborations, both actor and director created their most enduring works. The Infante-Rodríguez team created Infante's eminently charismatic image: alternately a devoted rural son in the two-part films *Los tres García/Vuelven los García* (The Three Garcías/The Return of the Garcías, 1946) and *La oveja negra/No desearás la mujer de tu hijo* (The Black Sheep/You Shall Not Desire Your Son's Wife, 1949), the fully urbanized, working-class trickster figure who transgresses and upholds social conventions in *ATM (A toda máquina)* and *¿Qué te ha dado esa mujer?* (1951), and the idealized devoted urban father figure in Rodríguez's urban trilogy beginning with *Nosotros los pobres* (We the Poor, 1947) and followed by *Ustedes los ricos* (You the Rich, 1948) and *Pepe el toro* (Pepe the Bull, 1952). When he portrayed a son or father figure, Infante's roles were fully imbued with sacrificial tendencies and a willingness to take whatever means necessary to ensure the well-being of his family and friends. His artistic legacy includes some 310 recordings and a total of 59 films, with 55 starring roles, made between 1942 and 1956. Only his contemporary Jorge Negrete rivaled his status as the Golden Age's preeminent singer. Infante's death in 1957, two years after Negrete passed away, also marked the end of the Golden Age of Mexican cinema.

The profound public affection for Infante is underscored by accounts of his extraordinary funeral services, with more than 150,000 mourning fans present and a riot at the cemetery.[12] The 1963 documentary *Así era Pedro Infante* (*Portrait of Pedro Infante*), directed by Ismael Rodríguez and narrated by actor Arturo de Córdova, includes footage of the masses of people lining the streets of Mexico City as their idol's body was transported in a hearse. In 1991 a commemoration of the anniversary of his death gathered some 15,000 fans in Mexico City.

Nosotros los pobres, one of the most commercially successful and loved Mexican films of all times, holds a cultural status in Mexico equivalent to that of *The Wizard of Oz* in the United States. Pepe el Toro, played by Infante in the trilogy, functioned as an alter-ego for many Mexican males as well as an object of desire for both genders because of the respect, authority, and physical and sexual prowess he demonstrated in his *vecindario,* the modest housing complex where he lived and worked.

The cult of Pedro Infante has produced a veritable cultural industry.[13] A Mexico City radio station has for years programmed a daily Pedro Infante hour. Tellingly, of all the performers of the classic period star system, Infante's films and those of the comedian Cantinflas are the only complete body of Mexican films available on video, for sale or rent, in both the United States and Mexico. Most importantly, Infante's films and his music are in constant circulation on television, video, radio, and compact disks, introducing new generations of spectators in Mexico and in the United States to his work. The commodification of Infante ranges from his image on national lottery tickets to, more recently, a brand of tequila that bears his name. Curiously enough, Infante preferred cognac because unlike tequila, it did not decrease his sexual stamina. Photographic reproductions of stills from Infante's films, live musical performances, and off-screen life continue to circulate in print media and on the Internet.

Infante's working-class origins, together with his many occupations and hobbies—including that of carpenter, with its Christ-like connotations—contributed greatly to the authenticity with which he portrayed charming and long-suffering migrant working-class men from northern Mexico. All these components facilitated mass working-class audience identification with Infante. His biographers repeatedly draw on his off-screen and on-screen image to emphasize how his popularity registers a profound identification between Pedro and *el pueblo* (Infante Quintanilla, 1992: 46).

How then can we explain this phenomenon? Anne Rubenstein argues that the Infante cult is associated with "moral and physical perfection as well as national pride" (2001: 126). She notes that Infante personifies four ideal models of masculinity: an urban *charro,* a sentimental macho, a working-class common man, and a wealthy and successful man. "In all of his guises," she writes, "Infante represents a living vision of what it might mean to be Mexican" (126). The Infante cult is a product of marketing and the commodification of *mexicanidad*. As symbolic capital, the Infante cult registers complex social processes and forms of identification. As mediator, Infante gave voice to the popular sector, since he was considered part of it.

Cristina Pacheco's *crónica* "Pedro Infante no ha muerto" (Pedro Infante Has Not Died), written in 1984, documents why his fans consider him *la voz del pueblo* (the voice of the people) as well as *el máximo representante del pueblo mexicano* (the ultimate representative of the Mexican people). The actor's first official fan club, the Club de Admiradores de Pedro Infante, was established in 1958, shortly after his death. Froylán Flores, president of the club in 1984, notes the membership requirements:

> To belong to this club you only need pay fifty pesos a month and have a profound admiration, from deep in your heart, for that incomparable man, for that unique actor, for that singer for whom I find no words to describe, and that we all know as Pedro Infante. (Cited in Pacheco 1992: 217)[14]

For this fan, Infante is both exceptional and beyond language. Don Froylán cannot find words that adequately describe the feelings Infante elicits.

The overriding common denominator of fan identification is class status, followed closely by his working-class on-screen occupations: auto mechanic, carpenter. Infante appeals to both men and women in equal degrees. An unnamed female fan interviewed by Pacheco in her *crónica* gives the following testimony:

> Look, for starters I need to tell you one thing. Mexico has had many idols known as the greatest in music. There you have Jorge Negrete, who people say even sang opera and everything. We do admire him, but we never really felt identified with him. Why? Well I'll explain it in a simple manner: Negrete ate bread, while Pedro ate tortillas like all of us. (Pacheco 1992: 220)

Another female fan identified by Pacheco as Gloria Juárez de González says,

> I saw Pedro for the first time in 1955 in the film *Nosotros los pobres*. I was so impressed by him! I think that Pedrito's work made us feel

we were on the same level. While I was watching the film, I felt as if I was reliving parts of my own life, moments from my history, my problems, and the sad moments in my life. . . . I completely identified with Pepe el Toro, especially during certain tragic moments in his life. For example, the scene where he is in pain after seeing his son's burnt body. I lived through similar experiences since my little boy almost died from drinking gasoline. . . . No other person in cinema spoke like us as much as Pedrito did. No other actor was capable of embodying and expressing the problems of the poor as much as he did. He interpreted us and represented us with a force that even politicians lack. (221, 224)

Fans identified with Infante because they themselves were struggling to adapt to modernity and the social problems caused by the urban explosion. Infante's performances clearly show how deeply he identified with the experiences of poor Mexicans. The dignity and strength that he conveyed in his roles uplifted and empowered his fans.

By the mid-1940s, Mexico City had a population of three million, while the population of the nation surpassed twenty-five million. The quintessential Infante urban melodrama of migration, the 1952 film *Un rincón cerca del cielo* (A Place Near Heaven), glorifies poverty, victimization, and family through narrative tropes of disillusionment, failure, suffering, and redemption. This film, along with *Nosotros los pobres* and others, is profoundly conservative. It naturalizes social inequalities and asks audiences to see poverty as more desirable than wealth, since the wealthy are stereotyped as a cold, callous, and unhappy lot.

Carlos Monsiváis notes that Infante served as the bridge between the abandoned traditions of the rural past and the adaptations required by the modern, industrialized, urban environment (1986: 2). Judging from his continued popularity, Infante, as screen ideal, continues to mediate the contradictions of modernity for mass audiences across the Spanish-speaking Americas.

III. A MEXICAN DON JUAN?

Neither Golden Age actors Pedro Armendáriz's noble macho nor Jorge Negrete's arrogant landowning *hacendado* brand of machismo, or even, for that matter, Arturo de Córdova's intense Freudian-inflected neurosis or his cosmopolitanism allowed the kind of gender and sexual transgressions found in Infante's buddy movies. Only Cantinflas's beloved underclass *peladito* (a picaresque figure associated with the urban poor and racialized as mestizo) competes with the melodramatic emotional excesses and the gender- and sexual-bending transgressions proffered by Infante's on- and off-screen star image. The characters portrayed by Infante were not afraid to display their emotions, particularly pain, anguish, and vulnerability. Again, it is instructive to pause when Monsiváis compares and contrasts Negrete to Infante, a comparison that hinges on how class difference and social status shape how each actor-singer performs his masculinity.

On one hand, Infante's star image signifies a radical departure from the dominant image of the aggressive, arrogant, *criollo* (Mexican-born but of "white" Spanish ancestry), upper-class Mexicans like Negrete. On the other hand, men from the popular sectors, often mestizo, are negatively coded as promiscuous, hard-drinking, and irresponsible; they are often not good family providers. Infante stands in the middle. The characters Infante plays are kind, humble, approachable, human, imperfect, rarely violent, playful, and emotionally expressive. Infante's version of the new macho both departs from and reinscribes stereotypical traits. Infante represents a positive machismo. The range of roles Infante embodied encompasses culturally specific differences between Mexican men based on class, ethnicity, age, and regional origins that challenge uniform and monolithic notions of an unchanging, essential Mexican masculinity and homogeneous understandings of macho and machismo.

The new model of masculinity proffered by Infante depends on his highly expressive qualities as an actor, on his plasticity. Infante's acting abilities span a full emotional spectrum of melodrama, musicals, comedies, tragedies, action-adventure, historical films. His repertoire includes excessive melodramatic moments depicting searing pain caused by the loss of loved ones, as in a sequence in *Vuelven los García* when he is shown crying at the graveside of his grandmother in the midst of a raging thunderstorm. In *Pepe el Toro,* Infante portrays a charismatic and playful father figure whose musical versatility is displayed through charming renditions of children's songs by the popular singer-composer known as Cri Cri. In *Islas Marías* (Emilio Fernández, 1950), Infante personifies the unselfish and long-suffering son who is willing to serve time in prison for the crimes of his delinquent brother. In *La vida no vale nada* (Life Is Worthless, Rogelio A. González, 1954) he portrays a philandering, alcoholic womanizer in need of domestication through marriage and monogamy.

Off and on screen, Infante embodies stereotypes of the Mexican macho as a Latin lover who is driven by his sexual instincts and who is a master of seduction. A recent study of *Nosotros los pobres* points out the operative gender double standards:

> The comments that characters make contribute to build Pepe el Toro's Juan Tenorio image. He is the "seductive" gentleman that all women chase and with whom they flirt. Men can do with their sexuality "whatever they please," even if they lose their reputation. Just like when Pepe el Toro tells the prostitute: "I lose nothing by talking to you because I am a man" (de la Peza 1998: 50).

A famous dream sequence in *Los tres García* depicts Infante dressed as a *charro* looking away in disdain from a group of women in mourning. He calls them *las abandonadas* (the abandoned women, meaning his ex-girlfriends). They kneel before him, their eyes cast upon him, imploring his attention and affection. The sequence is not without a sense of humor and a healthy measure of self-consciousness.

This film is a tongue-in-cheek celebratory fantasy about the alluring and irresistible charms of the Mexican macho man popularized by the Mexican film industry. It is not coincidental that *Los tres García* is the film that catapulted Infante to fame, for in it he plays a character who pretty much sums up the characteristics of the stereotypical cinematic Mexican macho. This film also stages the Mexican Oedipal narrative of the strong bond between mother and son, another distinctive component of the archetypal Mexican male.

Los tres García focuses on the relationship between three competitive and querulous cousins—Luis Antonio (Pedro Infante), Luis Manuel (Victor Manuel Mendoza), José Luis (Abel Salazar)—and their widowed grandmother, Doña Luisa García (Sara García), and the young men's attempts to win over the heart of their blonde Mexican-American cousin, Lupita Smith (Marga López), who is visiting. Each member of the trio has his unique traits that if combined would embody the ideal man. Doña Luisa plays a critical part in forming the opinions the audience can have about the male characters in the film. As the head of household she is overtly masculinized. She carries a cane and smokes huge cigars, a practice that separates her from the rest of the women in the film. As the figure of power and authority, she spends much of the film disciplining the young men when they get out of hand. She is the only person they both fear and respect.

Pedro Infante with his ex-girlfriends at his feet, *Los tres García*. Courtesy Centro de Investigación y Enseñanza Cinematográficas, Universidad de Guadalajara, Películas Rodríguez S.A. de C.V., and Cinematográfica Rodríguez S.A. de C.V.

Doña Luisa's favorite is Luis Antonio (Infante); he, in turn, is also the most attached to her emotionally. Luis Antonio is promiscuous, has many girlfriends, and is a playboy prone to partying (*parrandero*) who breaks into song whenever he becomes emotional. In *Los tres García* he is cocky, temperamental, emotionally immature, and highly expressive. At one point, he bursts into his grandmother's birthday celebration giving the classic Mexican *grito* (shout), swigging on a bottle of tequila; dressed in complete *charro* outfit, he is accompanied by a complete mariachi and performs "Mi cariñito." The song is a hymn to motherhood and a celebration of the deep bond between mother and son. Mexico's history and culture are profoundly shaped by *marianismo,* the institutionalized cult to Nuestra Señora de Guadalupe. Given this context, the mother is positioned as the most important woman in a Mexican man's life; she is valued above all other women, including wives and lovers. In *Los tres García* the grandmother gets so excited by Infante's musical performance and by his affirmation of his unbridled devotion to her that she returns the praises with the distinctive Mexican *grito*. As in other national projects, here motherhood functions to sustain and reproduce the patriarchal family structure.

Beginning in the 1930s, Mexico's burgeoning culture industry popularized the figure of the *charro* and the idealized pastoral life of the hacienda via the *comedia ranchera* and *ranchera* music, a trend begun with Fernando de Fuentes's film *Allá en el rancho grande* (1936). The *charro*, strongly associated with the pre-revolutionary landowning elite, is paradoxically celebrated, elevated onto a pedestal, and transformed into the quintessential embodiment of the post-revolutionary nation. Thus, the *charro* is at odds with the populist politics of the 1930s, notably agrarian reform. The *comedia ranchera*'s nostalgia for a rural past untouched by the class conflict ushered in by the Revolution is frequently interpreted as a sign of the anxieties felt by the Porfirian elite. The *comedia ranchera* registers the conservative, authoritarian, and paternalistic political strain that marks Mexico's political culture, especially after Lázaro Cárdenas's presidency.

The narrative focus on three highly differentiated Garcías—personality, style, and the manner in which they perform their masculinity—ultimately seeks to create a model of the most desirable man who would be a composite of the Garcías' most positive traits. The film is clearly slanted in favor of Infante. The two female characters are the vehicles that channel and promote desire for and identification with Infante. Infante is associated with new and old Mexican vernacular traditions including *ranchera* music, the *charro*, tequila, sentimentalism, virility, and an Oedipus complex. The film pointedly promotes the idea that the *charro* outfit separates the men from the boys. *Los tres García* promotes the *charro* as a romantic symbol of rural fatherland (*patria*), honor, and manliness. When one of the nephews appears in a *charro* outfit instead of the business suit with which he is identified, Doña Luisa declares: *Vaya, ya era día que te vistas como un verdadero hombre* (It's about time you started dressing like a real man). Infante's breakthrough film participates in elevating the *charro* as the quintessential symbol of masculine *mexicanidad*.

Infante is Mexico's first music and film performer of working-class origins to simultaneously hold a monumental heroic status in the popular national imaginary while being an erotic symbol at the same time. Infante circulated as a male pin-up, an example of the (im)perfect man. Photo spreads display Infante striking poses for the camera bare-chested, offering his body as product of the labor of weight lifting and sport (notably boxing), exhibiting his formidable musculature that is not bulging and overdeveloped as evidence that he earned his good health (although he had diabetes) and exquisite physique through hard work. These examples of Infante's investment in his physique also include the nude photograph discussed in the preface that was allegedly taken by his brother-in-law, Guillermo López Castro, in 1939 of a twenty-two-year-old Infante taking a shower in an outdoor patio or rooftop setting. Infante's body, particularly his muscular upper torso, is frequently displayed in his films. In *Nosotros los pobres,* playing the carpenter Pepe el Toro, Infante wears a tight striped shirt that accentuates his muscular build. We are not allowed to see his nude upper torso until near the end of the film when in three separate sequences he gets into a brutal fight with a ruffian who is responsible for the crime for which Pepe is incarcerated. Infante's films from the 1950s more frequently exhibit his broad bare chest and shoulders and back in moments of pure spectacle that clearly encourage the spectator to take pleasure in looking at his body as an erotic object. The shower sequence in *Pablo y Carolina* (1956) is a good example. In Pacheco's *crónica* about the Infante cult, female fans comment at length on his body and sexual appeal. A young fan explains why she prefers Infante to other contemporary youth idols:

> Singers are very different nowadays. Rene, the ex-Menudo, is handsome and everything, but I don't like it when he wears earrings and women's stuff. Pedro is another story: he is like more a gentleman, manlier, and very handsome. (Pacheco 1992: 218)

Similarly another female fan proclaimed, "No way, there is no comparison. Pedro was simple, handsome and had such a great body" (ibid.).

Both on screen and in real life, Infante was never a one-woman man. At the time of his death Infante's marriage to fifteen-year-old dancer Lupita Torrentera was annulled by the Mexican Federal Court, as he was still legally married to María Luisa León Infante. Furthermore, he was seriously involved with the actress Irma Dorantes. Criss-crossing screen life and real life, Infante's mythic status as a notorious womanizer and his well-publicized, tumultuous extramarital affairs, the subject of a number of biographies, resonate with popular stereotypes about the sexually aggressive Mexican macho (Franco Sodja 1992; García 1994; Infante Quintanilla 1992; Morales n.d.; Torrentera and Ávila 1991). Extra-filmic material on Infante's lifestyle and sexual history have aggrandized his status as the romantic, wise-cracking, and virile singing *charro,* comparable to the mythology that circulates about the legendary Puerto Rican singer Daniel

Santos, famous for boleros about male sexual promiscuity such as "La número cien" (My One-hundredth Woman). Infante's biographers revel in his legendary sexual conquests, while his love for gastronomic pleasures also circulates widely. His fans, both male and female, interpret his infidelity and promiscuity as signs of his humanity, as this man expresses:

> Yes, he did have a lot of wives, but we cannot judge him for that. . . . After all, Infante was a man just like us. And because of those things he did is why we identify so much with him. (Pacheco 1992: 219)

Another fan, identified as Gloria, says,

> Pedro was simple, honest, and fair. He was a decent man. Now, when people say he was immoral and that he had too many wives, I answer: We should not judge him as God. Let's just see him as a man. If we don't, then it stops making sense. He was just human. And as a human he had his defects, but he also had his greatness. (224)

His fans do not chastise him for his womanizing but instead choose to interpret his busy love life as a sign of his human imperfections. Infante can do no wrong in the eyes of his fans; for him, all is allowed.

Infante's performances merge his incorrigibly "infantile," free-spirited, and good-natured screen image with his off-screen private conduct. His only lawful wife, María Luisa León, some years his senior, noted that when she became aware of Infante's numerous extramarital affairs, his strategically employed alter-personality (El Nene—the baby) would kick in (García 1994: 2.32). It appears that in these moments of confrontation over his infidelity, he would act like a small child in order to excuse his unethical behavior and to evade his obligations as a husband.

Monsiváis notes one of the major differences between Negrete and Infante: the characters Infante played did not occupy the space of an authoritarian father figure, nor did he abuse the power he wielded.

> Generosity, humbleness, contagious happiness and a lack of power are the predominant characteristics of his persona. Infante never represented authority while Negrete did. (1986: 6)

Infante is constructed as prototype of the expanding working-class population, a representative of *el pueblo*. Infante's charisma and the blending of his eminently accessible on- and off-screen image facilitated the separation of authoritarianism from machismo. However, Monsiváis's assessment of the lack of authority projected by the characters that Infante played de-emphasizes the male privileges that all of Infante's characters possessed, regardless of the social class to which they belonged. The heroic figure of Pepe el Toro in the *Nosotros los pobres* trilogy nicely encapsulates masculine privilege when he asserts to the "fallen" woman of the housing complex (played by Katy Jurado), who is pejoratively nicknamed *La que se levanta tarde* (woman who gets up late because she stays out at night and therefore has dubious morals): "I don't lose anything by speaking with you because I'm a man."

Infante's whiteness was undoubtedly crucial to his mass appeal. Despite early efforts to put a positive spin on *mestizaje* by the likes of José Vasconcelos or the eroticization of the male mestizo body in Eisenstein's *¡Que viva Mexico!* (1931) and Adolfo Best Maugard's *Humanidad* (1934), white continues to be imaged as more beautiful and desirable than brown in the dominant cultural imaginary. The cross-racial, cross-class melodrama *Tizoc* (Ismael Rodríguez, 1956), also starring María Félix, is the only film in which Infante played an Indian, doing so in brown-face and completely stereotyped as childlike and superstitious. Although *Tizoc* was Infante's second-to-last film, it appears unlikely that he would have significantly expanded his repertoire of racialized characters given that his desirability and appeal was in no small measure also based on his whiteness. Infante's whiteness remains an unexamined subject. Critics never mention it, as if his whiteness conferred no privilege.

Indeed, many of Mexico's most popular and classic stars are *criollo*: Dolores del Río, María Félix, Jorge Negrete, Pedro Armendáriz, Arturo de Córdova, Marga López. The Soler brothers (Andres, Fernando, Julián, Domingo) were Spanish immigrants. Mario Moreno, "Cantinflas," was the only "brown" actor to become a superstar. Along with *Tizoc,* Infante's only other race melodrama is *Angelitos negros* (Black Angels, Joselito Rodríguez 1948), in which Infante's haughty and racist blonde wife, Ana Luisa (Emilia Guiú), is shocked and horrified when she gives birth to a *mulata*, whom she rejects with disgust and denial the moment she sees that the child is "black." She is equally patronizing and disdainful to Mercé (Rita Montaner), her *mulata* nanny who worships her. Infante is a foil for Ana Luisa, who is even more horrified when she discovers that Mercé is her mother. Infante is shown as not having prejudices in regard to blackness.

IV. THE 1950S: BARBARIC MODERNITY AND CROSS-CULTURAL BUDDY MOVIES

In her 1983 study of film in fascist Italy, film scholar Marcia Landy observes that the ideological aim behind the softening of masculine images in film masks attempts to consolidate political power. In 1950s Mexico, the social justice agenda promoted by former President Lázaro Cárdenas became a thing of the past. Under President Miguel Alemán, revolutionary nationalism was replaced by industrial developmentalist policies that sought to continue modernizing the nation's economy, at great social costs. Thus, the unthreatening façade of masculine power embodied by Infante's characters parallels the nation's efforts to mark a distance between the more radical socialist components of the 1910 Revolution and the bureaucratic and capitalist tendencies of the 1950s.

Mexican and U.S. scholars have critiqued the State's alliance with machismo (Bartra 1987; O'Malley 1986; Monsiváis 1997b; Ramírez Berg 1992) as a strategy for social co-optation and psychological compensation. In *La jaula de la melancolía* (The Cage of Melancholy, 1987), Roger Bartra periodizes the socially acceptable forms of subjectivity associated with the Mexican archetype of the lumpen *pelado* necessary for the creation of a modern labor force and for the legitimacy of the post-revolutionary political system. He maps the metamorphosis of the *pelado* figure from the innocent rural "primitive" during the *porfiriato* to the violent but heroic macho semiprimitive and revolutionary warrior to his domestication in the 1940s and '50s into a productive citizen-worker under the PRI.

Drawing out some differences and similarities in my use of the buddy movie as a transnational genre requires that I compare the Hollywood genre to its closest counterpart in the Mexican context: films about *compadrazgo*. Beginning with the Hollywood context, Canadian film critic and theorist Robin Wood has argued that the gay subtext in buddy movies is most clearly visible in the film's constant disclaimers.

If the films are to be regarded as surreptitious gay texts, then the strongest support for this comes, not from anything shown to be happening between the men, but, paradoxically, from the insistence of the disclaimers: by finding it necessary to deny the homosexual nature of the central relationship so strenuously, the films actually succeed in drawing attention to its possibility. Read like this, the films are guilty of the duplicitous teasing of which they have often been accused, continually suggesting a homosexual relationship while emphatically disowning it. (1986a: 229)

While the subgenre of "buddy movie" gained currency in the United States in the late 1960s with the success of *Butch Cassidy and the Sundance Kid* (George Roy Hill, 1969) and *Midnight Cowboy* (John Schlesinger, 1969), the Hollywood buddy movie dates back to the silent period with melodramas that celebrate male friendship and male bonding in war films such as *Wings* (William Wellman, 1927) and in the early sound films of comedians Laurel and Hardy (*Their First Mistake*, 1932), cross-dressing comedies such as *Some Like It Hot* (Billy Wilder, 1959) and *I Was A Male War Bride* (Howard Hawks, 1949), and Westerns such as *Red River* (Howard Hawks, 1948), all belonging to the classic Hollywood studio era.

Mexico also has a long tradition of films celebrating male relationships. From the classic period, films focusing on male camaraderie include Fernando de Fuentes's *¡Vámonos con Pancho Villa!* (Let's Go with Pancho Villa, 1933), Miguel Zacarías's *Me he de comer esa tuna* (I Will Have That Woman, 1944), and Rogelio A. González's *Tal para cual* (Made for Each Other, 1952). In both national contexts, the films focus on tight male-male friendships and introduce a homoerotic subtext. U.S. buddy movies, as noted by British cultural critic Richard Dyer (1993), insist on the male couple's separation when the growing bond between the men threatens to cross over into deeper emotional and erotic attachments. In contrast, Infante's buddy movies focus on achieving the unification of the male couple and on smoothing out the tensions that threaten to separate them. This usually translates into a mutual verbal agreement on the primacy of their relationship predicated on the decision that women occupy a secondary role in their lives. The bond between men is what is valued above all because within the narrative's masculinist heterosexual economy, women are treated as interchangeable sexual commodities.

Both Mexican and Hollywood buddy movies contain the potentially disruptive homosocial bond by employing women as a heterosexualizing ploy and elicit—while at the same time diffusing and mediating—the otherwise inexpressible declaration of the male couple's commitment to and love for each other. The treatment of female characters often crosses into misogyny, given that women are imaged as threatening and disruptive to the male bond. Women mostly circulate as sexual objects, thereby underscoring the men's heterosexuality, and in the Hollywood and Mexican buddy movies, women are treated as dispensable characters whose roles are marginal to the male-male relationship. By closely analyzing the triangulated relations, however, it can be seen how women's roles are central to the male bond. A final element shared by the buddy movie in both national contexts is the explicit or implicit disavowal of homosexuality structuring the same-sex friendship.

It is important to emphasize that I am not equating intimacy with sexuality. Rather, I propose that the narrative, visual, and aural codes register signs of deep emotional and physical attachment between men, including ways to "sabotage" the relationship in order to draw attention to the importance of the male bond. Thus sadomasochistic behavior in these films operates as a narrative strategy to divert the erotic drive into violence.[15] Sadomasochism, as played out in these films, simultaneously courts homoerotic elements and disavows them. In Infante's buddy movies, Eros meets Thanatos in a heady mix of melodramatic labyrinths.

My readings of Infante's buddy movies are grounded in determinants shaped by my position as a gay male spectator. While I want to emphasize how different audiences use and read cultural texts, my interpretations are informed by my interpretation of the filmic codes that introduce sexual ambiguity into the emotional, and erotic, dynamics between *cuates*. I am not wishfully reading sexual ambiguity into these texts. To cite B. Ruby Rich, "'queer' resides as much in the eye of the beholder as in the work itself and the intention of its maker" (1995: 1). Rather than confer an inherent meaning to any text, I choose to underscore how each spectator brings to a film his/her own cultural baggage. I invoke the term "queer" as an alternative concept to the heterosexual/homosexual binary in order to examine the interactions of historically and culturally specific forms of non-fixed, non-normative sexual desires, practices, and identities. Queer theory brings feminist and gay and lesbian studies insights on gender and sexual power relations to cinematic representation and reading practices.[16]

El gavilán pollero (1950)

In Infante's buddy movies, erotic desire is visually sublimated through various exploits including drinking, gambling, musical performance, and sports. In *El gavilán pollero,* two lovers, the ex-cabaret performer Antonia (Lilia Prado) and the trickster figure José Inocencio (Infante) pass themselves off as brother and sister in order to obtain employment at a ranch. Antonia catches José making out with the coquettish and seductive young wife of their much-older employer and in revenge takes off with their joint earnings. José, in turn, gets into a fight with their employer and must flee. He then meets Luis Lepe (Antonio Badú) in the town cantina during a card game at which Luis is caught cheating. Having met his mirror image, José comes to Luis's aid during the fight that breaks out among the card players. Victorious, they set out to celebrate at another cantina and later migrate to Mexico City, where they run into Antonia performing at a cabaret. Still seeking revenge over José's incorrigible sexual infidelity, Antonia seduces Luis. The rest of the narrative consists in how the men renegotiate their relationship in response to women's attempts to distract their interest from one another. At the film's conclusion, José and Luis literally ditch Antonia in favor of other women who are willing to take a back seat to the primary importance of the male friendship.

In this classic example of Mexican cinema's celebration of male bonding rituals, the characters played by Infante and Badú clearly prefer each other's company but acquiesce to the need to prove their masculinity through their affairs with women. As in most buddy movies, homoerotic anxieties are displaced onto a conventional heterosexual coupling. The musical number in the cantina sequence, celebrating their initial chance encounter, serves to reveal the intensity of their bond. Song, humor, and liquor are enlisted to facilitate the expression of emotionally charged, and potentially gender-transgressive, declarations of true and unfailing friendship.

Addressing the mythic stature of the cantina in Mexican film culture, Carlos Monsiváis characterizes this archetypal male space:

> The (preferably rural) cantina was the limit of experience, one of the three locales for suffering (the others were shadowy churches and the bedrooms of abandon). In the cantina, the male character was forged and his psychic collapse plotted, fatal resolutions were made, and songs became edicts of self-destruction. (1995: 118)

The cantina, over and above the confessional, is the preferred secular space for laying the soul bare. In a comedic sequence that takes place in a rural cantina, a moment of heartbreak and disillusionment over romance with women allows Luis Lepe and José Inocencio to make a prolonged friendship pledge. Interestingly, the pledge is couched in what could be described as lovers' discourse.

In this pledge, the language of male bonding and solidarity equates friendship as a form of pairing parallel to that of lovers. Between songs and drinks, José points out to his *cuate*, "God makes friends in the likeness of lovers and in unique ways. He puts them in the world so that they may find each other. And when they meet, they shouldn't separate." The religious solemnity of this statement recalls marriage vows. In this same sequence, however, the characters' heterosexuality is repeatedly reinforced through masculinist terms like *valiente* (brave), *Usted es muy macho* (You are very macho), and *Usted es muy hombre* (You are a real man), all conventional terms and phrases used both to describe the normative and hegemonic concept of masculinity and to police competing masculinities. The erotic dimensions of the friendship vows taken in the cantina are, however, not entirely contained by the masculinist terms used to seal their brotherhood.

ATM *(A toda máquina)* and *¿Qué te ha dado esa mujer?* (1951)

Sadomasochism is the driving impulse shaping the relationship between the two central male characters in *A toda máquina* (a toned-down version of the slang expression *a toda madre*, used to express approval and admiration) and its sequel, *¿Qué te ha dado esa mujer?* The narrative core of both films revolves around how the men sustain their relationship in spite of conflicts over women. The conflict-ridden friendship begins when the bachelor Luis Macías (Luis Aguilar) befriends the homeless vagabond and jinx Pedro Chávez (Infante). Luis offers Pedro room and board with the agreement that Pedro perform the domestic chores, an implicitly gendered division of labor that fixes Pedro in a feminine role and elicits from him expressions associated with a jealous lover, bordering on hysteria. For example, in a fit of jealousy over Luis's girlfriend, Pedro prepares a drink to poison or, at the very least, cause Luis severe discomfort. The gendered attachment displayed by both characters registers a misogynist and homoerotic subtext underpinning this relationship in which each man uses women to get the attention of the other *cuate*. Their rivalry is framed as a conflict over issues of power, honor, betrayal, and territoriality.

Pedro's infantile attachment to Luis and their mutual jealousy and loud protest over each other's attachment to a woman can be explained by Pedro's history as a man without a home, a vagabond who lived by his wits after having been released from prison for falsely being accused of murdering a woman. (No information is provided about Pedro's life before his incarceration except that he was innocent of the accusation.) Pedro finds in Luis the nurturing protection he lacked in his homelessness, hence the possessive attachment, coded as feminine, that Pedro expresses when a woman tries to displace him from being the center of Luis's attention.

As *A toda máquina* opens, Luis has just qualified to enter the elite Escuadrón Acrobático de la Dirección de Tránsito (Acrobatic Squadron of Traffic Police), motorcycle officers who occasionally perform daredevil stunts for public entertainment. Before the end of the film, Pedro also secures a job as a traffic officer in the same elite corps. Their on-the-job competitiveness will be an extension of their competition for women as well as a testing ground of superior virility.

The nightclub sequence in *A toda máquina* in which Infante performs the famous love song "Bésame mucho" in Spanish and English, illustrates how homosociality works, aptly visualizing what theorist Eve Kosofsky Sedgwick (1985) describes as "erotic triangles" in which two men compete for the same woman, underscoring a complex circuit of desire that is neither heterosexual nor homosexual. This ambiguous desire falls along a "homosocial continuum," which Sedgwick defines as "a strategy for making generalizations about, and marking historical differences in, the *structure* of men's relations with other men" (2). In her influential study of the representation of male friendships in mid-eighteenth- and nineteenth-century English literature, Sedgwick notes that male bonding may "be characterized by intense homophobia, fear and hatred of homosexuality" (1). Sedgwick examines "the ways in which the shapes of sexuality, and what *counts* as sexuality, both depend on and affect historical power relations" (2). Her feminist intervention is to show how the different manifestations of the male homosocial continuum promote the interests of men, thus reproducing inequality between men and women. Her Marxist historical contribution to the study of sexual politics is to show the links between sexuality and power. She does this by posing the question "What does it mean—what difference does it make—when a social or political relationship is sexualized?" (5).

She uses structuralist feminism and Marxist historical analysis to elucidate the changing meanings of sexual desire and the ways it shapes social and political relations. Her study is situated in the historical period when sexuality is reorganized and classified as either heterosexual or homosexual. Sex is a central category of analysis because, she argues, it is "an especially charged leverage-point, or point for the exchange of meanings, between gender and class (and in many societies, race), the sets of categories by which we ordinarily try to describe the divisions of human labor" (11). Sexuality becomes ideologically charged because patriarchy uses it to distribute power unevenly between men and women.

Summarizing literary theorist René Girard's analysis of erotic triangles in the European novel, Sedgwick notes that the bonds of rivalry and love between two men are equivalent if not stronger than the bond that either man has for the desired female member in this relationship. In a similar vein, feminist anthropologist Gayle Rubin, following the work of Claude Lévi-Strauss and others, describes power relations in patriarchal heterosexuality as being involved in the "traffic in women," where women function as exchangeable material and symbolic property for "the primary purpose of cementing the bonds of men with men" (cited in Sedgwick 1985: 26).

I borrow Sedgwick's discussion of how male homosocial desire circulates in heterosexual economies of desire to highlight various social and national anxieties expressed in power relations shaped by gender, class, race, and ethnic differences. I focus on men to examine the uniqueness of the culture of Mexican masculinities and to underscore the homoerotics of Mexican nationalism. Infante's buddy movies are rich sources for examining the ways the social experience of male homosocial desire is represented in Mexican films of the 1950s. In my readings of erotic triangulations in Infante's buddy movies I seek to contribute to antihomophobic and antimisogynist politics. But although I find Infante's buddy movies both sexist and homophobic, I do not mean to suggest that male homosociality is always necessarily homophobic and misogynist. On the contrary, I want to point to the contradictory impulses in the representations of male bonding rituals and male rivalry.

Thus, in the triangulated erotic rivalry between Pedro, Luis, and an anonymous blonde American (Amelia Wilhelmy) stereotyped as a naive *gringa,* the primary bond *is* between the men. Luis and Pedro meet the American woman by the roadside when they stop to help her change a flat tire. She functions in the scenario as the medium through which the men's competitive spirit will allow them to "get at each other." Pedro's performance of "Bésame mucho" intentionally incites his buddy's jealousy, since he is putatively performing the song to woo the American woman, who is on a date with Luis. *ATM* thematizes U.S.-Mexican political relations via gender and sexuality. Mexican men are idealized as being superior lovers to American men, who are commonly represented as effete, cold, frumpish, and/or clownish. *ATM* stages how easily Mexican men seduce American women.

Pedro attempts to woo the American woman through cross-national cultural codes, singing part of "Bésame mucho" in English. A key component of the performance/seduction resides in his imitation of Frank Sinatra's

English-language interpretation of the immensely popular bolero composed in 1941 by Consuelo Velázquez. Pedro's performance abruptly ends
Luis's flirtation with the American woman, thereby shifting the narrative
focus back onto Pedro and Luis through a series of montage-based shot-
reverse-shots, depicting the reaction of each man individually. Through
the editing in this sequence, the song's recipient oscillates ambiguously
between the American woman and Luis.

The sequence is visually organized around the exchange of looks between the men through a series of medium and close-up shot-reverse-shots.
In the tension created through the exchange of looks between the men, the
strength of their erotic rivalry is privileged to the point where the spectator
is led to question who exactly is the object of seduction. Throughout the
musical performance, Pedro is self-reflexively framed as the object of Luis
and the American woman's gaze through close-up facial shots of Infante
hamming up his Sinatra imitation. Pedro, together with female audience
members of all ages who clamber onto the stage to join him, becomes the
spectacle. Pedro's status as the desired star and center of the musical spectacle is underscored to the point of self-parody through his exaggerated
performance as the romantic crooner. The extensive use of close-up and
medium shot-reverse-shots between the two men foregrounds the playful
erotic tension underlying the rivalry in which the American woman both
disrupts and cements the male bond.

Along with musical performance, sadomasochistic behavior is the only
other socially sanctioned expressive modality for the men to articulate
their mutual affection. The sadomasochistic impulse shaping the narrative can best be illustrated by the closing sequence from *A toda máquina*,
a sequence marked as a reconciliatory moment between the two friends.
After having performed daredevil motorcycle stunts, including riding
through circles of fire, to outdo each other, the buddies lie side by side in
an ambulance, their faces tinged black by the fire, finally able to declare
their mutual love outside of a sadomasochistic logic. Pedro explains to
Luis: *Tanto odio entre nosotros no era odio. Era amistad* (All the hatred between us wasn't hate. It was friendship). Meanwhile, the male and female
paramedics, who sit in the background watching the two men with a look
of bewilderment, function as an ironic counterpoint as well as silent wit-
nesses to the buddies' queer behavior.

In the sequel, *¿Qué te ha dado esa mujer?,* Pedro and Luis pledge to
one another to remain bachelors and to swap their girlfriends once
they break up with them. Neither, however, is aware of the other's prior

"All the hatred between us wasn't hate. It was friendship." Pedro Infante and Luis Aguilar in *A toda máquina*. Courtesy Filmoteca UNAM.

commitments: Pedro has promised his girlfriend marriage, and Luis is deeply in love with his current sweetheart. These circumstances introduce jealousy and tension, once again testing the limits of their friendship. Thus, the principal trope structuring the narrative conflict again places women both as the force that disrupts male homosocial bonds and as the means for cementing the relationship between the men.

In this sequel, the musical sequences again function as a utopian space for the expression of male intimacy. This can be illustrated in the sequence when Pedro and Luis perform the title song, "¿Qué te ha dado esa mujer?" at a point in the narrative when they have broken their friendship for the sake of securing their girlfriends. Simultaneously the female rivals, Marianela (Rosita Arenas), Luis's fiancée, and Yolanda (Carmen Montejo), Pedro's girlfriend, have taken leave of the men because they both realize that their presence is tearing the men apart.

In a departure from realist conventions typical of musicals, special effects are deployed in a sequence that visually transports Pedro to the place he wants to be: in Luis's apartment, by his side. The sequence opens with a waitress at an open-air restaurant asking the sullen and uniformed Pedro, who is on his motorcycle in the foreground, if Luis has abandoned him and if he would like some *pozole* (a hominy-based stew); she then turns on the radio that sits on the counter. The usually voracious Pedro declines the offer of a meal, shocking the waitress. Up to this point, the sequence had been composed of mostly close-up and medium shot-reverse-shots of Pedro and the waitress. Once Pedro opts not to eat, the reaction shot of the waitress leads to a pan left and tilt down to a close-up of the radio speaker just as the soundtrack plays Lucha Reyes, the foremost female *ranchera* performer of the classic period, singing "¿Qué te ha dado esa mujer?" Cut to a track-in close-up of Pedro looking off screen to his right as he listens to the song. Cut to an extreme close-up of another radio speaker broadcasting the same song, and track out to a long shot showing the interior of Luis's apartment, where he is shown frantically pacing back and forth with a large radio in the foreground. Then, a medium-long-shot holds on Luis, who stops pacing and stands next to the radio on the left side of the frame with his head slightly bowed as he looks toward the radio listening to the song with a worried expression.

Suddenly, special effects magically transport Pedro into Luis's apartment, where he appears on the right corner of the frame standing next to the radio. The medium-long two-shot depicts Luis and Pedro facing forward with the large radio separating them. Pedro turns toward Luis and begins to sing the song that Lucha Reyes was previously performing. Cut to medium shot of Pedro as he walks closer to Luis, who has also joined in the singing. The camera then pans left to incorporate Luis into the same frame as Pedro. Cut to a close-up of Luis facing forward. As he turns his head to the right to face Pedro, the camera quickly pans right and holds on a close-up of Pedro. Cut to a medium-long shot of the buddies in the same frame. Following these scenes, there is a series of shot-counter-shots that individually depict them singing.

The men address each other in this unforgettable duet performance, which stages the glories of male camaraderie coached as a plaintive lament over a female heartbreaker. Their voices substitute the voice of Lucha Reyes, whose openly bisexual lifestyle, explored in the work of postmodern performance artist Astrid Hadad and by filmmaker Arturo Ripstein in *La reina de la noche* (*Queen of the Night,* 1994), lends an ironic extra-filmic queer nuance to the Infante-Aguilar duet. Reyes's reputation as a butch *machorra* (masculine woman) responsible for popularizing *rancheras* in the *mujer bravía* (strong-willed woman) style underscores the barely articulated homoerotic tensions between Luis and Pedro.

> What has that woman given you to leave you so lovelorn, dear friend?
> Dear friend, I don't know what she has given you.
> If you just made the effort to leave her, your fate is to understand her and then forget her.
> Every time I see her coming, she ducks and sidesteps me, dear friend.
> Dear friend, it is better to die.

The title of the song, with its subtextual distrust of women, almost demands that its homoerotic connotations be articulated: What has that woman given you that I can't give you? The frequent repetition of *querido amigo* (dear friend) in the refrain, the longing reproach in the intonation used in the lyrics, as well as the honey-coated looks the men exchange also suggest the ambiguous parameters of this putative platonic friendship. The lyrics emphasize and valorize the primary male bond associated with purity, transparency, and naturalness in opposition to the mysterious origins and dangerous effects women exert over men when they fall in love.

What is most interesting about this sequence is the absence/presence motif of women via the voice of Reyes, heard on the radio performing the title song, and the use of headshots of Marianela and Yolanda, their current girlfriends, superimposed over the radio speaker. The absence/presence of the girlfriends and the radio medium enables the reunification of Pedro and Luis, since it functions to defy spatial separation. The absence/presence motif also functions as a precondition for the reunion of the buddies. The presence of the radio in Luis's apartment is a substitute for the absent women, symbolizing how women both facilitate and block the highly charged male homosocial bond. Medium-long-range two-shots of Pedro and Luis depict them standing side by side with the radio simultaneously both separating them and symbolically bringing them together.

Interestingly, women, associated with the radio, become the vehicle for transmitting homoerotic desire via music. Musical performance as visual and aural spectacle allows the men to sing to each other, to express their love for each other, and to suspend the competitive nature of their relationship. The two-shot frame establishes a parallelism between Luis and Pedro that underscores equality, not difference and competition. In this space of equality, the men mirror each other, suggesting the ambiguous continuum between homosocial bonding and homoerotic desire. It is also significant that pans instead of cuts are used during the initial moments of the duet to convey a desire to reconcile and reunite the embattled friends.

Dos tipos de cuidado (1952)

The ingenious comedy of errors *Dos tipos de cuidado*—considered by Mexican film scholars as one of the most important *comedias rancheras*—brings together for the only time Infante and Jorge Negrete, the two leading singing *charros* of the classic period. *Dos tipos de cuidado* uses the narrative structure of erotic triangulation to comment not only on the affective bonds between men, ranging from hostility to devotion, but also on the shifting relations between genders in light of changes introduced by modernity and the incipient political enfranchisement of women as full-fledged citizens. Most importantly, the rivalry between the two male protagonists registers a crisis of masculinity that reflects social anxieties about the limits of the Mexican economic miracle of the World War II period, the huge social contradictions that the Revolution had not resolved, and the onset of the crisis of the film industry, which in effect marked the end of the Golden Age. In this film, Infante is inscribed once again as the archetypal Mexican macho womanizer, while at the same time his masculinity is also questioned, measured, and tested. At stake in this film is reestablishing both the primacy of the male homosocial bond and the unsullied masculine honor of the character played by Infante. It is notable that the loss of male honor and the lead character's subsequent, implicit effeminacy is played out in a sequence late in the film through the use of gendered narrative and visual codes.

The opening sequence in a rural setting introduces the central romantic couples whose eventual breakup causes a rift between the *cuates*: Jorge Bueno (Negrete) loves Rosario (Carmen González), who feels similarly, while Pedro Malo (Infante) loves María (Yolanda Varela), Jorge's sister, but she rejects him because of his womanizing. A year later, Jorge returns from a long trip and, to his surprise, finds that Pedro has married his sweetheart, Rosario, and that they have a baby. Feeling betrayed by his best friend, Jorge writes off Pedro and begins to court Genoveva (Queta Lavat), the daughter of a general (José Elías Moreno).

Jorge uses various tactics to humiliate Pedro in order to provoke a fight with him. Pedro resists stoically until Jorge cuts off the water supply to his property. At a cantina Pedro confronts Jorge, who proposes a duel to resolve the conflict. At this point, they lock themselves in a back room in the cantina to renegotiate the terms of their relationship. The audience, however, is not privy to the content or outcome of this off-screen meeting until the film's conclusion. At that point, we are informed that during that off-screen back-room meeting, Pedro reveals to Jorge that he married Rosario because she was pregnant, the result of a rape. The delayed revelation that Pedro married Rosario to save her honor retroactively reestablishes Pedro's status as a self-sacrificing, noble, and loyal friend. The happy ending pairs Jorge with Rosario and Pedro with María.

The night after their reconciliation, Jorge serenades Rosario, Pedro's wife, and Pedro serenades María, Jorge's sister. In this musical interlude a split-screen image is used to show the parallel serenades happening in different spaces. Simultaneously, the split screen also contrasts their different star images. The fundamental difference between Negrete and Infante hinges on class differences, as discussed earlier. In a review of the film, Jorge Ayala Blanco, an institution in Mexican film criticism, writes,

> Jorge Negrete is the wealthy macho who is a nice guy, yet also a petulant, aggressive and rancorous guy. Pedro Infante is the humble, submissive, stoic and noble macho. Negrete's boastfulness comes from a high social position. Infante's sympathy comes from a humiliated compensation. (1993: 66)

The split-screen special effect underscores the men's narcissism and, by extension, opens a Pandora's box that queers the bond between Pedro and Jorge. (This split-screen visual device and narrative trope was used several times in previous Infante films directed by Rodríguez, including *Los tres García*.) Ayala Blanco uses this film as an example to discuss the complex imbrication of Mexican-style machismo with homosexual desire in relation to the film's many veiled homosexual references.

Ayala Blanco's review also highlights the film's critical edge. He writes, "This enthusiastic compliment directed at the Mexican macho is also the greatest challenge to its myth" (66). So the film is unintentionally a critique of sexism by showing how women occupy a marginal and subordinate position and where the bond between men is celebrated to the detriment of relations between the sexes. Ayala Blanco notes that Jorge and Pedro's lack of sincerity and interest in their spouses underscores their misogyny and latent homosexuality.

The latent homosexuality that characterizes friendships between Mexican machos is manifest in dialogues such as, "when a woman betrays us, we just forgive her. After all, she is just a woman. But when someone we believe to be our best friend betrays us, damn, that really hurts. ...." Where does praise end and where does the insult start? The level of comedy Rodríguez handles, authorizes the question. (66)

Ayala Blanco suggests a facile link between misogyny and homosexuality. One does not necessarily follow the other, although it is not out of the question and does make sense, to a degree. I would argue for a more nuanced interpretation of the film's representation of machismo and the mixed messages about homosexuality. The sexual ambiguity activated by this comedy of errors emphasizes the contradictory impulses shaping this film's articulation of male homosocial desire and camaraderie. Furthermore, the narrative's playful, deliberate confusion and masking of the truth registers anxieties about Mexican heterosexual masculinity that borders on a homosexual panic. This homosexual panic is in large measure due to the changes in gender relations introduced by the Revolution's modernizing project. *Dos tipos de cuidado* strategically and self-consciously stages the uneasy transition from tradition to modernity by having elements associated with both coexist in a precarious balance.

The film's gender politics reinforce the sexist idea that all single women are sexually available for men who, according to the same logic, have insatiable sexual drives. An important and recurrent narrative trope is that Jorge is afflicted with a mysterious and unnamed illness. Jorge's affliction is referred to as an "incurable disease" that he attributes to "an old weakness." Because the disease goes unnamed and is kept a secret throughout the duration of the film, its definition and its referent remains unstable and thus accumulates multiple meanings.

The disease discussed only through allusions and veiled in secrecy as if it were a stigma thus functions as a double entendre, sliding between womanizing and homosexuality; men's sexual promiscuity and inability to be monogamous is associated with homosexuality and feminine-like excess. From the beginning, the narrative emphasizes that both men are womanizers. This is established in two parallel scenes at the beginning of the film. The opening sequence depicts Jorge Malo and Pedro Bueno's techniques of seduction: Jorge sings an aria to his conquest-to-be in an idyllic romantic setting, in front of a dramatic waterfall. In contrast to

Jorge's affectedness, Pedro is authentic and clear in his intentions. This sequence encapsulates each actor's star image and reputation for being men who are rarely satisfied with having just one woman and who possess all the charm and skills to seduce any woman they want no matter how much or for how long the woman might resist. The film's concealment of the secret affliction conjures up the idea of "skeletons in the closet." Furthermore, the number of times the narrative draws attention to the importance of not revealing the secret echoes Oscar Wilde's widely circulated characterization of social prohibitions against naming homosexuality, "the love that dare not speak its name." Promiscuity is treated in the film as a hereditary and natural tendency in Mexican men. Further, a trait of the Mexican national character is men's tendency to be *muy enamorados* (prone to falling in love easily), an allusion to chronic womanizing; stereotypically, manliness is measured by the number of sexual encounters of which a man can boast.

A sign of the film's contradictory impulses is that it celebrates male promiscuity and pokes fun at men's "natural" infidelity, while at the same time it explicitly critiques irresponsible fathers. For example, Pedro's father-in-law, Don Elias, constantly complains about Pedro's lack of responsibility and calls him *un padre desnaturalizado* (an unnatural father). The film's discourse on Mexican masculinity both castigates men's fickle treatment of women while at the same it asks the audience to indulge this weakness. Ideologically the film justifies, reinforces, and celebrates men's overheated sexual drive and their gender privileges.

The serenade sequence pointedly establishes the homosocial structure of the lead characters' friendship where romantic relationships with women are but a pretext for the men to get together. In this sequence, matrimony is mocked by a swapping of women that suggests that the men are trying to "get at each other" through their female partners. One must wonder if Pedro loves María because she is Jorge's sister and if Jorge loves Rosario because she is Pedro's wife. The serenade scandalizes the town and, in particular, enrages the general since his daughter, Genoveva, is engaged to Jorge. The sequence following the serenade confirms Pedro and Jorge's queer relationship. The sequence depicts the arch-masculine, authoritarian general confronting Pedro and demanding that he kill Jorge, who is engaged to marry Genoveva. If he fails to do so, the general threatens to kill Pedro, whom he has already dismissed as a coward and a homosexual. The general shouts at Pedro *el primero que debe morir eres tu por agachón* (the first person who should die is you for cowering). The physical action of cowering (*agachar*) connotes fear and a loss of honor and greatly diminishes Pedro's masculinity. The verb *agachar* also means to bend over or duck. In the general's opinion, Jorge has symbolically penetrated and feminized Pedro, since Pedro has allowed Jorge to serenade his wife. In the incredibly irreverent serenade sequence preceding the confrontation between the general and Pedro, Jorge serenades Rosario while Pedro serenades María.

The confrontation with the general foregrounds Pedro's status as a cuckold. The sequence begins with Infante walking past a group of townswomen congregated at a sidewalk *mercado*. A woman in the group suggestively asks him, "¿Qué tal, Pedrito? Su esposa, bien? Y su amigo Jorge Bueno, ¿está bueno?" (How are you, Pedrito? Is your wife well? And your friend Jorge Bueno, is he good?) This bantering registers the tainted masculine and (hetero)sexual dishonor that now stigmatizes Pedro, since his honor also depends on his wife's virtue. But this bantering, replete with homosexual innuendos, has deeper resonances. The multiple layers and ramifications of Pedro's dishonor can also be traced to the off-screen meeting between Jorge and Pedro. By not allowing spectators to watch and listen to what takes place inside the cantina, we are playfully and falsely led to believe that Pedro made major concessions to Jorge, concessions that implicitly disempower and emasculate Pedro.

The magnitude of Pedro's dishonor is addressed through a highly playful mise-en-scène. Director Ismael Rodríguez frames Pedro in a medium-to long-range shot in front of a plant with big round leaves at crotch level to foreground his effeminacy. Additionally, Pedro is imaged with a portrait of the Virgin of Guadalupe on the wall directly behind him. The anatomical shape of the flowers, combined with the use of the Virgin of Guadalupe, playfully connote Pedro's effeminate status. Additionally, his refusal to accede to the general's demands codes him as a coward. In contrast, the general is placed in front of a plant with a large, phallic extended flower that curves up to his crotch. These playful visual motifs again place Pedro in a feminine space that is also homosexualized.

In *Dos tipos de cuidado*, homosexual connotations linked to the feminization process described above emerge as a sign of masculine dishonor and are coded as the result of farcical misunderstanding. The queer threat is largely evacuated at the film's conclusion during a folkloric *kermés* (bazaar) sequence in which the heterosexual couples celebrate the unraveling of the film's multiple melodramatic twists. However, a hint of the primacy of the male-male relationship resurfaces in the final scenes when the men

Male friendship takes center stage. Pedro Infante and Jorge Negrete accompanied by their on-screen girlfriends, Yolanda Varela (far left) and Carmen González (far right), in *Dos tipos de cuidado*. Courtesy Filmoteca UNAM.

are paired at the center, side by side, with their female partners at the edges, once again troubling the film's attempt to provide unambiguous heterosexual narrative closure.

Dos tipos de cuidado is both traditional and irreverent. One the one hand, it promotes family values through the narrative of Pedro sacrificing in order to pose as father of Rosario's child when he is not the biological father; and on the other hand, the film mocks marriage as a sacred institution.

V. CONCLUSION

In this chapter I examined the meanings and symbology of Infante's stardom and fandom in the period in which he was still making films and after his death. In dialogue with Richard Dyer's rich study of the star phenomenon, I've situated the layers of meaning that Infante-as-star text has accumulated across different historical periods and viewing contexts (Dyer

1986: 4–5). Infante continues to be as highly revered an ethnic, national, and sexual cultural icon today as he was during his lifetime for Mexicans inside and outside the boundaries of the nation-state. References to Infante in Chicana/o literature are not uncommon and include *Loving Pedro Infante*, Denise Chávez's novel-homage to Infante and his fans.

I have also attempted to situate him in relation to the specific ways of understanding ethnic, (trans)national, and sexual questions that were available in the '40s and '50s but with an emphasis on what he means to me. I have looked at Infante through the lens of an urban gay male fan subculture, using a queer and feminist lens, but rooted in my experiences growing up as a first-generation Mexican immigrant in San Francisco's heavily Latino-populated Mission District, which borders the Castro neighborhood, the "gay mecca" of the West, where I feel both at home and out of place among the predominantly white, middle-class, Anglo-American gay men.

If there are two stereotypical ideas associated with *mexicanidad*, they are surely machismo and a taste for suffering. Achieving consensus on a definition of macho and machismo, however, is very difficult because it changes over time, and its meaning hinges on the context in which it is used. If during the brief reign of Infante, one particular model of masculinity was hegemonic, yet still contested, by the 1960s, the macho stereotypes remaining were unsuccessful in stemming the crisis embroiling Mexican male identity. Masculinity, like patriarchy, is a system of power. As Ramírez Berg (1992) has cogently argued, a crisis of masculinity was only one part of the political collapse produced by the events in Mexico of 1968. In the 1970s the State stepped in, sponsoring cinema, to resuscitate national gendered mythologies and re-legitimate the political system.

In the next chapter I attempt to address the unstable boundaries of heterosexual masculinity vis-à-vis its relationship with homosexual desire in this fraught national climate. In particular, I am interested in the increased emphasis on suffering, humiliation, and shame in cinematic production. What function do homosexuality and same-sex desire serve in popular culture, and how are they expressed? How do shame and suffering shape gender? Far from being excluded or even marginalized, male homosocial relations figure prominently in the new cinema of the '70s, but are featured much more ambivalently and are more charged with tension and violence than the representations of relations between men in the classic period.

⚛3⚛

The Last Dance

(Homo)Sexuality and Representation in Arturo Ripstein's
El lugar sin límites *and the* Fichera *Subgenre*

✛ ✛ ✛

Pero un beso de amor, no se lo da a cualquiera.
[You don't give a kiss of true love to just anybody.]
EL RELICARIO (THE RELIQUARY)

I love the night, I love night people, I love the downtrodden, I love
the licentious, I love the lecherous, I love the lonely and lost . . . losers,
people in states of desperation, people at the end of their rope, sinners
in the broadest aspect, and people who bear guilt in suffering . . . and
despair . . . I like the great sufferers because they make for great story-
telling. Great sufferers are ambiguous and mysterious and that is what
art should ultimately be.
ARTURO RIPSTEIN (QUOTED IN DE LA MORA 1999)

*O*f all the lonely and tortured losers and dreamers in Arturo Ripstein's
extensive filmography, La Manuela, the aging and somewhat grotesque transvestite star of *El lugar sin límites* (Hell Has No Limits / The
Place Without Limits, 1977), stands out as his most memorable character.
La Manuela embodies the abject and quintessentially flamboyant effeminacy intimately linked to how male homosexuality has historically been
perceived and represented in Mexican society and culture. La Manuela,
as portrayed by the late actor Roberto Cobo, is both heroic and pathetic.
She is admirable for her tenacity in conquering Pancho, a virile married
man, whose conflicting homoerotic fears and desires make him dangerous.[1] In her pursuit of her object of desire, La Manuela plays with fire.
The highly charged desire that circulates throughout the film foreshadows

La Manuela's inexorably violent murder at the hands of Pancho and his brother-in-law, Octavio. This circuit of desire takes various forms: Pancho's red truck and his big hands, both prominently shown during the opening sequence; La Manuela's treasured, body-hugging red flamenco dress; the red thread she looks for early on in the film to sew her badly torn dress; and the pool of blood where lies her savagely beaten body in the concluding sequence.

Perhaps it is not coincidence but fate that Cobo—who played El Jaibo, the orphaned, love-starved teenage troublemaker in Luis Buñuel's *Los olvidados* (*The Young and the Damned*, 1950)—gave the most memorable performances of his career for two directors who were close friends and soulmates of sorts.[2] Buñuel bought the rights to film José Donoso's novella *El lugar sin límites* (1965). According to Ripstein, however, Buñuel did not pursue the project because he was unable to cast a particular Spanish actor he had in mind to play La Manuela. Upon hearing this, Ripstein informed Rodolfo Echeverría, head of the government-funded film sector and the brother of President Luis Echeverría (1970–1976), that he wanted to pursue the translation to the screen of *El lugar sin límites*. Echeverría acquired the rights from Buñuel and passed the project on to Ripstein (García Riera 1988: 183).

Ripstein shares with Buñuel a sensibility that is iconoclastic, irreverent, and fond of the absurd. Both Ripstein and Buñuel engage Mexican cinema's rich tradition of melodrama and find ways to subvert its conventions. Born into a prominent filmmaking family, Arturo Ripstein inherits Mexican cinema's melodramatic tradition, its cinema filled with emotional turmoil, secrets, betrayal, guilt, tears, and above all suffering.[3] However, Ripstein unsettles Mexican melodrama's genre conventions. His debut film *Tiempo de morir* (*Time to Die*, 1965), based on a screenplay by Gabriel García Márquez and directed when he was just twenty-one years old, exposes the destructive shortcomings of rigid male honor-bound traditions and features a central male character who is imperfect and vulnerable and thus not conventionally masculine: he likes to sew and he wears glasses. Ripstein's dictum, following French surrealist André Breton, is that "art should be convulsive." He uses the structures of melodrama to confront audiences with everything that should not be said or shown. Ripstein's melodramas (scripted since 1985 by his partner, screenwriter Paz Alicia Garciadiego) explicitly question, unsettle, and expose family values and religious morals, gender expectations, sexual norms, as well as vernacular forms and practices intimately associated with Mexican national identity.

They desecrate holy spaces and institutions and thereby often alienate and enrage Mexican audiences. His films do not have happy endings. Ripstein takes pride in critic J. Hoberman's characterization of his work as "feel-bad movies." In Ripstein's films, including *El lugar sin límites*, the family is not the idealized, nurturing, and protective cocoon typical of family melodramas from the classic period such as Alejandro Galindo's *Una familia de tantas* (A Family Among Many, 1948) or Juan Bustillo Oro's *Cuando los hijos se van* (When the Children Leave, 1941). Instead, Ripstein sees the family as a "nucleus of destruction and horror."

Families can be very demanding and very castrating. Families can, of course, be a source of protection and serenity, but serenity and protection have a very high price. What I've tried to do is to demolish the basic values of certain bourgeoisie who believe that religion, family, and country are the most important factors one has. I believe in the freedom of the heart and of the mind that does not include these very closely knit nuclei. I try to tread on them and make room for other possibilities. (In de la Mora 1999: 9)

Like Buñuel, Ripstein also found ways to stay true to his artistic convictions while working in commercial filmmaking. While Ripstein's work is in dialogue with classic Mexican melodramas, his films take an entirely different route in terms of narrative, visual style, and ideology. His dark melodramas end tragically and without a glimmer of hope. Like other members of his generation (such as Jaime Humberto Hermosillo, Felipe Cazals, and Jorge Fons), Ripstein breaks with the ideological conventions of Mexican cinematic melodramas. He exposes, lingers, festers in the dark and disturbing underside of sacred icons, institutions, and sensibilities that are part of Mexican national identity: family, paternal and maternal representatives of authority and power. Long takes and extended tracking shots, a sparse use of close-ups, claustrophobic, tawdry, dark, enclosed interiors, often kitschy mise-en-scène, characterize his frequently predatory, relentlessly voyeuristic, and impassively detached gaze. Ripstein revisits the familiar territory of Mexican melodrama and runs a bulldozer right through it. The brothel in *El lugar sin límites* is a site of pleasure, but it is also a third-rate, dead-end watering hole that has seen better days. Claustrophobic, dilapidated, and fraught with tensions and danger, it imprisons its inhabitants, for whom there is no possibility of a better future. The brothel is thus a prison, as is the space of the home in several of his films before and after *El lugar sin límites*.[4]

In this chapter I analyze how Arturo Ripstein's *El lugar sin límites* comments on the social construction of heterosexual masculinity in Mexico and how this film addresses the dilemmas of homoerotic desire. I focus on the ways in which Ripstein's film contests the cinematic codes used to represent gay men in *fichera* films of the 1970s by arguing that the tropes of transvestism and drag facilitate a discussion of homoeroticism, homophobia, and their links to misogyny. A semiotic reading defines the function of the figures of the male transvestite (drag queen) and the effeminate gay male (*el joto*) in commercial Mexican cinema as enabling the construction of male heterosexuality, most notably the Mexican macho.[5] Simply stated, I argue that the macho needs the *joto* to define his identity. Furthermore, I examine how Ripstein's film comments on the codes used to render male homosexuality visible and intelligible in Mexican film as well as in popular culture. I argue that the consistent inclusion of gay male characters and/or references to homosexuality in many Mexican films since the sound period and across various genres (from prostitution melodramas to family melodramas to classic revolutionary melodramas) indicate that male homosexuality is an integral component of national erotics. Furthermore, the foundational and enormously influential studies on Mexican identity by Samuel Ramos (1934) and Octavio Paz (1950) both acknowledge the prominent place male homosexuality holds in the particular models and expressions of masculinity ascribed to men from the popular and marginalized sectors of Mexican society—such as the *pelado*—while at the same time homosexuality is just as frequently denied, sublimated, or repressed. This tension distinguishes Mexican masculinities from other national models of manhood. Below I discuss the links Ramos makes between hypermasculinity and homosexuality in relation to the lumpenproletarian *pelado* figure. The literal meaning of *pelado* is someone whose skin has been flayed and is thus hypersensitive and tends to be on the defensive. The *pelado*, a close cousin of the leper, is a prominent figure in the Mexican picaresque tradition. Actor Mario Moreno, "Cantinflas," is often credited for popularizing the wily *peladito*.

Recent research about male sexual practices and what it means to be a man in Mexico (Almaguer 1991; Alonso and Koreck 1989; Carrier 1995; Carrillo 2002, 2003; Castañeda 2002; Girman 2004; González Block and Liguori 1993; Gutmann 1996, 2003; Irwin 2003; Irwin, McCaughan, and Nasser 2003; Mirandé 1997; Monsiváis 1998, 2000, 2001, 2002a; Novo 1998; Núñez Noriega 1999, 2001; Prieur 1998; Wilson 2000) has emphasized that masculinity is less rigid and much more complex and ambiguous than is suggested by canonical studies of *mexicanidad*. I draw from humanities, social science, and cultural studies scholarship to analyze the representations of male heterosexuality and homosexuality in Mexican films from the early to mid-1970s, as these are shaped by the spatial politics and poetics of the brothel-cabaret. As in the previous chapters, I argue that the brothel-cabaret is a crucial site for understanding social relations, gender, and sexuality in Mexican culture. Theatrical and musical performances are marked as the sites/sights for the reinscription and contestation of gender and sexual norms.

I. THE BROTHEL-CABARET AS CLOSET: IMAGES OF MEXICAN HOMOSEXUALITY

A veritable altar for male virility and femininity, the brothel-cabaret provides a stage to enact the myth that men's sexual prowess, their capacity to penetrate and dominate, reinforces power over women. The ubiquity of brothel culture is intimately linked to Catholicism. The brothel is that private space where repressive religious ethics about sexuality can be left at the door. The extremely lucrative *fichera* subgenre is the early 1970s variation of Mexican cinema's continuing effort to reproduce patriarchal heteronormativity as well as to preserve the institution of the family and bourgeois morality.[6] The *fichera*'s consistent inclusion of male or female transvestites (both heterosexual and homosexual), drag queens, and effeminate gay men is symptomatic of larger social changes taking place in the politically uncertain years leading up to and following the massacre at Tlatelolco Plaza in 1968, changes shaped by growing social disparities, the government authorities' lack of respect for civil liberties, the impact of Mexican feminism and the women's movement, and the homosexual liberation movement.[7]

Fichera films dominated Mexican cinema from the early '70s to the mid-'80s and as a whole were the most commercially successful films of their time.[8] The dance with a *fichera,* a female cabaret dancer/prostitute who receives a *ficha* for each drink her customer consumes, is frequently the prelude to a sexual encounter. The subgenre has its origin in the mythology of the prostitute, which can be traced to Federico Gamboa's novel *Santa* and its various film versions.[9] The foundational features of *Santa*—seduction, abandonment, descent into prostitution, and redemption—have been taken up by subsequent prostitution melodramas across Mexican film history as I discussed in Chapter One.

The foundational texts of Mexican prostitution melodramas establish the interdependent opposition of two of the most iealized figures in Mexican society and culture: the mother and the whore, the latter being the sexual escape valve that patriarchy finds necessary to maintain the "virginal purity" of the desired familial woman. As I discussed earlier, the virgin/whore binary is folded into the character of Santa, literary and cinematic symbolic mother of Mexican prostitutes. These early filmic representations of prostitution uphold a rigid morality which asserts that transgressions of established sexual conventions be paid for by women, as "woman" symbolizes moral ideals. Such representational strategies work to contain female sexuality within a repressive patriarchal order. The sexual permissiveness that the brothel facilitates for men also recruits "deviant" sexualities. In Mexican film history, the gay male is placed in the brothel often enough as a bartender, waiter, entertainer, and sex worker, a figure signifying sexual difference and excess. Like cantinas and cabarets in Infante's buddy movies, the brothel-cabaret is a place where male homosociality and heterosexuality are reinscribed while at the same time, conflicting desires and anxieties about masculinity surface.

The hybrid *fichera* subgenre draws from the prostitution melodrama, vaudeville-like sketches, and soft-core pornography, although its immediate antecedents are the *cabaretera* films of the 1940s and '50s. Critic Jorge Ayala Blanco (1986) has written that the film *Tivoli* (Alberto Isaac, 1974) anticipates *fichera* films.[10] One of the principal elements that this film contributed to the *ficheras* is a nostalgic remembrance of irreverent, vaudeville-like popular theater (*género chico* or *teatro frívolo*), which, as noted by Ana M. López, developed in working-class neighborhoods and in tents (*carpas*) in urban areas. Before cinema became the principal visual medium to represent the popular classes, the *género chico* served this function. López notes,

> While the *género chico* and its carnivalesque ribaldry attracted a socially but not sexually mixed audience, the cinema was family entertainment . . . By the late 30s and through the 40s and 50s, the national cinema manifested itself as an efficient way of life, granting access not only to entertainment but to vital behaviors and attitudes. . . . There was not much room for the carnivalesque celebration that continued to take place in the *teatro frívolo*: the cinema helped to transmit new habits and reiterated codes of behavior, providing the new nation with the common bases and collective ties

necessary for national unity. In fact, the cinema helped make a new post-revolutionary middle class viable. (1993: 152–153)

In the nondominant *género chico*, representations of sexuality and popular culture momentarily invert established hierarchies, but similar representations (although more audacious) in the *fichera* subgenre give little cause for celebration. The subgenre is largely devoid of a critical edge.

Ayala Blanco argues that *fichera* films exploited the lifting of cinematic censorship over "bad words," female nudity, and sex scenes. He claims that producers lured an audience lost to the amenities of television back to the cinema through the spectacle of silicone breasts and a barrage of vulgar language posing as the authentic voice of the popular classes (1998: 119). He argues that the *fichera* subgenre's representation of Mexican popular culture involves a reductive focus on the most salient picaresque elements from an urban working-class milieu. He sees the sexuality in these films, which abound with female striptease, as "the simple reproduction of spectacles which exploit sexual frustration" (119). As of the mid-1980s, the production, distribution, and exhibition of hard-core pornography was still prohibited in Mexico; this ban was lifted in the early part of the '90s. This prohibition helps to explain the proliferation of proto-pornographic *fichera* films. In 1981 alone, out of a total production of ninety-seven films, some thirty were *ficheras* (García Riera 1986: 325). *Fichera* films serve as a cultural index for various sex-related transformations in modern Mexican society. Among these changes are the public recognition of homosexuals, the growth of the sex industry via film and video, a greater objectification of the female body, and an increased tolerance for the open use of "bad words."[11]

With this in mind, one might ask what is at stake ideologically in the *fichera* subgenre? *Fichera* films provide an occasion to stage five potentially contradictory phenomena: the narrative agency of the hypermasculine leading man; the phallic vigor of heterosexual male characters in general; the frenzied visual display of the sexual availability of the female characters; the sanctity of the heterosexual couple; and the delineation of the parameters that male sexuality and behavior can take.

What draws me to a subgenre that offers me little visual or narrative pleasure is the urge to demystify an enigma—not the commercial success of the subgenre, since the sexual titillation and the picaresque humor alone can account for the high revenues, but rather the inclusion of a gay male character in every *fichera* film. Considering the limited yet symbolically

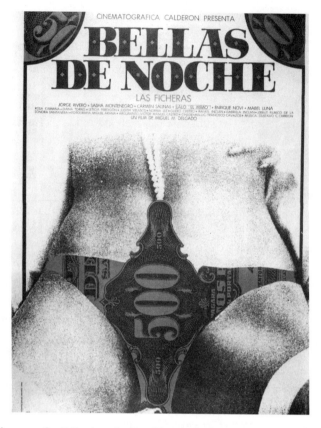

Sex for sale: poster for *Bellas de noche* (*Las ficheras*), the "sexy comedy" that launched the lucrative *fichera* subgenre. Courtesy Centro de Investigación y Enseñanza Cinematográficas, Universidad de Guadalajara.

important historical visibility of gay male characters in Mexican film, it is curious that a subgenre that is so clearly marketed to a working-class male heterosexual audience would consistently include a homosexual in its cast of characters. This inclusion is double-edged. On the one hand, it makes male homosexuality visible; on the other, this visibility is only possible at the price of stereotyping gay men with negatively coded characteristics, including weakness, frivolity, and narcissism, attributed to "femininity" by misogynist discourse.

To begin to answer this question, it is necessary to explore some issues concerning the representation of male and female homosexuality. In his groundbreaking essay on gay and lesbian images in visual culture, Richard Dyer (1993b) examines how the stereotyping of homosexuals opens space for the visualization of queers. Through the taxonomy of sexual types, he identifies signs in behavior, clothing, and social environments that serve as cultural markers for homosexual subcultures. Dyer proposes that stereotyping is bound up with the construction of sexual identities, especially ideas regarding gender and the naturalization of gendered psychosexual predispositions, i.e., active male/passive female. The efforts to differentiate between male and female are related to the drive to identify male homosexuals through a fixed representational system that links them with femininity.

Homosexual types cannot be understood outside of the cultural context in which they are produced. Dyer identifies four homosexual types: the In-between, the Macho, the Sad Young Man, and Lesbian Feminism. All representations of male homosexuality in *fichera* films fall into the first category. The In-between type refers to both the queen and the dyke, classic representations of homosexuality that subvert the idea that gender proceeds from biological sex because their behavior and dress do not correspond to their anatomy: the queen is effeminate and the dyke is mannish. They stand on a border between genders. When used pejoratively, the "In-between" type designates a lack in gender authenticity and an assumption that reveals the notion that "true masculinity and femininity are in large measure defined in heterosexual sexuality" (Dyer 1993b: 36). English homosexuals used "In-betweenism" ("invert" is the historically specific nomenclature) at the end of the nineteenth century, however, as a medical category for the purpose of establishing "a third or intermediate sex." By not performing their culturally ascribed "biological" gender roles, the queen and the dyke resemble the opposite gender. In gay and lesbian cultures, these types embody the refusal to play the neat, unambiguous gender roles constructed by the heterosexual libidinal economy.

The meanings that these types have in dominant culture, however, are very different. By not being a "real" man or woman as defined in heterosexual terms (rigid gender-role playing, opposite-sex object choice, for example), the queen and the dyke represent failed masculinity and failed femininity (Dyer 1993b: 37). The queen is a biological male who acts like a woman yet is (generally) not "feminine" enough to pass for a "real" woman. This failed realness is what prompts film narratives to represent queens and dykes in extreme terms—from tragic to comic. For Dyer, In-between homosexual typology represents both regressive trappings and a potentially radical statement in the rejection of proscribed gender roles.

While the inclusion of gay men (reified as queens) in the *fichera* sub-genre openly acknowledges the existence of a homosexual subculture in Mexico, the recourse to flat, one-dimensional representations connotes an increasing anxiety over heterosexual male identity. This pervasive inclusion of the queen homosexual type is indicative of a cultural obsession with distinguishing and fixing the look and behavior—and thus the sexual identity—of heterosexual and gay men. Consistent with the belief in Mexican culture and society that (most) gay men are effeminate, the *fichera* film never admits representations of the other extreme of gay types, the macho gay man, for in this system of representation the macho image would threaten to collapse the binary logic that permits homosexual and heterosexual categories to operate as stereotypes that are polarized and have easy-to-identify visual differences. Stereotyping as a system for categorizing and differentiating self from other demonstrates how the terms "homosexual" and "heterosexual" are interdependent. The "macho homosexual" emerges most notably in Jaime Humberto Hermosillo's *Doña Herlinda y su hijo* (*Doña Herlinda and Her Son*, 1987).

Stereotypes have a more complicated relationship than being self-contained oppositions, as a structuralist analysis would have it. A deconstructive methodology demonstrates the dependent relation between two terms that are diametrical opposites and independent of one another. In the context of my argument regarding the function of the homosexual stereotype in *fichera* films, on one level the identity of the heterosexual male could not be secured without the inclusion of the scandalous difference of the queen, who provides the defining contrast of an In-between gender, neither man nor woman but a "failure" to be either. Queens are men who deliberately reject conventional male behavior by "acting like women."

II. THE *JOTO*: THE MACHO'S SEXUAL OTHER

Before analyzing gay male stereotypes as they relate to the deployment of homophobia in *El lugar sin límites* as a vehicle for social control, I shall briefly outline the different ways that the subgenre in general and Ripstein's film in particular (which works within the *fichera* milieu) utilize stereotypes of male homosexuality. In *fichera* films, flamboyant queens are rarely narrative agents.[12] They seldom move the plot forward or control events and thus are not constituted as active historical subjects. Rather,

Roberto Cobo as La Manuela in *El lugar sin límites*. Courtesy Centro de Investigación y Enseñanza Cinematográficas, Universidad de Guadalajara.

they are represented as clowns and entertainers present in the diegesis as a mere source of comic relief.[13] I propose a different function: the figure of the *joto* as the effeminate queen is indispensable for the subgenre because his difference is essential for defining the overdetermined "stability," "normalcy," and supposed superiority of heterosexual masculinity.

In Ripstein's film, structured as a three-act tragedy, the figure of the effeminate homosexual is a vehicle to critique homophobia, a tool used to regulate male relations and to challenge the purity of the prevailing hegemonic gender system. The plot focuses on the sadomasochistic relationship between the aging gay man La Manuela and the hypermasculine Pancho (Gonzalo Vega). The narrative is set in contemporary Mexico in the fictitious rundown rural town of El Olivo. Don Alejo (Fernando Soler), an aged landowner, controls the town and all its property except for the brothel. The brothel is run by La Manuela and her daughter, La Japonesita (Ana Martín), product of her seduction by the brothel's madame, La Japonesa Grande (Lucha Villa). We find out in the film's long second-act flashback segment that Don Alejo makes a bet with La Japonesa Grande that if she can make La Manuela take the "man's" role during a planned seduction, both "women" will be owners of the brothel. The film's first sequence begins with medium shots of the brothel's interior, then cuts to another interior; this time it's a close-up of Pancho's hands on the wheel of a pickup truck he is driving through town in his grand return after a year's absence. Cut to a bedroom in the brothel where La Manuela shares a bed with her daughter. In this sequence La Manuela, awakened by the pickup's noisy clanking, listens with fear and anticipation and recalls the last violent encounter with Pancho, when in a fit of homophobic/sadomasochistic desire, he attempted to rape her. Pancho's reunion with La Manuela ends in her eventual murder when Pancho's brother-in-law, Octavio (Julián Pastor), forces Pancho to reassert his heterosexual identity in outraged response to the "spectacle" of seeing Pancho kissing La Manuela.

The imaging of male homosexuality in this film breaks with the cinematic codes of the *fichera* subgenre. La Manuela mobilizes a series of tensions and ambivalences that unmask the contradictions of heterosexual masculinity. To my knowledge, this is the only instance in Mexican cinema in which a gay male is invested with such a degree of subversive power in terms of challenging the dominant gender and sexual system. From *Bellas de noche* (Night Beauties, Miguel M. Delgado, 1974), the film that inaugurates the *fichera* subgenre, to *Zona Roja* (Red Zone, Emilio Fernández, 1975), which revisits the mythic victimized prostitute narrative, to *El día del compadre* (Buddy Day, Carlos Vasallo, 1981), all the gay male characters in *fichera* films are made to hype the artifice of their faggotry. They are excessively concerned with their appearance, as their highly stylized clothing, mannerisms, and high-pitched voices connote; they are represented as being bitchy and wise-cracking, weak and cowardly. Like Vito Russo's sissy, they are perfect "yardsticks for measuring the virility of the real men around them" (1987: 16).

Yet, on another level, some *fichera* films flirt with acknowledging that a heterosexual male identity can be maintained only by repressing feminine or homosexual impulses already present in the "heterosexual" male. *Noches de cabaret* (Cabaret Nights, Rafael Portillo, 1977), for instance, is a comedy of errors in which the space of the cabaret elicits a chain of confusion regarding the gender and sexual identities of a handful of heterosexual men who enter it. For example, actor Jorge Rivero (an ideal embodiment of conventional masculine good looks, including a massively muscular body and hard, angular facial features) plays a character who falls in love with a false male transvestite (played by the busty Sasha Montenegro) who performs at the cabaret as a member of the Unisex troupe; "he" is really a woman in male drag. The Rivero character immediately goes into a state of crisis and sees a doctor because he fears he is becoming a homosexual. In the end, his heterosexuality is firmly reasserted (minutes before attempting suicide) once the "male" transvestite reveals her true gender identity. *Noches de cabaret* deploys what Simon Watney calls the "contagion theory of homosexuality" (1982: 110) whereby the mere presence of a number of queens and transvestites destabilizes the rigid gender and sexual boundaries of those with whom they come in contact. This contagion theory oscillates between viewing homosexuality as an inherent sexual tendency just waiting to surface upon contact with a homosexual and viewing homosexuality as a danger coming from the homosexual who threatens the heterosexual's fragile identity.

The following year, in *Muñecas de medianoche* (Midnight Dolls, 1978) director Rafael Portillo again deploys both male transvestism and homosexuality, at first to momentarily put at risk (for comedy's sake) the monolithic construction of heterosexual masculinity, which admits no slippage in object choice or "feminine" behavior in men, and to reconfirm and privilege the "normality" and "superiority" of heterosexual masculinity. This is achieved by narrative framing devices in which homosexuality and transvestism are treated as ridiculous and comic elements; in contrast, heterosexual romance is coded as serious drama. Actor Jorge Rivero (the perennial stud in *fichera* films) and his buddy, actor Rafael Inclán, must dress in drag in order to hide from the mafia, which is out to kill the character played by Rivero. Both begin to work at a cabaret—Rivero as the personal assistant to the female star performer at the cabaret (Sasha Montenegro), an ideal embodiment of conventional feminine beauty. His buddy, however, is mistaken for a *fichera* by the gay manager of the cabaret and is forced to *fichar*. While Rivero immediately falls in love with the character played by Montenegro, re-establishing his "real" gender identity and his unwavering heterosexuality in the obligatory sex scene, his buddy, on the other hand, takes a liking to his feminine masquerade—to the extravagant dresses and jewels, the emotional histrionics, and the attention of male customers—and refuses to perform his "real" gender.

Although *Noches de cabaret* and *Muñecas de medianoche* in the end narratively evacuate any "homosexual tendencies" that surface after the heterosexual identity of the male characters is established at the start of the films, it takes a woman or a feminine-identified gay man to reconfirm their "authentic" identity. Although the visual and narrative strategies used in both films are conservative, both point to the interdependency of the categories of masculinity and femininity, heterosexuality and homosexuality. The coded-as-positive categories of masculinity and heterosexuality could not take on the meanings and privileges they hold in isolation from the coded-as-negative categories of femininity and homosexuality. *Fichera* films thus highlight how male heterosexuality is constructed through self-other relations where homosexuality plays a constitutive role.

The flip side of conferring this central role to the homosexual in structuring male heterosexuality is that by always reducing the gay character to narrative marginality and/or one-dimensional comedian, such films make it clear that homosexuality is something to be laughed at, that gay men are not worthy of being taken seriously, of being fully fleshed-out characters. The gay men function as minstrel figures, the source of comic relief mediating and servicing the heterosexual characters' dramas but at the cost of diminishing themselves. In commercial Mexican film, in contrast to art and independent cinema, the price of gay visibility is segregation into the sexual ghetto of the brothel-cabaret. In this socially sanctioned space, moral codes are allowed to be broken and non-heterosexuality is permitted. Prostitution melodramas and *fichera* comedies confine gay characters to the brothel-cabaret and reduce their existence to carnivalesque *relajo* and to the realm of the exclusively sexual, as if their entire existence revolved around sexual activities and frivolous partying. The gay male character in *fichera* movies is never shown to have a life outside the space of the brothel-cabaret; he is virtually closeted and contained there, whereas the male heterosexual characters participate in a more multifaceted life. The gay character is made into a spectacle—all emotional histrionics and primping. The hysterical behavior of the *joto* as flamboyant queen foregrounds the desirability of heterosexual masculinity along with the narrative control that comes with the territory. The anxieties of heterosexual masculinity—sexual impotence is just one example—played out in *fichera* movies, can also be read as political allegory. The Mexican political system and the legitimacy of the PRI begin to fall apart in light of the government's intransigent and authoritarian response to the student movement of 1968. The new social movements that emerge in the 1960s and '70s—including the gay and lesbian movement and women's participation in politics—gain visibility and power and thus unsettle patriarchal values.

III. *EL LUGAR SIN LÍMITES* AND THE POLITICS OF SEXUALITY BETWEEN MEN

Ripstein's *El lugar sin límites* is one of the better-known Mexican films to focus on dilemmas concerning male homosexuality.[14] It places homoerotic desire and homophobia at the center of its narrative. The film is a ferocious indictment of intolerance and *caciquismo* (pre-modern landownership system headed by an authoritarian rural political leader). Transvestism and drag, as employed in the *fichera* subgenre, operates by reconfirming the binary gender system. In contrast, throughout Ripstein's film, transvestism is deployed as a destabilizing element. My exploration of representations of male transvestism in this film illustrates how male homosexuality operates as an ideological battleground in the redefinition of restrictive gender and sexual identities. My reading of *El lugar sin límites,* hence, focuses on how Mexican heterosexual masculinity and erotic desire are problematized, rendered unstable, conflicted, deeply ambiguous, and always in crisis.[15] The film clearly links compulsory heterosexuality, sexism, and homophobia to authoritarian and patriarchal *caciquismo.*

Locating the specific national and cultural context of Ripstein's film is fairly straightforward. The rural setting of José Donoso's novella easily allows for a geographic relocation to almost anywhere in Latin America. A major theme in Donoso's text is the modern persistence of neofeudal *latifundismo* (large-scale land and plantation ownership). Concomitant with this economic system is the problem of *caciquismo* (the abusive power of the local authority, usually the *latifundista,* the plantation owner) and authoritarian patriarchal rule. *Latifundismo* and *caciquismo* are socioeconomic and political problems that persist throughout Latin America, even in countries like Mexico where major social upheavals have brought significant changes in these areas. Despite socioeconomic and political problems common to most of Latin America, linguistic and musical elements serve to clearly mark Ripstein's film as Mexican.[16]

Not until the films of Jaime Humberto Hermosillo (1971–present) did Mexican cinema break with its tradition, most notable and sustained in the *fichera* subgenre, of coding male sexual identities with the corporeal accoutrements of butch and femme polarities.[17] The difference is always consistent: the body of the heterosexual is marked as masculine, while the homosexual's body is effeminized. In modern Western and imperial societies, the male body often signifies the power to control women, other men, nature, technology, and itself. It also constitutes an object of desire and often a site of identification for the spectator. The male body type that is the repository of these signifiers is the athletic build, the ideal most closely associated with activity and strength. In *El lugar sin límites,* Gonzalo Vega, the actor who plays Pancho, has the kind of sculptural, hunky body that exemplifies virile heterosexual masculinity as imaged in most contemporary Mexican films. This follows an acute recent shift in modern, Western visual arts (especially notable in advertising, photography, and music video) toward an eroticization of male power symbolized in physique culture. The principal attribute used to characterize masculinity is muscularity. This muscularity resides mainly in the torso and arms: bulging biceps and pectorals, broad chest, flat stomach. Vega's body is accentuated by his always being in tight clothing, T-shirts, and blue jeans, as in an early sequence when Pancho arrives at his brother-in-law's gasoline station. Concealment of the body through clothing works to highlight the round, firm contours of the muscles. Pancho's red T-shirt fits so tightly over his muscular torso that it lends to the image an almost tactile quality.

In his classic essay about the male pinup, Richard Dyer argues that the ideology to be read in male muscularity is one that naturalizes male physical strength and domination, given that until recent developments in female bodybuilding and sports, visibly developed muscles were principally understood as characteristically male. Dyer notes that although muscles are a biological reality and are hence considered natural, visibly developed muscles are not. They are developed either through labor, exercise, or rigorous bodybuilding. Dyer argues that the potential achievement of a muscle-bound body articulates and corroborates the legitimacy of male power (1992: 114).

Gonzalo Vega's body is a model of pronounced virility. Modern, Western concepts of masculinity dictate that the more muscular the body, the more masculine the man, since muscularity multiplies the signs of strength and power. The film features a jarring and sustained close-up shot of Vega's crotch, unprecedented for its day in Mexican cinema. Vega's hard body functions as a metonym for the penis that the spectator is not allowed to see.

Canonical treatises about Mexican masculinity and machismo, beginning with Samuel Ramos in the 1930s, argue that Mexican men belonging to the lowest social classes construct what manhood means to them primarily with phallic symbology. Psychologist Rogelio Díaz-Guerrero, following Ramos's primitivist characterization of the *pelado*'s hypermasculinity, argues that "through the entire life of the male virility is measured by sexual potency, and only secondarily in terms of physical strength, courage or audacity" (cited in Ramírez Berg 1989: 70). In his discussion of Díaz-Guerrero's work, Charles Ramírez Berg writes, "These secondary characteristics are believed to originate in the male's sexual potency. . . . The focus is on the male sexual organs, with emphasis on their physical size and, more importantly, their functional size" (70). Here lies the origin of the pathologized stereotypical hypersexual Mexican *macho,* one who believes that sexual potency enables social status and power. The theorists of the oversexed macho stereotype reveal layers of class discrimination and racism as well as an ambiguous mixture of fear, desire, and pride. Ironically, as theorist Robert Irwin perceptively stresses, "Although Ramos's intent is clearly to critique the *pelado* stereotype, his articulation of it in a book that was to achieve great renown, in fact, serves to establish the stereotype as the basis for any discussion of national identity. *Lo mexicano* would . . . from 1934 on be synonymous with the overstated masculinity of masculine protest" (2003: 191).

Two sequences in *El lugar sin límites* explicitly associate male genitalia with power, a power that, in the film, is structured around economic independence, ownership of property, and control over women and men. Only when there is a lack of economic stability (as in Pancho's case) do physical strength, bravado, an excessive sexual drive, and the need to blatantly subjugate and humiliate women and other men surface as compensatory mechanisms. The characters of Don Alejo and Octavio, two older males, are employed as powerful economic models that Pancho must (futilely) emulate. Don Alejo, the aging local *cacique,* a patriarchal figure, owns all of El Olivo with the exception of the brothel. His master plan is to sell the entire town to a financial consortium; he has cut off all electricity in an attempt to prompt folks in town to leave the area.

In a conversation with La Manuela, Ludovina (played by Emma Roldán), an old woman who worked for Don Alejo, provides background information crucial for understanding the dynamics of power between Don Alejo and Pancho. She informs Manuela that Pancho is the son of Don Alejo's oldest peon and that the *cacique* loves Pancho as if he were his own son. When Pancho was a boy, Don Alejo would force him to play with his daughter Moniquita, who was often ill. The games consisted in Pancho pulling her cart as she rode in it, "as if he were a horse." Don Alejo still regrets that Pancho did not follow his plans for him. Instead of studying to become a doctor, Pancho ran away but later returned and asked

Don Alejo to lend him money to buy the red cargo truck he arrives in at the beginning of the film.

This background information regarding Pancho's childhood functions as a psychosocial history of the origins of his anxieties about his masculinity. Because Pancho is the son of a peon, he is immediately placed toward the bottom of the economic hierarchy, with Don Alejo on top. The fact that he is under Don Alejo's "benevolent" tutelage, in an extremely unequal power relation, only serves to foster Pancho's resentment, not only for being controlled by the *cacique* and surrogate father figure—Pancho also resents Don Alejo for depending on him to move up the economic ladder. The childhood anecdote about Pancho being obligated to play with the sickly Moniquita is relevant on many levels. The anecdote underscores the gendered humiliation and shame likely felt by the "sensitive" boy when he played the beast of burden in their games; thus humiliation and shame contribute to Pancho's anxiety regarding his male identity in relation to the rich girl. His implicit feminization is characterized as both negative and "unnatural" by the revelation that Moniquita died prematurely. These games also foreground class-based subordination and accentuate gender differences, both between men and between men and women. This background is loosely framed around the myth of the prodigal son: Pancho, after avoiding El Olivo for some time, is again returning to Don Alejo because he needs his intervention to secure clients for his incipient transport business.

Octavio, Pancho's brother-in-law, although not as important for Pancho's psychological development, is the economic model toward which he is supposed to aspire. They apparently share similar class origins, though Octavio did not have the economic privilege (or the psychological handicap) of being pampered by a wealthy *cacique*. Despite this important difference, Octavio has made good: he is now owner of two gasoline stations and doesn't hesitate to set himself up as a model of economic success.

Octavio also functions as the male heterosexual regulatory figure. That is, he is instrumental in drawing the boundaries of what it means to be "a real man." Thus, Octavio is instrumental in the formation and policing of Pancho's wavering masculine heterosexual identity. He tests Pancho's strength, questions his economic independence, and defines what differentiates a *maricón* from a "real" man. *Un macho* is aggressive and fearless (standing up to Don Alejo); machos are capable of inflicting violence on others (the punishment and eventual murder of La Manuela); machos must limit their sexual desire to women, at least in public. In the realm of male bonding, Octavio articulates the ritualized language meant to glue men: *cabrón* (bastard), *chingar* (to fuck or fuck up), *maricón*. He is an accomplice to Pancho's extramarital infidelities. Octavio is also the one to suggest that they go to the brothel run by La Manuela and his daughter, La Japonesita, enabling the extended sequence that constitutes the film's climax. He encourages Pancho to drink. At the brothel, he also attempts (unsuccessfully) to convince his buddy to go with their respective partners from the dance floor to the bedrooms. Octavio, the elder mentor figure, both guides and controls the neophyte.

Pancho's type of masculinity can be read as what Lynne Segal terms "working class aggressive masculinity," a stylized persona performed and shaped by class differences. It is a manual labor–produced masculinity that emphasizes "physical toughness, endurance and male bonding" (1990: 94). Working-class aggressive masculinity takes on a compensatory function for men who are subordinated to other men, helps to build self-respect and acts as a form of resistance to the economic power they do not possess. Recall that Pancho was born to a peon. Although the narrative period is set in post-revolutionary Mexico (most likely in the early '70s from the clothing worn and the cars shown), the fact that Don Alejo still equates Pancho's social status with that of a peon, even going to the extreme of stating in a confrontation between the two men early in the film that he "gave him his freedom," signifies the survival of pre-revolutionary neofeudal structures. And although Pancho is self-employed, he still owes Don Alejo a substantial amount for his cargo truck. Pancho's ongoing economic peonage is the cause of the nasty confrontation, which I will shortly discuss. Thus Pancho's class background and his association with peonage racialize him as mestizo while Don Alejo, especially as played by Fernando Soler, is racialized as *criollo*. Casting Soler as Don Alejo is strategic given that Soler's career in Mexican film has marked him as the prototype of the authoritarian *criollo* patriarch that he perfected in films such as the classic family melodrama *Una familia de tantas* (Alejandro Galindo, 1948).

Pancho overcompensates for his lack of economic power with bravado. Although Pancho is technically a self-employed small businessman, his class identity is firmly anchored in working-class physical labor. Thus among Pancho's assets are his body, physical strength, and sexual prowess. Like the mythic mestizo *pelado* described and pathologized by Samuel Ramos as a "primitive" and animal-like lumpenproletarian, Pancho hides his intense feelings of socioeconomic inferiority and his unstable and ambiguous gender and sexual identity behind a mask of virility. The *pelado*'s devalued "feminine-like" social vulnerability drives him to employ signs of masculinity to conceal his lack of social status. For the *pelado*, virility as signifier of masculine power is located in and surges from his genitals. His phallic obsession manifests itself, as Ramos notes, in expressions such as *tengo muchos huevos* (I have a lot of balls), meant to signify his bravery, and *Yo soy tu padre* (I'm your father), meant to assert patriarchal authority (1997: 55). Both verbal expressions strongly connote an active and aggressive sexuality and physical dexterity. The *pelado*'s phallic obsession reveals a belief—both fictitious and real—that male genitals confer both sexual potency and social power; it is real in the sense that his gender provides him with some (minimal) privilege over women and fictitious because his lumpenproletariat status makes him economically expendable and, at a metaphoric level, physically weak. Ramos suggests that without economic power, physical strength and bravery cannot be made real, have no valid currency, and thus cannot be socially recognized because the *pelado*'s phallic masculinity is a mask (a fictitious persona) to conceal his actual impotence and feelings of inferiority.

The idea of the male genitals as source of masculine strength is strategically indexed in *El lugar sin límites* at narrative points that highlight Pancho's weak economic status, his slippage into behavior considered unmanly, or both. In the first sequence, at his gas station Octavio verbally castigates Pancho for still being in the "inferior" economic position of truck driver. Then he challenges him to move some heavy barrels. After complying, Pancho cups his crotch as if to register his genitals as source of his manly physical strength but also to assert his masculinity at an instance in which it is being both questioned and measured. This crotch-squeezing gesture, which can go by almost unperceived, is important because it anticipates and echoes another similar sequence that will be crucial for the film's denouement. Furthermore, it is not uncommon to see men in Latin America belonging to various social classes frequently grabbing their crotches.

The second visual reference to Pancho's genitalia follows his virtual emasculation by Don Alejo. Their confrontation, which revolves around Pancho's delinquent payments on the money he owes Don Alejo, warrants close textual scrutiny. The sequence takes place in the public space of a train station warehouse. The elderly *cacique* humiliates Pancho in front of Octavio, Lila (the secretary at the train station with whom Pancho had been flirting), Reinaldo (Don Alejo's right-hand man), and La Japonesita, who, hidden from the others' view, is also watching the leveling of Pancho's masculinity.

Don Alejo boasts not only that he arranged the alfalfa contract for Pancho, but that he has since had it cancelled. Don Alejo characterizes Pancho as a *sin vergüenza, un bruto de nacimiento* (a shameless brute), likens him to an animal, and calls him a *bestia* (beast)—all adjectives used earlier by all the other main characters to describe Pancho. He also gives himself paternal authority over Pancho by stating that he knows him as if he had fathered Pancho himself (*como si te hubiera engendrado*). The next remark is indicative of the devastatingly vicious tone and intent of Don Alejo's verbal assault: *Si te di la libertad fue para ver cómo reaccionabas. Pero contigo es inútil—eres una bestia. Y pensar que un día supuse que pude hacer de ti un señor, mandarte a estudiar. Pero si vergüenza debías dar* (If I gave you your freedom, it was to see how you would react. But with you it's useless, you're a beast. And to think I imagined I could make a gentleman out of you by sending you to school. You are a source of shame.) He not only positions himself as the source of Pancho's freedom and attacks his intelligence, but also reduces him to an animal-like condition. Adding insult to injury, Don Alejo also suggests that Pancho is something less than a man for allowing himself to be addressed in such derogatory terms: *Además de ingrato ¿eres cobarde? Tu padre no hubiera aguantado que yo le hablara así. Era un hombre de veras. Y mira el hijo que le salió* (In addition to being ungrateful, you are also a coward? Your father wouldn't have let me talk to him this way. He was a real man. And look what you've turned out to be). Throughout the confrontation Pancho barely utters a word, finding himself so overpowered by his elder's paternal authoritarianism.

Their unequal power positions are visually registered in the final scene of this sequence through the dynamics of the act of looking and the use of light and framing. Pancho's eyes are alternately lowered or looking fearfully up at Don Alejo from a subordinate position, since he maintains his head bowed. In contrast, Don Alejo, with his prominent hat, does all the looking, and most of the talking, in a sustained, controlling, fearless manner. He is shot in high contrast (half of his face lit, half in shadow), giving him an intimidating aura. Don Alejo is also shot with more of his torso in the frame so that he looks more imposing, though his aged figure is slight, almost bowed. Their vocal timbre is also polarized. Don Alejo's voice is loud, firm, and reprimanding, signifying authority, while Pancho's is low, meek, and pleading, signifying disempowerment. The confrontation is coded in familial/socioeconomic terms: the threatening, all-powerful patriarch/*cacique* castigating a fearful, subordinate son/peon whose needs are dependent upon the other's favors.

It is at this narrative point, when Pancho's hypermasculine persona has been almost obliterated, that his genitalia are again enlisted to serve as a visual reference to phallic power, or lack thereof. A close analysis of this sequence indicates how this discourse of the phallus links male sexuality to power. Pancho, alone in the warehouse, lies crying face-down on a pile of sacks. La Japonesita, witness to his humiliation, approaches him and tells him he is not to bug her or her father (she never refers to La Manuela as a woman), as Don Alejo had already warned him. He then turns around, uncovering his face. *Estás llorando como una mujer* (You're crying like a woman?) she queries. With this remark she reveals her *machista* belief in a gender-polarized emotional spectrum: "Real men don't cry" is the ideology she invokes here. Pancho, infuriated by her remark and at finding himself exposed and vulnerable—"like a woman"—lunges at her, throwing her back against the sacks, pressing at her neck as if to choke her, and pushing his weight against her body. A short but fierce struggle ensues before he lets her go.

Pancho curses Don Alejo, then she reprimands him for his ungratefulness. He denies it and again begins to whimper. At this point there is a cut from a medium two-shot of the couple to a close-up of Pancho's blue jean–clad crotch. La Japonesita's hand enters the frame. She cups his crotch and firmly squeezes. Her ego stroking could not be less subtle: she goes directly to the mythic source of phallic power. With this gesture, she seemingly reaffirms his previously deflated macho identity. This gesture is also significant because it suggests the complicit role women sometimes play in upholding male domination, similar to her characterization of crying as a feminine act.[18] From this moment on, some aspects of Pancho's masculinity do indeed seem to be greatly recuperated, namely his physical strength and his phallic sexuality. As she masturbates him in off-screen space, his facial expressions change in a series of quick reverse shots from weepy insecurity to self-assured determination.

By the time Pancho's orgasm is cut short by Octavio's off-screen voice calling him, his macho bravado seems renewed, as his comments to La Japonesita imply: *[Don Alejo] se va arrepentir. Eso no se dice en frente de la gente. Da mucha vergüenza que le digan bestia a uno. Te mato si le dices a alguien que me viste chillando* (He's going to regret it. You shouldn't say things like that in front of people. It's embarrassing to be called a beast. I'll kill you if you tell anyone you saw me crying). She, apparently unperturbed by this warning, retaliates with: *Y tú acuérdate lo que te dijo el viejo. Que a La Manuela y a mí no nos andes molestando* (And you remember what the old man said. That you shouldn't harass La Manuela or me). This exchange sets up a tension and an oscillation of power between them that will play itself out in the culminating sequence of the film when he attempts to rape her before turning his attention to her father, La Manuela.

Pancho's acute crisis of masculinity, however, has clearly surfaced. Pancho obviously lacks the economic power to command respect and to be independent, his emotional state wavers close to unmanly femininity, and even his sexuality has been brought into question to some degree, since it is a woman who has taken on the active role. La Japonesita, coded as "mannish"—moved by disdain, erotic desire, and pity at seeing this "virile" man weep—corroborates in the recuperation of Pancho's phallic power by conflating it with his genitals.[19] But she achieves this by inverting conventional gender roles.

The crotch shot sets a transgressive precedent in Mexican cinema. To the best of my knowledge, this is the first close-up (although veiled) framing of male genitalia. Not until the films of openly gay filmmaker Jaime Humberto Hermosillo (beginning with *Naufragio* [Shipwreck], 1977) is a film audience permitted to look so willfully at a man's crotch. This shot marks the man as object, not subject, of erotic investment. A woman is given sexual agency (albeit around the phallus), a prerogative conventionally reserved for the man. La Japonesita, however, does not act on a masculine visual economy but rather on a nondominant economy of touch, smell, and sound. She listens to Pancho's "confession" and grabs his crotch in a symbolic gesture, a mixture of disdain, pity, and erotic desire. After their mutual masturbation has been cut short by Octavio's call off-screen, La Japonesita smells her hand after touching herself between her legs. La Japonesita is specifically empowered in this sequence because Pancho is at a moment of crisis and hence has been weakened. The eroticization of aggressive masculinity makes this sequence profoundly disturbing since the film as a whole critiques sexualized male violence.

The static formal quality of the entire film doubles the narrative content. Ripstein's use of a static camera works as a metaphor for the "stagnant world" the film depicts (García Riera 1988: 188). This stagnation is twofold. First, it registers the neofeudal *caciquismo* still operating in the geographic space where the narrative unfolds; and secondly, it registers the regimentation of gender/sex roles that are simultaneously reinforced and interrogated in the film. Starkly contrasted against the rigidity of the camera is the animated movement of the actors, for their body language unmasks the male heterosexual anxieties played out in this film. I employ the metaphor of unmasking to refer to Ramos's concept of the *pelado's* mask of virility as a compensatory mechanism to conceal his socioeconomic impotence and to underscore how hypermasculine behavior and expressions mask insecurity and conflicting desires.

It is the figure of the transvestite, La Manuela, who enables this unmasking. Her dance performance spotlights Pancho's unstable gender and sexual identity as fraught with conflicting impulses. The narrative point at which this takes place has Pancho and Octavio at the brothel in direct defiance of Don Alejo's dictates, celebrating Pancho's belated economic independence from Don Alejo. (His brother-in-law has lent him the money in order to save the family's honor.) At the brothel, Pancho demands to see La Manuela and threatens to rape La Japonesita in the main room of the brothel, where others can watch, because she had earlier caught him crying. La Manuela hides out in the patio with the chickens (while the men cavort inside with the prostitutes) to avoid another confrontation with Pancho. Upon seeing her daughter physically struggling with Pancho, La Manuela courageously reenters the house to prevent Pancho from raping La Japonesita and because La Manuela is getting jealous that he is showing interest in her daughter.

La Manuela makes her grand reappearance in the red flamenco dress Pancho damaged the last time he was in the brothel. She announces proudly, *Yo soy el plato fuerte* (I'm the main dish). La Manuela then performs "La leyenda del beso" (The Legend of the Kiss), a variation on the Sleeping Beauty theme but set to the music of "El relicario" in a camp reference to Spanish diva Sarita Montiel, who performs this song in the tragic musical melodrama *El último cuplé* (The Last Song, Juan de Orduña, 1957), a cult film that is especially popular with queer audiences in Mexico and in Spain (as is her classic film *La violetera* [The Violet Vendor], Luis César Amadori, 1958). Quoting Montiel's performance in *El último cuplé* foreshadows Manuela's death, since the character Montiel plays in that film dies of a weak heart after giving the greatest performance of her career with her rendition of "El relicario." "La leyenda del beso" is the story of a divinely beautiful woman who while walking through a forest spots "the most vigorous man in the world" asleep. Her kisses awaken him from his state of enchantment, bringing him back to life. This story mirrors and elicits Pancho's barely repressed homoerotic desires for La Manuela and the fascinating dissolution of Pancho's macho posturing.

Roberto Cobo and Gonzalo Vega during the seduction sequence in *El lugar sin límites*. Courtesy Centro de Investigación y Enseñanza Cinematográficas, Universidad de Guadalajara.

With La Manuela's reappearance, he becomes like a euphoric, giggling little boy, utterly enchanted by the aging transvestite's playful and creative imagination, appropriately hyped up for their long-awaited reunion. Played out in this sequence is the inversion of the active heterosexual macho/passive feminine homosexual dichotomy, giving way to La Manuela's control and authority over Pancho and thus challenging binary stereotypes of gender and sexuality. Although she will dance for him because that is what he wants to see, La Manuela's dance does not become the traditional visual spectacle of woman's subordination to man's controlling gaze (nor for that matter is she made a mere spectacle as is the case with the queeny gay male character customarily featured in *fichera* movies). She directs Pancho to where she wants him to be seated. She also controls him at the discursive level, that is, she commands the narrative and gets him to respond to her requests to kiss his eyes and knees. After playing hard to get, eventually the amused Pancho responds affectionately, almost pleading: *bésame la rodilla, Manuelita* (Kiss my knee, Manuelita). Note that Pancho uses the affectionate diminutive to address Manuela.

After her flamenco performance, La Manuela and Pancho dance together thrilled at again being together and finally in each other's arms.[20] Pancho even ends up calling her *mi reina* (signifying both "my queen" and "my love"). But the most dramatic moment occurs when Manuela gives him a quick kiss on the mouth. Pancho's face first registers a bewildered surprise but then gives way to a smile. He says to her, using the formal "usted" form of address: *Un hombre tiene que ser capaz de todo, ¿no cree?* (A man should try everything, don't you think?). Then follows the passionate kiss that would make Mexico's most conservative, sexist, and homophobic guardians of heterosexuality and family values stare in a state of shock.

This unprecedented man-to-man kiss signifies the release and full expression of Pancho's homoerotic desire. In the mythology of the culture of prostitution, kissing remains the one intimacy reserved for the partner for whom the prostitute really has "feelings." In this instance, the sight of two men kissing, one visibly marked as young, virile, and "heterosexual," the other an aged, worn-out, and abject gay male in female drag, ruptures the norm of screen kisses. The entire sequence, culminating with the kiss, effectively represents a seduction.

La Manuela, in this sequence, is clearly the active partner who elicits Pancho's repressed homoerotic desires. He sits while she performs, discursively and physically, for him, on him, slowly drawing out the tender manifestations of love and desire that previously had been sublimated and expressed through violence. During Pancho's previous visit to the brothel, he attacked La Manuela, viciously beat her, tore her red flamenco dress, and almost raped her. (This event takes place outside the film's narrative frame so that when La Manuela narrates to her daughter what happened during the beating at the beginning of the film when Pancho returns to El Olivo, the spectator experiences the event indirectly through its mediated recounting.)[21] That remembered and traumatic incident establishes Pancho's sadistic homophobia, a repulsion and desire for La Manuela. La Manuela describes Pancho's ambiguous behavior and facial expression when he beat her as: *Yo le ví la cara de quererme hacer quien sabe qué* (I saw on his face a desire to do who knows what to me). From the hindsight of the unraveling of events in the final portion of the film, one can interpret this first instance of Pancho's homophobia as a twisted manifestation of repressed homoeroticism.

Another important example of homoeroticism translated into sadistic impulses occurs in the second part of the film in the long flashback that

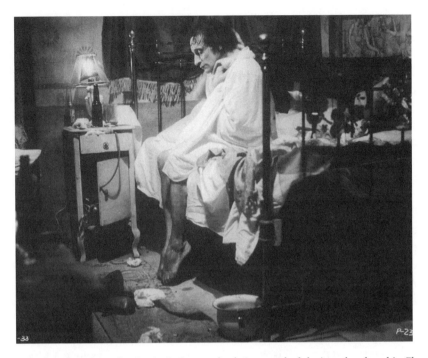

Roberto Cobo takes refuge in the bedroom after being assaulted during a bacchanal in *El lugar sin límites*. Courtesy Centro de Investigación y Enseñanza Cinematográficas, Universidad de Guadalajara.

constitutes the middle of the film. La Manuela, decked out in her fabulous flamenco dress, does a flamenco song and dance performance of "El relicario" for a large group gathered at the brothel to celebrate Don Alejo's election to the senate. The initial reactions from the men are the expected homophobic epithets: *joto, maricón,* and degenerate. These insults halt the performance, since La Manuela complains that her audience cannot appreciate her art. Don Alejo begs her to continue and she obliges. This time the reactions could not be more contrasting. The men literally line up to dance with La Manuela, fight over her, and nibble at her shoulder. La Manuela squeals with pleasure, thrilled with her success at converting her audience into participants. But soon the entire group exits from the brothel to an open field, ostensibly to "refresh" La Manuela because she is "hot" (as if their own behavior didn't also express sexual desire). In this arresting sadomasochistic sequence, the men, still in a celebratory spirit, dump her into a shallow body of water and tear off her dress. This is an urge to get behind La Manuela's feminine masquerade and see her "real" anatomical gender.

This attempted rape sequence is highly ambiguous because La Manuela seems to take such pleasure in being humiliated by the men, who are no longer participants but now are positioned as spectators of her naked body. La Manuela's behavior in this sequence can be characterized as oscillating between submitting to the men's sadistic pleasures and rebelling against them. One can argue that her pleasure is in part derived from her own masochism. Such an overdetermined interpretation would be in line with the ideological circumstances depicted in the film. That is, one can read La Manuela's masochism as partly accepting the culturally scripted behavior of ostensibly heterosexual men living in a patriarchal regime that circumscribes the forms sexual desire can take. Hence, she apparently takes great delight in getting dumped into a large water pit and having her dress torn off, to the point that she squeals and even willfully displays her buttocks. She perhaps realizes that under the homophobic circumstances, the predominant form homoerotic desire can take is sadism.[22]

Presumably, had Octavio, the brother-in-law, not intervened as the narrative agent who polices desire and reinstates the rigid codes of compulsory heterosexuality and its accompanying homophobic ideology—*Orale cuñado, no sea maricón usted también* (Hey there brother-in-law, don't be a faggot), La Manuela's seduction of Pancho would have been completely successful. Nevertheless, the seduction is successful to the degree that it calls into question the social norms that construct gender and sexual identities as uniform polar opposites. Pancho and Octavio end up beating La Manuela to death after a harrowing chase as she attempts to seek refuge at Don Alejo's estate. Although Don Alejo realizes what is happening, he does not stop the killing.

IV. CONCLUSION: TOWARD AN ANTIHOMOPHOBIC MASCULINITY

El lugar sin límites reflects upon what it means to be a man in Mexico. The film represents how masculinity is policed, bounded by showing who is and who is not a *joto*. *El lugar sin límites* explores how sexual desire crosses borders and stages the limits of sexual expression by showing how rigidly drawn is the border of the public display of sexual desire between men. Heterosexual masculinity is revealed as conflicted and contested.

The film underscores the hierarchy of differences between men that are grounded in power differentials such as class, race, ethnicity, occupation, age, sexuality, body type, and health. These differences shape how men embody, live, and feel their gender. Hypothetically, Pancho can be sexually intimate with La Manuela in private without compromising his heterosexual masculinity, but he cannot kiss her in the regulatory presence of a representative of the patriarchal family without causing alarm and repression.

El lugar sin límites illustrates the extent to which sexual practices between men in Mexican society are closeted into the most confined and private spaces of the brothel. Simultaneously the institutions of the brothel, the cantina, and the cabaret enable the visibility of male homosexuality. The tensions in the Pancho-La Manuela-Octavio triangle represent how homosexual practices carried out by an ostensibly heterosexual male pose a threat to patriarchal divisions of sex and gender when they become public knowledge. Homosexual practices are accepted so long as they are not explicitly flaunted in public spaces. *El lugar sin límites* contests familiar stereotypes of homosexuality via the figure of the abject queen whose visibility simultaneously defines what the heterosexual is not and also exposes the ambivalent and contradictory impulses that shatter the cohesion of binary categories. As I noted earlier, in a number of *fichera* and post-*fichera* movies, homosexuality is represented as a constitutive element instrumental in reestablishing a heterosexual masculine identity and in structuring desire between men. Ironically enough, Mexican film culture displays the degree to which heterosexuality is co-articulated with homosexuality. Ripstein's film shows that the macho needs the *joto* to shore up his power. Mexican film makes a spectacle of the "heterosexual" male's flirtation with the *joto* and unveils the constitutive pleasures of the *mayate* (a heterosexual who has sex with men) and the distinctive flavor of Mexican masculinities.[23] Needless to say, this vital structuring presence accorded to the male homosexual is a dubious honor at best.

Within what I read as the film's antihomophobic project, *El lugar sin límites* foregrounds the danger posed by any public transgression of masculine codes of behavior by an ostensibly heterosexual man. La Manuela's ultimate victimization can therefore be read not as a product of Pancho's homoerotic and homophobic desire for her but rather as a result of heterosexist oppression that polices sexual desire. Indeed, a gay liberationist take on Pancho and La Manuela's sadomasochistic relation would read it as a metaphor for heterosexist oppression. That La Manuela does elicit such strong homoerotic feelings from Pancho is a radical critique of compulsory heterosexuality. That Pancho and Octavio kill La Manuela for exposing the contradictions and instability of a seemingly fixed concept of masculinity does not legitimate a victimization all too frequently experienced by transgender and gay men, especially those who are feminine. Instead, the film's conclusion functions as an arresting critique of machismo and homophobia. In *El lugar sin límites,* the function of stereotypes as markers of what one is not fail to distinctly draw the border between self and other since the male homosexual is shown to be an integral part of the fears and desires of heterosexual masculinity.

In the next chapter, representations of *mexicanidad* are explored in a case study of the State's neoliberal and free-trade agenda as reflected in unpredecented changes in film policy and shifts in the gender conventions of the revolutionary melodrama *Como agua para chocolate* (1991). In the 1990s the Mexican State aggressively marketed its national cinema as a crucial component of cultural diplomacy and political legitimacy. Filmmakers returned to popular genres associated with the Golden Age, a legendary period interpreted by historians and cultural critics as "a metonym for a nostalgically depicted bygone era, a period when lo mexicano still invoked a series of roughly shared assumptions about cultural belonging and political stability under a unifying patriarchy" (Joseph, Rubenstein, and Zolov 2001: 9). While the preoccupation with Mexico's gendered international image resurfaces in the '90s, the United States is no longer represented as the threat it posed in films from the Golden Age. Instead, new concerns about individualism, U.S.-Mexico relations, female domesticity, women's sexual agency, and Mexico's legendary macho image displace narratives of class struggle and national unity.

Mexico's Third-Wave New Cinema and the Cultural Politics of Film

✛   ✛   ✛

Mexico has an expansive cultural tradition. It is in our interest to increase the presence of our values, our culture, and the art of Mexico. These will benefit from having a privileged status in our international policy. At the same time, we wish to reevaluate our patrimony and promote our exceptional heritage and our rich future.
CARLOS SALINAS DE GORTARI, 1994

*I*n the 1989 to 1994 administrative period, the ambitious initiatives of IMCINE Director Ignacio Durán Loera in collaboration with various national and international private and state cultural institutions carried out controversial changes to deregulate and privatize the film industry. Government investments in the film industry were drastically reduced, while at the same time IMCINE aggressively promoted a new generation of filmmakers who formed a putative "new cinema" that heralded an uneven and discontinuous and controversial renaissance in Mexican film culture. This renaissance was augmented by high-profile exhibitions of Mexican art and culture globally, but especially in the United States. Most notable among these events were two major touring retrospectives of Mexican films from the classic and contemporary periods: one took place at the Georges Pompidou Center in Paris, the other at the University of California, Los Angeles. The touring blockbuster fine arts exhibition "Mexico: Splendor of Thirty Centuries," held in conjunction with more than 150 cultural events across the United States, was designed to explicate Mexico's history and culture to U.S. audiences and to reinforce the sense of Mexico as an equal business partner.[1]

In the early 1990s, cultural theorist Néstor García Canclini reexamined state-cinema relations and asked several provocative questions, most importantly: Is it necessary for the state to continue to fund Mexican films, and are the current levels of state funding allocated for film productions viable and desirable?[2] This broad reevaluation was expanded to include the pertinent topics of the importance of cinema in protecting and promoting Mexican national identity as well as the very desirability of government regulation and promotion of national film culture. The 1990s "new" Mexican cinema is the third "new cinema" promoted by the state and the film industry.[3] The previous two "new cinemas" emerged in the mid-1960s and in the 1970s, both part of early State and film industry–sponsored initiatives to promote quality "art" films in light of a prolonged crisis in the film industry that paralleled a sociopolitical crisis in Mexico and waning State legitimacy.[4] The contemporary cinema-state relationship in Mexico was borne of early 1990s restructuring of State involvement in film through IMCINE. Cinema was envisioned as an integral component of government diplomacy and was particularly important to both the Salinas de Gortari administration and his beleaguered party, the PRI.

This chapter focuses on the role of film in light of the Mexican government's promotion of globalization, including the deregulation of the market. I discuss Néstor García Canclini's questions concerning the necessary protection of the film industry via a case study of changes in the representation of *mexicanidad* in the revolutionary melodrama film genre, for decades the privileged genre for representing national history. I focus on the film adaptation of Laura Esquivel's novel *Como agua para chocolate* (*Like Water for Chocolate*, Alfonso Arau, 1991), the most commercially successful Mexican film of the early '90s. The film is a genre hybrid, blending romance, border drama, and revolutionary melodrama; it is simultaneously a family saga and a woman's picture. *Como agua para chocolate*, along with several other features and short films, carved an important niche in the competitive U.S. film market, around the world, and in film festival circuits. Beginning with *Como agua para chocolate*, Mexican film become "an international film critics' darling" and "audience favorite," according to B. Ruby Rich, film critic and programmer for the Sundance Film Festival (2001). Arau's film almost single-handedly paved the way for the success of *Amores perros* (2000) and *Y tu mamá también* (2001), which caused an international splash with audiences and critics alike. Close readings of the *Como agua para chocolate* phenomenon, both novel and film, reveal how the neoliberal policies adopted by the Mexican government in the late 1980s contributed in no small measure to the marginalization of narratives and images of the Revolution in state-funded film production. I argue that these shifts are consistent with how the rhetoric of the Mexican Revolution has been selectively re-elaborated by successive political regimes and its attendant institutions.

During the Salinas de Gortari administration (1988–1994), IMCINE actively promoted classic and contemporary Mexican cinema globally, opening new spaces for distribution, exhibition, and scholarly research. The emphasis accorded to State film policy in this chapter stems from my contention that the radical transformations of this period will prove pivotal for the future of Mexico's film industry and its national cinema. Having viewed the sixty-one feature-length films and most of the shorts funded and promoted by IMCINE during Durán Loera's administration, I contend that contemporary state-funded Mexican film is engaged in a process of rearticulating the official national discourse of *mexicanidad* in order to project a highly exportable image of a changing, but immediately recognizable, modern Mexico, a country ripe for business and tourism, a quaint, demasculinized, and romantic paradise for the weary postmodern consumer. Accordingly, the origins of *mexicanidad* are no longer tied up by the macho mythology of the Revolution.

I. THE GOALS AND ACHIEVEMENTS OF IMCINE, 1989–1994

IMCINE was created in 1983 under the administration of President Miguel de la Madrid to (co-)produce, distribute, and promote quality cinema ("cine de calidad") within and beyond Mexico.[5] Under de la Madrid, IMCINE provided full funding for films and established, in collaboration with the University of Guadalajara, the Muestra de Cine Mexicano in Guadalajara (renamed the Guadalajara International Film Festival in 2005) as the principal venue to launch its productions.[6] As of 1989, IMCINE is part of the Consejo Nacional para la Cultura y las Artes (Conaculta), the state institution responsible for formulating and administrating national cultural policies. Conaculta is, in turn, a branch of the Department of Public Education. The Secretaría de Gobernación (roughly equivalent to the U.S. Department of the Interior) previously administered state-funded film. This shift means that IMCINE was freed from certain types of censorship to which it was previously susceptible and frequently subjected. The censorship scandal that emerged when IMCINE tried to prevent the exhibition of *La ley de Herodes* (*Herod's Law*, Luis Estrada, 1999), a political satire critical of the PRI, is talked about as heralding a new age in cinematic free speech.[7] The claim is dubious, however, as the president and the military are still taboo subjects in Mexican film.

Between 1989 and 1994, six central objectives constituted the core cultural politics of Conaculta, the most important being the stipulation to support and promote audiovisual communication. Conaculta's inclusion of audiovisual media as part of the national cultural patrimony underscores how film continues to be a key site for staging and preserving narratives of national identity and for producing and reproducing the hegemonic political system. Since the late 1940s, film joined the ranks of public education, archeological sites, museums, and the popular arts in meriting the active promotion and protection of the State. Government control in this area also underscores the intention of the State to reshape the national identity in collaboration with the local power elite and transnational corporations. It is important to note also that the Federal Film Law, enacted in 1992, explicitly states that national identity and culture be "strengthened, stimulated, and promoted" via state-funded film.

Ignacio Durán Loera's administration at IMCINE charted controversial new directions to revitalize Mexican cinema by privatizing or liquidating State-owned properties and deregulating the film market (eliminating film quotas and ticket price controls). For Durán Loera's administration, this restructuring was integral, on the one hand, to the State's modernizing efforts, and on the other, to the need to make the national film industry more competitive on a global scale, especially in the U.S. market. For prominent members of the film industry and film critics—including Jorge Ayala Blanco (1991, 1994), Marcela Fernández Violante (1998), Gustavo García (1996), Gerardo Sandy Ochoa (1994), and Juan Carlos Vargas (2003a, 2003b)—the changes in film policy and the withdrawal of the State from film production, distribution, and exhibition was the logical final phase in the destruction of a film industry that took sixty years to build. I will discuss these changes and responses to them in what follows.

This restructuring of IMCINE accounts for six major changes, reflected in policies that were in place between 1989 and 1994 and have been modified since then. First, in contrast to the previous three presidential administrations, the State is no longer the sole producer of individual film projects. IMCINE provides up to 60 percent of a film's total budget, while the director or producer must secure the remaining 40 percent from other sources. The one exception is that projects by first-time filmmakers are given full funding by IMCINE. Other funding sources have included funds from regional states (such as Veracruz, Jalisco, and Durango) as well as the University of Guadalajara, the British Film Institute, the U.S. Corporation for Public Broadcasting–American Playhouse, and Spanish Film and Television. IMCINE has also signed a number of international co-production agreements with Canada, France, Cuba, Argentina, and Bolivia.[8] The number of feature-length films co-produced by IMCINE has fluctuated from an annual average of sixteen in the 1989–1994 period to an average of eight from 1995 to 2000. In 2004 IMCINE announced it would fund eleven films. Since Durán Loera's administration, IMCINE's cultural policy focuses much more on promoting rather than producing films, a significant break from the past, especially in the 1970s, when the State funded films through the National Film Bank (The Banco Nacional Cinematográfico, BNC). The BNC was dismantled in 1978.[9]

Second, IMCINE assumed many of the responsibilities that were previously distributed among various state companies, including production, distribution, exhibition, programming, and cultural promotion at the national and international levels. Following neoliberal dictates to reduce the role of the State in regulating economic policies, companies deemed no longer efficient or financially viable were either privatized or shut down. IMCINE coordinated the merger of Churubusco and Azteca studios, as well as stimulated the production of short and feature films by film students at the Centro de Capacitación Cinematográfica (CCC), one of two major film schools. IMCINE also oversaw the sales of COTSA (Compañia Operadora de Teatros), the State-operated theater chain, and Películas Nacionales, the most important film distribution company. Durán Loera's administration also promoted a new legislative agenda that included abolishing film quotas, which (in theory) had previously guaranteed 50 percent screen time to Mexican films. In 2001, President Vicente Fox signed into effect important changes made in 1999 to the 1992 Federal Film Law (Ley Federal de Cinematografía), promoted by actress María Rojo when she was a member of the House of Representatives, that allocates 10 percent screen time to Mexican films.[10]

IMCINE's third achievement has been to draw Mexican and international audiences, particularly in the United States, back to Mexican films, thereby reestablishing Mexico, along with Spain, as a leading producer of Spanish-language films. The self-consciously political State-funded films produced during the 1970s second-wave new cinema were modestly successful. The once-popular, privately funded picaresque *fichera* and action films about drug trafficking had, by the late 1980s, saturated both the video and commercial theater markets and consequently lost much of their audience. The early 1990s renaissance in Mexican filmmaking changed this bleak landscape. The "new cinema" of the 1990s showed that the Mexican film industry was able to produce quality films with national prestige and popular commercial appeal.

During Durán Loera's administration, Mexican film achieved a level of global commercial and critical success unprecedented since the Golden Age. In the first half of the 1990s, largely as a result of IMCINE's aggressive marketing strategy of combining art film qualities (such as films of personal expression) with a broad commercial appeal, four films obtained a specialized market ("art film") release in the United States: *Cabeza de Vaca* (Nicolás Echevarría, 1990), *Danzón* (1991), *Como agua para chocolate*, and *La invención de cronos* (*Cronos*, Guillermo del Toro, 1991). These films established Mexico as a producer of "world-class quality" films for export (Moore 1994: 58), in contrast with the exploitation and B-quality movies (sex comedies, border action films about immigration and drug trafficking) that before the 1990s were the bread and butter of the film industry and were made largely for domestic consumption and for the U.S. Spanish-speaking Latino market. Such a high profile of Mexican films with theatrical distribution in U.S. arthouse cinemas had never before been achieved. This was the case because the exhibition of Mexican films had been limited to theaters catering to Spanish-speaking audiences, mostly in the Southwestern states, Chicago, and the New York City metropolitan area. To the best of my knowledge, exclusively Spanish-language theaters in the United States no longer exist; they began disappearing in the 1980s, making it necessary for the Mexican film industry to produce films that would appeal to "mainstream" audiences within the subtitled foreign-language cinemas in the United States as well as other international markets. Two decades later, it is interesting to read in film historian Jorge A. Schnitman's study *Film Industries in Latin America: Dependency and Development* (1984) that according to an article published in *Variety*,

> the sustained and continuous access to foreign markets . . . was and continues to be a basic aspect of the success of the Mexican film industry, that can also count on the large Latino population in the U.S., perhaps the only growing market for Spanish-speaking films in the 1980s. . . . The U.S. is the fastest growing market in the Latin world

... with ... 650 theaters. Most of the films for this market come from Mexico. ... Country-wide billings have been estimated to reach $20,000,000. ... This might be a relatively short-term market, however, as future growth might be limited by youth assimilation (1982: 110).

Indeed the audience for Mexican films has changed considerably since the 1980s. The audience for Mexican films in the United States has diversified and is no longer primarily a Spanish-speaking audience. The place of film consumption has also shifted considerably so that now theaters share the viewing space with video/DVD, cable, and television. Film consumption at home has considerably changed the communal experience of film spectatorship.

The major transformations in the patterns of distribution, exhibition, and consumption of Mexican films in the United States underscore that the audience for Mexican films in the United States is no longer exclusively or even principally native Spanish-speakers. In an interview in 1994, Durán Loera noted that "without neglecting the Spanish-speaking market, it is very important that Mexican film should aspire to the mainstream. Films should be made which could appeal to audiences across the U.S." [11] Mexican films co-produced by IMCINE in the period surveyed here have been sold to distributors in more than fifty countries.

IMCINE's fourth achievement is that it incorporated three generations of filmmakers dating from the late 1940s to the present, thus ensuring continuity while encouraging innovation. The high investment in promoting a new generation of mostly film-school-trained directors is registered by the fact that twenty-six films out of the sixty-one produced—that is, 46 percent of total state-funded production—were feature debuts.

A fifth objective was the promotion of films directed by women. The new generation of filmmakers includes several women directors. Women made twelve of these sixty-one features, four of which were directorial debuts. Among the most outstanding feature films by women filmmakers are: Guita Shyfter's *Novia que te vea* (*Like A Bride,* 1992) about European Jewish immigration to Mexico during the World War II period; Dana Rotberg's *Ángel de fuego* (*Angel of Fire,* 1992), a grim tale of a young woman who works in a circus; Marysa Sistach's *Los pasos de Ana* (*Ana's Steps,* 1990), and María Novaro's *Lola* (1989) and *Danzón* (1991), the last two being women-centered melodramas about single mothers. There is also a greater diversity in women's roles. For example, female characters no longer have to negotiate the virgin/whore dichotomy explored in Chapter One; women can now be both mothers as well as act on their sexual desires, as is the case in *Danzón*. Additionally, women are no longer represented primarily as victims but increasingly as empowered social agents.

IMCINE's final accomplishment is that, after many years, a large body of Mexican films again participated and received top honors at leading international film festivals. During the 1989–1994 period, Mexican films received an unprecedented number of major international awards, totaling well over 130.[12] The awards at national and international film festivals served both to legitimate Mexican cinema of the 1990s and to reconfirm the State as one of its principal promoters.

II. NEOLIBERAL NATIONALISM: THE 1910 REVOLUTION IN THE NAFTA ERA

In his survey of revisionist histories of the Mexican Revolution, historian Enrique Florescano observes that the Revolution

> is not just the series of historical acts that took place between 1910 and 1917, or between 1910 and 1920, or between 1910 and 1940; it is also the collection of projections, symbols, evocations, images and myths that its participants, interpreters, and heirs forged and continue to construct around this event. (Quoted in Mraz 1997: 93)

More than sixty films in as many years have promoted the official interpretation of the Revolution, in which the PRI is the legitimate heir to the warring factions that deposed the Porfirio Díaz dictatorship and guided the nation into modernity. In light of Florescano's conclusions, it is not surprising that film historian Andres de Luna (1984) describes the revisionist scholarship about the Mexican Revolution as an interpretive problem. He argues that official history has constructed the Revolution as a monolithic, unified, and abstract event.

Hence, in Mexico, cinema made history in more ways than one. On the one hand, documentary filmmakers from all over the world refined their craft in Mexico filming the fratricidal war that in several years took the lives of more than a million people in what would be the most important period in the modern history of Mexico. On the other hand, narrative films about the Revolution were instrumental in fixing the official interpretation of these social, cultural, and political events from the perspective of the ruling classes.

For Carlos Monsiváis, "the most vigorous repertory of nationalist feelings has been evoked by the Revolution, the central national event of the 20th century" (1995: 118). The cinema was largely responsible not only for promoting distorted and simplified narratives of this period of the nation's history; the cinema also produced nationalist models of manhood and womanhood, a gendered patriotic affect, and a Mexican film school. "The Mexican Revolution genre produced definitions of the epic, archetypes of the male, scenarios of fatality, and a programmatic pictorialism" (Monsiváis 1995: 18). Monsiváis notes that the film genre of the Revolution began as a critique of the co-opted bloody civil war (as in the films of Fernando de Fuentes), but after the progressive presidency of Lázaro Cárdenas the genre turned into a spectacular "folk-show." He substantiates this claim by arguing that

> the typical films presented only one enemy (the troops of the dictator Victoriano Huerta), propagated the sermons of Revolutionary idealists, trivialized the specific causes that led to the armed uprising, and focused only on a brief period of the Revolution (1910–17) . . . not even Fernandez's remarkable Revolutionary films . . . were exempt from the prevalent superficiality. The other filmmakers used the 1910–17 period to take advantage of the box-office appeal of "historical" settings and events. (119)

A significant difference in feature film production in the period being surveyed here is that, with the exception of *Como agua para chocolate*, the romantic comedy *Mi querido Tom Mix* (*My Dear Tom Mix*, Carlos García Agraz, 1990), and the children's adventure-melodrama *Bandidos* (*Bandits*, Luis Estrada, 1990), State-funded films produced in the 1989–1994 administrative period are not set between 1910 and the late 1920s, roughly the era when the most intense struggles for State power took place.[13] Significantly, none of the three aforementioned films addresses the goals, achievements, and shortcomings of the Revolution. This absence is a major break in Mexican film culture because the revolutionary melodrama has been one of the key narrative frameworks for imagining stories about national origins and national subjectivities.

Como agua para chocolate is the only film of the 1989–1994 period that, in part, can be classified as a revolutionary melodrama. Yet here, the genre's narrative focus shifts from the public events of the Revolution to gendered narratives concerning transformations in the domestic sphere, especially the family, changing cultural traditions, and U.S.-Mexico border relations. These changes signal a fitting and timely adjustment to national narratives given the neoliberal policies involved in the implementation of NAFTA, the broader globalization processes, and the recent critical interrogation of essentialist categories taking place in light of the accelerated flow of capital, labor, technology, and communication between nations. While historically, the Revolution has been selectively re-presented in film according to the governing party's political agenda, now the iconography and rhetoric derived from the Revolution is steadfastly disappearing from official culture, a process that accelerated after the 1968 student movement. How this privileged narrative of national origins has almost disappeared from State-funded Mexican film reveals an intriguing shift in the nation's cultural politics, beginning with the Salinas de Gortari regime.

This break from a long tradition in Mexican cultural nationalism both suggests a repositioning of the Revolution in official (State) discourse and reasserts the State's role as guardian of the nation's historical memory and cultural patrimony. This shift away from official discourses on the Revolution coincided with the restructuring of the Mexican economy to facilitate both foreign investment and the privatization of State-owned businesses, all changes made in accordance with Salinas de Gortari's efforts to prepare Mexico to join NAFTA. It is not by chance that the veritable renaissance in Mexican film culture (in production, exhibition, and scholarship) coincided with the signing of NAFTA and the privatization of a large number of State-owned businesses, including banking and telecommunications, all part of the putative benefits of Mexico's opening itself up to global and U.S. transnational economic investment.

Before the grim underside of Salinas de Gortari's regime was fully revealed to be a mirage—and on the threshold of the signing of NAFTA—the third-wave new cinema packaged Mexico as a young, modern, changing, affluent, and attractive place to invest. This transnational interpenetration—a strategic post-*malinchista* willingness to sleep with the enemy, so to speak—is no surprise given that Latin American political and intellectual history, since the nineteenth century, is marked by an admiration and fear of U.S. institutions and dominant ideologies. At the same time, Mexican nationalism stands in opposition to the historical proclivities of the United States toward imperialism, thereby positing the Mexican State as the protector of national sovereignty and cultural identity. Anti-Yankee sentiments, once an integral component of post-revolutionary Mexican cultural nationalism, are attenuated in the State-funded feature-length co-productions of the early 1990s, complementing Salinas de Gortari's self-proclaimed "new nationalism" that encouraged up-front partnerships with the United States instead of masking these transnational economic class alliances, which had, in fact, existed under various guises for decades, regardless of anti-Yankee nationalist rhetoric.[14] On December 8, 1991, Ernesto Zedillo, in his role as Secretario de Programación under Salinas de Gortari, defined the components of Mexico's "new nationalism" as it was articulated by President Carlos Salinas de Gortari as

a new direction so that with Mexican nationalism we can cross the threshold into the twenty-first century. The feelings we have for our nation have taken on a new vigor that will bind together our society in solidarity for our future. This new nationalism articulated by Carlos Salinas de Gortari is helping us secure a sustained economic development, political stability that is the fruit of our freedom to exercise widespread liberties, as well as the construction, for our children, of a society founded on fairness and justice. (Quoted in Acosta Córdova 1995: 6)

For Zedillo, the political economy of Mexico's "new nationalism" is based "fundamentally on the principles and goals of the Mexican Revolution" (ibid.). What he has in mind as the principles and goals of the Revolution remain unarticulated and thus abstract. Mexican critics consider *Como agua para chocolate* the paradigmatic film of the Salinas de Gortari presidency and, I argue, a good example of the "new nationalism" he promoted.

Arau's film contributed considerably to the wider dynamic that situated Mexican cinema at a vibrant and historically critical juncture, unparalleled since its Golden Age, according to *Variety,* in its annual issue focusing on Latin America.

With the breakout arthouse hit *Like Water for Chocolate,* Mexico has reached a watershed in its film history. Because of the impressive numbers chalked up by the 1993 film . . . nearly $20 million at the U.S. box-office. . . . America's southern neighbor appears ready to enter a new age in the international film scene, unrivaled since its Golden Age of the '40s and '50s. (Moore 1994: 37)

The theatrical exhibition of *Como agua para chocolate* broke box-office records around the world, including in Mexico and the United States. In Mexico, more than 100,000 saw the film during the first weeks after its release on April 16, 1992.[15] Distribution rights for the film were sold to thirty-four countries. The film was also a box-office success in Argentina, Brazil, Chile, Colombia, Italy, and Spain. Arau's film won ten Arieles, Mexico's Academy Awards, including best film, director, actress (Regina Torné), supporting actress (Claudette Maille), screenplay (Laura Esquivel), cinematography, and musical score. Despite its popularity in the United States and the almost unanimous critical praise it received worldwide, the film was not nominated for a Best Foreign Language Film Oscar. The success of the film drew attention to the "untapped potential of the largest, single-language market in the world" with more than 400 million Spanish speakers, including Spain and the U.S. Latino market (Moore 1994: 58). This success underscores the realization of many that Mexico's film industry can never capitalize on this achievement without an infrastructure and preferential tax incentives such as that extended to film producers in Argentina and Brazil.[16]

As Arau's fifth feature, (after *El águila descalza*, 1969; *Calzonzin Inspector*, 1973; *Mojado Power*, 1980; *Tacos de oro, chido guan*, 1985), and with a budget over three million dollars (including the promotional campaign), *Como agua para chocolate* is by far the film from the Salinas years that has generated the most scholarship and critical debate (Ayala Blanco 1994; Bejel 1997; Burton-Carvajal 1994/1995, 1997; Escarcega 1992; Gabilondo 2002; Lillo 1994; Rivera 1994; Saragoza and Berkovich 1994; Shaw 2003; Shaw and Rollet 1994; Wu 2000). A handful of other hits at the Mexican box office, such as *Danzón, Sólo con tu pareja* (*Tale of Love and Hysteria*, Alfonso Cuarón, 1991), *La tarea* (*Homework*, Jaime Humberto Hermosillo, 1991), and *La invención de cronos* (*Cronos*, Guillermo del Toro, 1993), as well as a high profile of Mexican films at international film festivals, sparked an interest in contemporary and classic Mexican films.

Laura Esquivel's *Como agua para chocolate* (1989) is part of an international boom in Latin American literature by best-selling women writers.[17] Within three years of its publication in Mexico by Planeta, one of the largest publishing houses in the Spanish-language book market, Esquivel's novel had been translated into at least twenty-eight languages. The novel remained on the *New York Times* top ten best-selling list for thirty-nine consecutive weeks, making it the only Latin American book to remain among the top ten for such an extended period. The extraordinary success of Esquivel's novel started a trend among major publishing houses in the United States to issue simultaneous English and Spanish editions of best-selling authors (such as Isabel Allende, Gabriel García Márquez, Manuel Puig, Sandra Cisneros, Cristina Garcia, and even "pulp romance" queen Danielle Steele) in order to tap into the large U.S. Spanish-language market. For example, Doubleday published Esquivel's novel in translation and in Spanish for the U.S. market, printing 750,000 hardcover English translations and 70,000 in Spanish; a mass-market paperback edition by Anchor Books was later also published in both languages. In Mexico alone, novels by women—including Esquivel, Guadalupe Loaeza, Ángeles Mastretta, Sara Sefchovich, and Elena Poniatowska—are credited for creating a new community of female readers akin to the large female readership of the nineteenth-century sentimental novel. These authors rework literary genres such as the novel of the Revolution, as is the case with Mastretta's *Arráncame la vida* (Mexican Bolero, 1985). Mastretta revisits Martín Luis Guzmán's novel *La sombra del caudillo* (*The Shadow of the Leader,* 1929), a sobering portrait of military corruption and political opportunism in post-revolutionary Mexico, introducing a critique of gender relations and a female point of view that, with notable exceptions (Elena Garro, Nellie Campobello), had largely been absent from this otherwise masculinized genre. In a backlash against the success of writing by women, Mexican critics coined this best-seller phenomenon as "*literatura* light," ostensibly because many of these works are, generally speaking, romantic novels and therefore are considered neither serious works nor high literature. Speaking on the subject of "*literatura* light," Esquivel has noted that best-selling novels by men such as Humberto Eco and García Márquez are not put into this category (cited in Rivera 1994: 51). For Esquivel, whether a novel is considered light or heavy is not a matter of how well an author sells, but rather the determining factor rests with the author's gender.[18]

When taking into account the integration of the North American economies and the growing U.S. Latino population and market, it is important to emphasize how the *Como agua para chocolate* phenomenon (again, both novel *and* film) promotes Mexican culture as eminently consumable.[19] A heterosexual romance targeted for a female audience—including beautiful men marked as objects of desire, abundant edible delights, and a magical realist aesthetic—the film clearly aims for international consumption, especially the U.S. market. Thus it is no surprise that the film is co-produced with private funds (Arau Films International) along with State funding agencies that include IMCINE, the Consejo Nacional para la Cultura y las Artes (National Council for Art and Culture), and most importantly various State agencies that promote tourism (Secretaría de Turismo, Fondo Nacional de Fomento al Turismo). *Como agua para chocolate* packages Mexico's history and culture as quaint, "colorful," exotic, festive, feminine, nurturing, and desirable. Infused with and marketed through the lens of magical realism, Mexico in *Como agua para chocolate* is associated with exotic and sensual food, given the narrative's structural and thematic organization around the cookbook genre and national cuisine; each episode (or chapter in the novel) opens with a recipe. The spatial focus on the kitchen recuperates this maternal-feminine space as the location of female empowerment.

Mexico in this film is gendered female while the United States is gendered male, although both non-threatening and hardly virile, thereby foregrounding a "natural" pairing of U.S.-Mexican intercultural relations. Gastón Lillo writes that the border zone in the film is framed within a discourse of the free circulation of goods and people, and he convincingly argues that the film presents a harmonious, hybrid U.S.-Mexican identity to the detriment and subordination of the Indian (1994: 73). This interpretation of national history and cultural identity is significantly different from the work of Fernández and Figueroa, whose work celebrated Mexico's indigenous population and for the most part did not include U.S. citizens as part of the national family.

Just as some literary critics have interpreted the success of writing by women as empowering women because it tells stories from "the margins," others disagree.[20] The explicitly female gendering of the film has also provoked some scathing criticism from Mexican critics. For Ayala Blanco *Como agua para chocolate* is the paradigmatic film of the Salinas de Gortari regime because,

> for all its pretense, blending a magical realist saga for fat and homely women with an anodyne mentality, with a pseudo-feminism reminiscent of my grandmother's failed love affairs . . . it is the perfect Salinista deception. It is a *Gone with the Wind* á la picturesque small town Mexican style, with silly jokes and a lyrical ending. All the confusion of the Salinas presidency is contained in this aberration. (Cited in Sandy Ochoa 1994: 50)

The success of *Como agua para chocolate* resignified the political function of the discourse and the conventions of the revolutionary melodrama that the film and the novel engage. The revolutionary melodrama was one of the master narratives of Mexico's modernization process, entailing the conflictive transformation of a largely rural society into an urban, capitalist, consumer society. As I discussed in Chapter One, this genre has been a staple of Mexican film history since the silent period when the documentary flourished as a consequence of the bloody upheavals. Narrative films about the Revolution date back to the early sound era in films such as *Maguey* (Cactus), the second episode in Sergei Eisenstein's uncompleted *¡Que viva México!* (1931),[21] and Miguel Contreras Torres's *Revolución, la sombra de Pancho Villa* (Revolution, the Shadow of Pancho Villa, 1932). The visual economy of the revolutionary melodrama consists of idealized tragic and "primitive" peasant Indians and mestizos (*los de abajo*) as noble savages, ruthless and authoritarian *caciques*, virile and determined military leaders and soldiers, faithful-to-their-man *soldaderas* (female camp-followers), and heroic female schoolteachers (*maestras rurales*). Revolutionaries enter towns and cities and pillage the homes of the wealthy and are depicted in rambunctious fiestas and orgiastic drinking sprees and spilling from train roofs, all shot in dramatic deep focus, long shots of billowy clouds, and landscapes dotted with maguey cacti in the foreground of the frame. Notable exceptions include director Fernando de Fuentes's trilogy of the Revolution (*El prisionero trece* [Prisoner Thirteen, 1933], *El compadre Mendoza* [1933], *¡Vámonos con Pancho Villa!*, [1935]); Emilio Fernández's *Flor silvestre* (Wildflower, 1943); Julio Bracho's *La sombra del caudillo* (1960); José Bolaños's *La soldadera* (1966); and Paul Leduc's *Reed: México Insurgente* (*Reed: Insurgent Mexico*, 1971).

This classic Mexican aesthetic was created by the collaborative team of director Emilio "El Indio" Fernández and the cinematographer Gabriel Figueroa, whose dynamic framing and poetic composition are among the most internationally accomplished.[22] This classic Mexican aesthetic, developed by the leading exponents of cinematic cultural nationalism, is drawn largely from a variety of national and international sources such as Renaissance painters, Mexican visual artists including the landscape paintings of Dr. Atl (a.k.a. Gerardo Murillo), the popular graphic art of José Guadalupe Posada and Leopoldo Méndez, and key figures in the muralist movement including José Clemente Orozco, Diego Rivera, and David Alfaro Siqueiros.[23]

In *Como agua para chocolate*, the Revolution occupies a backdrop space, one evocative of the carnivalesque and the exoticizing excess that Octavio Paz confers on the ritual of the fiesta in his canonical work *El laberinto de*

Where the U.S.-Mexico border meets the Pacific Ocean in *El jardín del Edén*. Courtesy IMCINE.

la soledad (*The Labyrinth of Solitude*, 1950). In *Como agua para chocolate* and *El laberinto de la soledad* alike, the Revolution signifies a moment of unbridled, primitive extravagance, one in which social conventions and hierarchies are transgressed and inverted. The marginalization and folk-lorization of the 1910 Revolution in *Como agua para chocolate*, together with the resounding absence of references to this historical event in the feature-length films co-financed by IMCINE during the Salinas de Gor-tari administration, suggests a cultural politics that erases U.S. imperi-alist interventions in Mexico. The contemporary filmic (post)nationalist discourse reframes the giant to the north's global economic and cultural hegemony in favor of a rhetoric of friendship, partnership, collaboration, and equal two-way exchange between both nations.

State-funded films of the 1990s favor a new rhetoric of progress, soli-darity, and transnational partnership evident in films like María Novaro's utopian, woman-centered, U.S.-Mexico border-focused melodrama *El jardín del Edén* (*The Garden of Eden*, 1994), with its final sequence of U.S.-bound Mexican migrants standing on the Pacific coast next to the metal fence that separates the two nations and where the border gives way to the boundless ocean, and Gabriel Retes's *Bienvenido-Welcome* (1994), a self-reflexive take on moviemaking, the AIDS crisis, and romance at the dawn of the new millennium whose dialogue moves freely from Spanish to English. From his speeches, Salinas de Gortari's "new nationalism" (consisting largely of the privatization of State-owned enterprises and economic integration with the United States and Canada) was still firmly anchored in the modernization framework of the 1910 Revolution.[24] Agrarian reform and social justice especially for the poor and indigenous populations, which were integral components of the ideals of the Revolution, have along the way been selectively placed outside the frame of social justice. Mexican cinema of the 1990s is overwhelmingly middle-class, urban, and white; the indigenous population figure mostly as local color and secondary players.

The rhetoric used in the sixty-one feature-length films produced during the third wave of new Mexican cinema shifted from the populist discourse developed during the classic period, which generally did not revolve around individualist, middle-class, gender-based issues that are evident in films like *Como agua para chocolate*. It is notable, however, that representations of the myths and folklore of the Revolution in *Como agua para chocolate* are not significantly different from their visual counterparts made during the 1940s and 1950s. Up to a certain point, it can be argued that *Como agua para chocolate* does pay homage to the classic melodramas of the Revolution, especially the collaborative projects produced by the Fernández and Figueroa team. One can detect traces of Figueroa's precious pictorial qualities in the cinematographic work of Emmanuel Lubezki and Steve Bernstein: a low angle shot of revolutionaries mounted on their horses racing past the camera, past the de la Garza hacienda, and into the warm orange-tinted horizon photographed at sunset; the low angle underscores the photogenic clouds reminiscent of Figuroa's famous skies and billowy clouds, set against tall, thin trees that recall the *ahuejote* willows which line the floating gardens at Xochimilco.

The soft and intimate lighting used in the closing candlelit sequence where the film's lovers finally consummate their perpetually deferred sexual encounter recalls a technique Figueroa used in the magnificent Day of the Dead sequence in *Macario* (Roberto Gavaldón, 1959) and earlier in *Maclovia* (Emilio Fernández, 1948).

Conspicuous similarities between *Flor silvestre* and *Como agua para chocolate* are also worthy of mention. Both use a prologue and epilogue as narrative framing devices to tell the story retrospectively and to show how

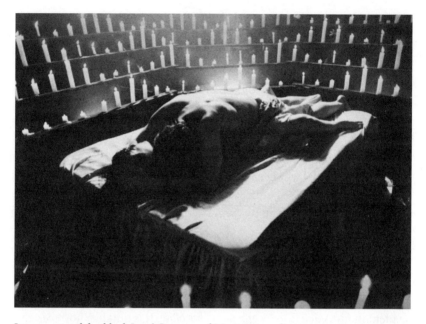

Lovers nest and deathbed: Lumi Cavazos and Marco Leonardi consummating their love in *Como agua para chocolate*. Courtesy Centro de Investigación y Enseñanza Cinematográficas, Universidad de Guadalajara.

the past paved the way for the present. Both also use a female narrator. The latter is narrated by Tita's great-niece (played by Arcelia Ramírez) and opens in the welcoming setting of a modern kitchen shown in medium shot and narrated in a direct camera address, emulating the familiar televisual language of cooking shows and curiously reminiscent of advertisements for Doña María brand *mole,* as noted by Ayala Blanco in his review of the film (1994: 328). *Flor silvestre* opens with a long point-of-view shot that pans almost 360 degrees, showing the vast landscape in the Bajío region of central Mexico that, before the Revolution, belonged to a single family, the Castros. The voice-over narrative later attributed to Esperanza (Dolores del Río) tells us that "the love for the land is the greatest and most painful of all," as her grown son, dressed in a military uniform, the beneficiary of the Revolution, stands by her side. *Flor silvestre,* Fernández's foundational revolutionary melodrama, tells a story of love between the son of a hacienda owner, the sensitive José Luis Castro (Pedro Armendáriz), and Esperanza, the daughter of a *campesino.* José Luis's sympathies with the

Dolores del Río and Pedro Armendáriz, the paradigmatic post-revolutionary couple in *Flor silvestre*. Courtesy Filmoteca UNAM.

Revolution result in a complete rupture with his family and ultimately lead to his death. This sacrifice, in turn, paves the way for the development of a more just and egalitarian Mexican society. The lofty goals of *Flor silvestre* are not echoed in *Como agua para chocolate*.[25]

Other conventions belonging to the revolutionary melodrama employed by *Como agua para chocolate* include the character Gertrudis, Tita's rebel sister, who after running away with a fiery revolutionary returns halfway into the story having turned from prostitution to becoming a general in the Revolution. The latter is a trope patterned after the masculinized *generala* characters made famous by María Félix in films like *La Cucaracha* (Ismael Rodríguez, 1958). However, *Como agua para chocolate* does introduce significant changes at the level of the representation of gender relations during the Revolution and in the placement of this historical event as a backdrop to the overall narrative.

Unlike classic revolutionary melodramas, *Como agua para chocolate* is curiously demasculinized. This woman-centered narrative focuses on three generations of female members of the de la Garza family who reside on the Mexican side of the U.S.-Mexico border, spanning nearly four decades, from 1895 to 1934. The Revolution in this film is treated as a folkloric and peripheral event, a colorful backdrop. The narrative focus is not on the social transformations ushered in by the armed struggle, nor on the fight against feudal *caciquismo,* nor on the familial divisions caused by cross-class, cross-ethnic, cross-regional romantic alliances, as can be seen in the classic revolutionary melodramas of director Fernández, such as *Flor silvestre* and *Enamorada* (*Woman in Love,* 1946). In *Como agua para chocolate,* the public events of the Revolution have seemingly little bearing on the film's central narrative conflict: how Tita (Lumi Cavazos) breaks from the family tradition of the youngest daughter being obligated to remain unwed in order to care for the dictatorial Mamá Elena (Regina Torné) until the latter's death. Tita's role as caretaker and reproducer of tradition proves to be a vantage point in her quest to wed her sweetheart, Pedro Múzquiz (Marco Leonardi), who, given Tita's unavailability, marries her older sister Rosaura (Yareli Arizmendi) to be near his loved one. With the kitchen as center of the home, Tita's culinary skills give her power over family members and friends. The kitchen then is recoded from being a prison of domestic servitude to a space of empowerment. Magical-realist elements are used to convey the central theme of transubstantiation, where food is the principal vehicle for transmitting and expressing personal emotions and physiological states of mind. The narrative thus underscores the supernatural and ritual function of food as a privileged code for communication.

Esquivel's text seems to emphasize the old feminist adage that the personal is political. Hence, the privileged site for individual transformation is in the domestic sphere, although, ironically, Tita's desire to be wife, mother, and cook is hardly the stuff of radical feminist politics.[26] In reality, Tita is so firmly anchored in the kitchen that the only other significant spaces she is permitted to inhabit are an informal insane asylum—where she is sent to recover from the trauma of the death of Pedro and Rosaura's firstborn, whom she raised, and the bedroom where she commits suicide in the final sequence after confirming that her Romeo died of a stroke. The Revolution provides the historical moment for representing shifting gendered power relations and generational tensions, but without the events of the Revolution having much bearing on the domestic sphere, with the exception of Gertrudis (who is most transformed by her time spent in a brothel rather than on unmentioned accomplishments that made her a general). Little to no importance is attributed to the violence and social disruption generated by the Revolution, resulting in bandits raping Mamá Elena and Chencha, the house servant (played by Pilar Aranda) who is both infantilized and prone to superstition. Neither is given any screen time to acknowledge the trauma of their sexual violation. Through the omission of historical reflection, the film nonetheless elicits discussion of changes in women's social roles and subjectivities during this crucial historical period. This women-centered narrative is rife with tensions and contradictions and lacks clarity concerning how the Revolution changed the social roles of women.

An important narrative trope in many of the revolutionary melodramas from the classic period is the Revolution's civilizing mission. This theme is especially prevalent in Fernández's films. The civilizing mission takes various forms. In *Río Escondido* (*Hidden River*, 1947) it is clearly about educating the marginalized native Indian population and eradicating tyrannical *caciques* who fail to integrate themselves into the new Revolutionary family and to the new centralized political system. In *Enamorada* (1946) the civilizing mission is about domesticating and "feminizing" female characters deemed to be too independent, too disobedient, and thus too masculine, as is the case in most films starring María Félix, dubbed *la devoradora de hombres* (the man-eater), including the aforementioned film. In *Enamorada*, famously based on Shakespeare's *Taming of the Shrew* and on an episode in Don Juan Manuel's Spanish medieval era narrative *El conde lucanor*, in order for the cross-class lovers to form part of the Revolutionary family, they both must undergo major transformations. The proud, feisty, and arrogant upper-class Beatriz Peñafiel (Félix) needs to be less rebellious and more obedient to the new Revolutionary patriarchal order. General Juan José Reyes (Pedro Armendáriz) needs to less brutish, less macho, and more spiritual and meek. Unconditional love tames the ex-seminarian General Reyes, as does his recovered spirituality, achieved through his gradual respect for the Catholic Church. General Reyes's spiritual rebirth is represented in a stunning sequence filmed in the interior of a baroque church. He must renounce his threat of taking by force the conservative city of Cholula (famous for its 365 churches). Beatriz must surrender her class privileges, renounce her marriage engagement to a U.S. suitor, admit that General Reyes has indeed won her over, and join the Revolution by taking her place behind General Reyes's horse as a *soldadera*.

If the classic revolutionary melodrama was a fertile ground for staging narratives that reinforced the nation's newly secured post-colonial

Who's prettier? Lumi Cavazos and Marco Leonardi in *Como agua para chocolate*. Courtesy Centro de Investigación y Enseñanza Cinematográficas, Universidad de Guadalajara.

masculinity, especially in the period following the nationalization of the country's natural resources and key industries that significantly altered Mexico's neocolonial status in relation to the United States, in *Como agua para chocolate* men are represented as one-dimensional objects of desire, boy-toys, and are frequently overly accommodating, weak, and somewhat feminized. In contrast, the characters who tend to display traits associated with masculinity are some of the women (Mamá Elena and Gertrudis). Given my focus on representations of masculinity, I will limit my discussion to the ways men are portrayed in this film, especially since the models of Mexican masculinities offered in Arau's film mark a radical departure from the gender conventions of the classic revolutionary melodrama.

I will begin with the leading man, Pedro, who is portrayed by the demure, pretty-boy Italian actor Marco Leonardi, who earlier catapulted to international fame with *Cinema Paradiso* (Giuseppi Tornatore, 1989).[27] Several factors tend to demasculinize Pedro: his inability to marry the woman he loves tends to infantilize him; Leonardi's boyish good looks make him look like an adolescent well into his adult life; the intertextual resonances linked to Leonardi's role as the adolescent Toto, the apprentice projectionist in *Cinema Paradiso,* make it difficult to disassociate Pedro from Toto, especially since *Como agua para chocolate* was released shortly after *Cinema Paradiso.* Pedro also lacks depth. We are given very little information about him; we know the bare minimum about his psychological motivations; he has very few lines; and, for the most part, he appears as a mannequin. The fact that Leonardi's voice is dubbed in a far-from-seamless manner reinforces this association of Pedro with an empty vessel, just another pretty face. Just when Pedro is set to take a more active role in Tita's life, he dies of a sudden stroke during their long-awaited sexual consummation.

His passivity and receptiveness is highlighted in the novel in Chapter Three when Tita, marked as the active and penetrating subject, cooks quail in rose petal sauce, which has the effect of rousing everyone's sexual appetite.

> She entered Pedro's body, hot, voluptuous, perfumed, totally sensuous. With that meal it seemed they had discovered a new system of communication, in which Tita was the transmitter, Pedro the receiver, and poor Gertrudis the medium, the conducting body through which the singular sexual message was passed. Pedro didn't offer any resistance. He let Tita penetrate to the farthest corners of his being, and all the while they couldn't take their eyes off each other. (Esquivel 1992: 48)

Gertrudis's assistant, the bumbling and servile sergeant Treviño (Joaquín Garrido), is emasculated. An index of his feminization is that he figuratively wears an apron, since Gertrudis, his military superior, orders him to prepare her favorite dessert during a visit to her family home. Doubling as a comic sidekick, sergeant Treviño is a pale version of comics from the Golden Age, such as Chicote and Agustín Izunza, who also portrayed popular types of comedic figures who were servant-like figures. Finally, Gertrudis's handsome partner, the Villista Captain Juan Alejandrez (Rodolfo Arias), is little more than a hunky boy-toy. He is shown engaging in two pleasure-related activities: having sex with Gertrudis while both are mounted on a horse and dancing "Jesusita en Chihuahua" with her.

The codes used to represent gringos continue the conventions used in the classic period. These conventions are stereotypes that fall into two categories: unscrupulous and greedy villains (*La perla,* Emilio Fernández, 1945) and inoffensive and unmanly objects of ridicule (*Enamorada*).

Dr. Brown, Tita's suitor, falls into the latter category. He is what my mother would call a *buen cristiano*—overly generous, naïve, gullible, verging on stupid. Critic Ayala Blanco appropriately calls Doctor Brown "a nerd" (1994: 330). Dr. Brown, as portrayed by the white-complexioned Mexican actor Mario Iván Martínez, does not exude sex appeal. He sports three-piece suits, a bow tie, and wire-rimmed glasses. He is positively inconspicuous, tame, and desexualized. Dr. Brown is also a cuckold; he is aware that Tita and Pedro are having an affair and is fantastically understanding of the dynamics that compel Tita.

This strategic displacement and resignification of the Revolution in contemporary State-funded Mexican film parallels the nation's recent neoliberal economic policies and represents a rejection of some of the basic tenets of the Revolution. These shifts encompass a neo-*porfirista* trend, enabling the historical rehabilitation of the Porfirio Díaz regime, a villain in modern Mexico's narrative of origins for his receptiveness to foreign and ruling-class economic interests. This rewriting of history is clearly evinced in the epic telenovela *El vuelo del águila* (*The Eagle's Flight*, 1991), focusing on the life of Díaz, produced by the mega-multimedia conglomerate Televisa, a major power broker in the Mexican political system belonging to the business empire of the late Emilio Azcárraga. Televisa, along with Brazil's TV Globo, are the largest audiovisual corporations in Latin America. *El vuelo del águila* forms part of a larger revaluation of Díaz's contribution to the industrialization of modern Mexico. The starkest signs of the shortcomings of the Revolution, not addressed in any films produced by the State during the current period of global economic integration, are the continuing ethnic, racial, and class-based social inequalities and the failure of effective agrarian reform exemplified by the ongoing armed struggle of the Zapatistas in Chiapas since 1994.

III. CONCLUSION: MEXICAN FILM CULTURE OF THE 1990S

In light of Mexico's current political, economic, and social problems, it is difficult to be celebratory about the remarkable achievements of Mexican State-funded film. Given the bleak sociopolitical context, it is clear that one function of State-funded Mexican film culture is to legitimize the reigning government's mandate. Funding the arts underscores the humane side of a fairly ruthless economic program whose primary beneficiaries are national and transnational corporations. By investing in what circulates as Mexican cultural capital at international film festivals, universities, museums, and art film circuits, the Mexican State showcases a selective national film heritage and selectively fosters national traditions, thereby reinforcing and reproducing its political institutions.

The function that film festivals, museums, and universities play in marketing national cinemas is to situate, in this case, Mexico's place in the family of nations that have been embraced by a world film culture canon defined by Euro-American standards, thereby symbolically positioning Mexico as an equal economic and cultural partner along with other leading First World nations. Mexico has officially been on the brink of achieving First World status since the Olympics were held in Mexico City in 1968, amidst mass social protests and escalated government repression not seen since the Revolution. In addition to functioning as cultural capital and political diplomacy, the films co-produced by the Mexican State also serve to stimulate private investment in an industry that during the height of its classic period (1943–1946) was the second-largest Mexican exporter, surpassed only by petroleum.

With this in mind, one might well ask if Mexican "art film" production will survive without the intervention of the State. Jorge Ayala Blanco has been proclaiming for some years that Mexican cinema is dead, in light of the drop in production and ineffective film policy that according to many analysts has only perpetuated structural problems that impede the growth of the film industry (Costa 1976; Sánchez 1982). Contrary to Ayala Blanco's opinion, Arturo Ripstein, Mexico's most renowned film auteur and one of the few established directors whose projects have consistently received State support since 1985, claims that art film production in Mexico cannot survive without the State's institutional support.[28] Perhaps a more telling question regarding the changing government involvement in cinema would be: How might Mexican national film fare without State funding, protection, and promotion? Televisa, a major player in the national economic and political culture, along with the Mexican government, is poised—along with Banamex, Bancomer, IBM de México, Pedro Domeq, and others—as a leading patron of the arts. Like IMCINE, Televicine, Televisa's film production branch, also promoted the work of various generations of filmmakers and has the capacity to take a leading role in "art film" and commercial productions, as can be gauged by the commercial and/or critical success of films such as *Mujeres insumisas* (*Untamed Women*, Alberto Isaac, 1994), *Sin remitente* (*No Return Address*,

Carlos Carrera, 1994), *Entre Pancho Villa y una mujer desnuda* (1995), and *La primera noche* (*The First Night*, Alejandro Gamboa, 1997).

In 1994, when Jorge Alberto Lozoya assumed the directorship of IMCINE, film production declined precipitously. Lozoya repeatedly expressed that IMCINE was not primarily an institution to promote production but rather to promote exhibition.[29] Accordingly, Lozoya's two-year term (1994–1996) increased the international exhibition of films funded by IMCINE compared to the preceding administration. There was renewed optimism in the industry when filmmaker Diego López Rivera, who previously directed Churubusco Studios, replaced Lozoya as head of IMCINE in the fall of 1996.[30] This optimism, however, proved erroneous. Feature film production at IMCINE dropped from an average of sixteen films annually during the 1988–1994 period to an average of eight films annually between 1995 and 2000, a pattern that confirms the government's lack of commitment to the promotion and protection of the national film industry. Since the 1970s during the Echeverría presidency, when the State became the major player in the film industry, State support for cinema has varied drastically according to the political imperatives of each administration. For Lynna Valdéz, who worked approximately from 1994 to 2000 at IMCINE in the department in charge of international promotion, the international success of a handful of Mexican directors and films from the 1990s is not a result of "a cohesive state project since IMCINE has never had continuity with its projects nor has it ever articulated a clear political agenda in regards to production, exhibition, and the distribution of its films" (2000: 71). She concludes that it is very necessary to establish a viable network for the commercial distribution and exhibition of films funded by IMCINE because without this, films risk being seen only by the limited audience to which IMCINE has access through its Mexican embassies, consulates, national and international film festivals, and other film-related cultural events (ibid.). The economic recession that hit Mexico in 1994 and the devaluation of the peso negatively affected the film industry. Feature film production has dropped to levels not seen since the 1930s, a period prior to the international expansion of Mexican film. Consider this: Mexico produced an average of one hundred features a year during the late 1940s and 1950s. In the 1980s, called the "lost decade" for many reasons, not the least of which was the low quality of feature films, the average number of annual feature film productions was ninety. Since then, overall feature film production has varied from as few as five in 1995 to fifteen in 1997 to thirty-two in 2000 to fourteen in 2002 (Vargas 2003a).

The impetus IMCINE gave to various generations of filmmakers emerging from Mexico's two principal film schools in the late 1980s and 1990s, as well as to established directors, combined with the international commercial and critical success of contemporary Mexican films, suggests some answers to the questions posed by Néstor García Canclini about the viability of promoting a national identity via art and about the future of Latin American cinema. Evaluating the impact that Mexican cinema has on its national and global audiences is a crucial way to assess the strengths and weaknesses of IMCINE's cultural politics.[31] Assessing the accomplishments of IMCINE during the period 1989–1994 shows how global politics shaped Mexican film policy and created the context for the "renaissance" in Mexican filmmaking, exhibition, and scholarship, an impact that was significant in local and global terms. This orchestrated renaissance displays the political function of film in shaping the legitimacy of the presidential mandate.

Filmmaking in Mexico has entered its second century of existence. Given Hollywood's persistent strength in many national film markets, findings from my field research on IMCINE, and other scholarly research on film policy and cinema-state relations in Latin America, suggests that in order to ensure the survival of a varied and diverse national film industry, a proactive and substantial level of State protection, funding, and promotion is crucial, as is the case with the Canadian and European culture industries, which have opted to exempt these from trade liberalization agreements in order to safeguard national culture and identity.[32] Another point of contention lies in who should administer dwindling State funds for film and how they should be distributed.[33]

I have outlined how cultural products are mediators of political ideologies and how audiovisual space constitutes a crucial site for the production and reproduction of power. The attention that Mexican cinema has received in the past decade clearly shows how "art films" are an integral part of Mexico's political culture as well as a crucial tool for diplomacy, as Carlos Salinas de Gortari makes explicit in the epigraph to this chapter. The crisis that the Mexican film industry currently finds itself in yet again reminds us how often crass political expediency overtakes a structural commitment to nourish and expand the national film industry and to sustain its huge potential. Without the collaboration of State, domestic, and foreign private investment, Mexican film runs the risk of becoming increasingly marginalized and overshadowed by Hollywood. Given the vital educational role that film plays in the formation of our social identities (how we perceive ourselves within our communities), and considering Hollywood's hegemony over the most lucrative international film markets, it seems of utmost urgency that national film cultures receive the State's full support to stimulate the development of a diverse national cinema that responds to the needs of its citizens while reaching out to audiences around the globe.

Mexican Cinema is Dead! Long Live Mexican Cinema!

✛   ✛   ✛

Necrophilia is culture.

JORGE AYALA BLANCO, 1990

It's hard to explain; it's a Mexican idiosyncrasy. . . . you're more macho
if you fuck men, you know?

GAEL GARCÍA BERNAL (QUOTED IN *RANTS & RAVES*, 2002)

*N*ot every actor inspires poetry. But for San Francisco Bay Area
resident Marina García-Vásquez (2004), Gael García Bernal is

the sparkle in onyx
an invincible eye-smile
obsidian against metallic

lips waves folding into each other
boca de cielo

charisma
a dahlia in full bloom
deep water-thrust of an octopus
a lone white kite lifting over Bombay
sun pressed against the moon
an eclipse.

The poem "For Gael" by the managing editor of *Planet,* a San Francisco-
based cultural magazine, appeared in an issue carrying the theme of

"man & woman." The text occupies the right edge of a full-page black and white mug shot that is lightly tinted with a mix of blue, green, and gray, reminiscent of the actor's eyes; in the layout, the poem sits on García Bernal's shoulder. In the close-up soft-focus photo by Brooklyn-based photographer Miguel Villalobos, García Bernal candidly looks out at the viewer. The photograph captures the actor in a moment that feels casual and spontaneous, relaxed, and intimate. The poem, like the photograph, evokes many of the perceived qualities that make García Bernal an international star, a sex symbol, a progressive and a kindred spirit, and an icon for a new generation of young Mexicans, Chicanas/os, Latinas/os, and Latin Americans—an immense critical mass beaming creativity and vitality—who see in the young actor a sign of hope ("a lone white kite lifting over Bombay"). García Bernal represents a young, modern, and cosmopolitan middle-class Latin/o American youth: multifaceted, multilayered, expressive, sensitive, sincere, intelligent, articulate, "real," down-to-earth, capable of expressing complex desires, and boyish. He is both feminine ("a dahlia in full bloom") and phallic ("deep water-thrust of an octopus"); a precious gem, he embodies both traditional objects associated with *mexicanidad* (obsidian used by Aztecs and other Native Mesoamericans) and global modernity (metallic, Bombay). His full lips are "waves"; his mouth is as heavenly as "Boca de Cielo," the idyllic seaside Oaxacan location where most of *Y tu mamá también* takes place; his eyes are like sparkling onyx, with its array of alternating colors.

García Bernal hails from Zapopan, part of Guadalajara's metropolitan area, the capital of Jalisco, home to *mariachi,* tequila, and *charros,* the horsemen who serve as the emblem for the region's agribusiness, all symbols of Mexican cultural and racial hybridity. Constructed as a synonym for *mexicanidad* during the Golden Age of Mexican cinema as well as in vernacular music, Guadalajara is ironically also famous for its manly macho men and for its large gay and lesbian population. It is a perfectly congruent birth origin for an actor who played in the same year two completely opposing models of masculinity. In *Los diarios de motocicleta* (*The Motorcycle Diaries,* Walter Salles, 2004) he plays the young Ernesto "Che" Guevara, the foremost icon of a virile Latin American revolutionary tradition.[1] In the second film, *La mala educación* (*Bad Education,* Pedro Almodóvar, 2004), he plays a strung-out transvestite who seeks a sex change by blackmailing the priest who sexually abused him as an adolescent.

It says a great deal about García Bernal's acting skills that he is credible as Che Guevara. As a Mexican national, García Bernal's participation in

Gael García Bernal. Photograph by Miguel Villalobos. Courtesy of Miguel Villalobos and *Planet.*

this biopic of the famous road trip taken by Guevara across South America with his friend Alberto Granado reminds us that the boat carrying Fidel Castro, Guevara, and others sailed across the Gulf of Mexico to Cuba on the eve of the Cuban Revolution. García Bernal playing Che, who was transformed into the legendary revolutionary in Cuba, also reminds us of the long tradition of cultural exchange between Mexico and Cuba. Like Che, García Bernal is a well-known traveler; both are transnational social actors of different sorts. It is paradoxical that this most recent cinematic commodification of Che inspires us to travel and consume rather than to critically reflect on the dire social conditions facing the millions of inhabitants of the vast lands south of the U.S.-Mexico border and throughout the "third world."

To his credit, García Bernal looks equally beautiful and authentic playing a sexy and vulnerable young man straddling a motorcycle and speeding past awe-inspiring landscapes in Brazilian director Walter Salles's road movie; playing a flirty fledgling writer of pulp screenplays who, in a memorable scene in Almodóvar's film, slips out of a pool in tight, wet, white briefs, revealing just enough to make his fans pant; and playing a Spanish transvestite in the aforementioned film. *La mala educación* is a film about films in which Almodóvar pays respect to Hitchcock and Spanish musical melodramas. García Bernal is positively seductive and coy in a sequence playing Zahra, an homage to the Spanish diva Sara Montiel, who starred in a number of films opposite Pedro Infante—with whom he is compared for his ability to seduce fans around the globe and for how profoundly audiences identify with him. García Bernal's breathy rendition of the classic *bolero* "Quizás quizás quizás," dressed in a tight-fitting silver sequin dress, is as sexy as Marilyn Monroe's "Happy Birthday, Mr. President."

In an interview, Almodóvar noted that

for Gael, I had to explain the period in Spain when the story took place and how to become a transvestite from that period, which is completely opposite of a drag queen nowadays. . . . Spanish and Mexican cultures are very different and he had to lose his Mexican accent. He also went through femininity classes and physical training to wear high heels. (Garibay 2004/2005a: 40–41)

In fact the issue of adopting a Spanish accent proved to be a sticky point for García Bernal. Commenting on the five-month training program he underwent to play the three roles he performs in *La mala educación*, García Bernal notes in an interview with the *New York Times*,

What was most difficult was losing my Mexican accent. Pedro insisted on that, and frankly, I thought it was ridiculous. He wanted a Spanish accent and that is a colonialist thing. The Spanish accent sounds to me like . . . Flemish. . . . But Pedro is a very specific person with a very personal point of view. It can be difficult to digest that information and meld it with your own interpretation, but in the end, it was very rewarding. (Quoted in Hirschberg 2004: 70)

Indeed, this wasn't the first time García Bernal adopted a non-Mexican accent. Like other Mexicans stars before him, García Bernal has played an entire gamut of ethnic nationals. His filmography is abundant in Latino roles that often typecast him as the all-too-familiar Latin lover. In English-language films, he has played an Italian in *I'm with Lucy* (John Sherman, 2002), an Argentine in *Fidel* (David Atwood, 2002), a Brazilian in *Dot the I* (Mathew Parkhill, 2003), and a Puerto Rican in *Dreaming of Julia* (Juan Gerard, 2003). In Spanish-language films that are not Mexican productions, he has played a Spaniard twice: first in *Sin noticias de Dios* (*Don't Tempt Me,* Agustín Díaz Yanes, 2001), followed by *La mala educación*. He has also played an Argentine in two films: *Vidas privadas* (*Private Lives,* Fito Páez, 2001) and *Diarios de motocicleta*.

The ease with which García Bernal mimics Latin accents underscores his capacity to transform himself into multiple embodiments of *latinidad* and to sound authentic, a key ingredient for audience identification.[2] His seduction of journalists—who are charmed by his unassuming manner, sincerity, and "natural" realness—and of film spectators around the world have made him the most sought-after Latin American movie star in recent memory, leading a Mexico City-based newspaper, *El Nacional,* to make the improbable claim that he is the Pedro Infante of the twenty-first century.[3] Infante's working-class roots and his appeal to ordinary Mexicans alone differentiate him from García Bernal and make the comparison between the two stars a stretch of the imagination.[4]

Similarly, U.S. journalists drool over the reluctant sex symbol. Kimberly Chun's feature story covering García Bernal's whirlwind San Francisco publicity tour for *Diarios de motocicleta* and *La mala educación* carried the headline "Y tu hottie también" (Chun 2004: 44). She remarks in her opening paragraph, "He's the only man who could have passed for Che, a delinquent priest, and the most grog tranny on the block—and now actor Gael García Bernal has done the impossible: he's reduced a set of hardened female ink peddlers, kept waiting in the lobby of a Union Square hotel, into pools of warm goo and fits of school kid giggles" (ibid.). Not surprisingly, the story focuses a great deal on sexuality, from the difficulty of filming sex scenes to the grueling grooming process required to transform Gael into Zahra. Not surprisingly, the requisite anecdotes about Guadalajara's dual, gender-bending identity are raised; Guadalajara's sex culture is symbolized by the image of professional soccer players in drag. García Bernal tells Chun that drag is "an everyday occurrence in Guadalajara . . . where football players dress as women for monthly matches" (ibid.).

Underscoring the significance of García Bernal's transformative capacity and his commitment to social justice, reporter Lisa Garibay (2004/2005a) argues that his political beliefs are congruent with the roles he takes and the way he presents himself in public and to the press. He scored points with many of his fans in the United States and abroad for his antiwar remarks at the Academy Awards ceremony in 2003, the year *Y tu mamá también* was nominated for Best Original Screenplay, *El crimen del padre Amaro* (*The Crime of Padre Amaro,* Carlos Carrera, 2002) earned a Best Foreign Language Film nomination, and his compatriot Salma Hayek received numerous Oscar nominations for her much-publicized film project *Frida* (Julie Taymor, 2002), the biopic about the celebrated Mexican painter Frida Kahlo. At the 2004 Academy Awards ceremony, García Bernal again made a political statement by refusing to attend the event in protest against the organizers who did not allow Uruguayan singer and composer Jorge Drexler to perform his Oscar-nominated song "Al otro lado del río" from *Diarios de motocicleta.* The organizers instead chose the Spanish actor Antonio Banderas to perform the song, accompanied by Carlos Santana on guitar. But this story had a happy ending because Drexler made history by winning the Oscar for Best Original Song, the first time a Spanish-language song triumphed at this English-centered event—yet another sign of the big impact Latin/o Americans are making in Hollywood and beyond.

García Bernal is different from other actors. He actively promotes Latin American and Spanish-language cinema. Reporter Jessica Hundley highlights his allegiance to Latin American and Mexican cinema: "He considers himself to be a Mexican actor, first and foremost" (2004: 130). He is as far removed as possible from the typical twenty-something Hollywood actor and rejects the superstar syndrome. As a case in point, it is uncommon for film actors to discuss race and class inequality in interviews with U.S. journalists. However, in an interview with *SOMA,* a New York-based magazine catering to the upwardly mobile, he explained how at age fourteen he underwent an "inner journey of self-awareness" when he joined a literacy program for Huicholes, a native indigenous population of northern Jalisco who were not conquered by the Spanish because the community fled to the mountains. His experience with the Huicholes was a transformative moment.

This inevitably awakens you to realize we share the same place. You find yourself in a more privileged situation just because you're born the way you are and they're underprivileged because of who they are. Yet we share the same territory and it's ridiculous. (Quoted in Garibay, 2004/2005a: 40)

With five film hits under his belt in just four years, the twenty-six-year-old has been featured on the cover of most cutting-edge and popular U.S. film and culture magazines. With the press he positions himself as both a cultural activist and a promoter of Latin American cinema. The press talks about him as an international film sensation. García Bernal comes off in interviews as being a somewhat reluctant star who is baffled as to why people think he is sexy. Hundley describes him as "a kind of anti-celebrity, a poster child for independent success and for achieving fame outside the carefully constructed, bleach-blond mainstream" (2004: 130).

With García Bernal's help, Mexicans seem to be slowly shedding their inferiority complex about their national cinema. Until recently, Mexican cinema received little international attention, most notably in English-speaking parts of the world. Since the 1990s Mexican films have become trendy with audiences and critics. In 1993 *Como agua para chocolate* broke box office records not only in Mexico but, most importantly, in the United States, becoming the highest-grossing foreign-language film at that time. *Amores perros* and *El crimen del padre Amaro* earned Oscar nominations for Best Foreign Language Film. The last Mexican movie to be nominated previously for Best Foreign Language Film was more than three decades ago.[5] *Amores perros* was released in thirty countries and *Y tu mamá también* in forty. In Havana there was so much buzz about *Y tu mamá también* during its premiere screening at the 2001 International Festival of New Latin American Cinema that a riot almost broke out among people waiting in line outside the Yara theater, as I can attest. I witnessed more than fifteen hundred people standing in line for over two hours waiting to get into the screening. As the crowd grew beyond normal proportions and more film fans pressed against the glass doors at the lobby of the Yara, the pressure caused the glass to shatter. When the police arrived, the screening was cancelled and the huge crowd was dispersed into the rain-slicked streets of La Habana on that memorable overcast evening in December.

The five films starring García Bernal have had an immense international impact and created a buzz about Mexico's new cinema. García Bernal's international appeal has been vital to the expansion of Latin American cinema as a whole. Since 2000 García Bernal has starred in "innovative narratives that have simultaneously spawned and defined a new era in Latin American cinema" (Hundley 2004: 130). Indeed, García Bernal is deeply aware of the dimensions of his own contribution to new Latin American cinema when he gushed at being part of a film trend that is "telling our stories as Latin Americans" (ibid.).

As a fervent supporter of U.S. Latino and Latin American cinemas, I feel fortunate to be an active participant in this surge of interest in film cultures that I call my own. This book is an appreciation and a celebration of a national cinema that has profoundly shaped me and my understanding of the world. My approach in this project has been to demonstrate how deeply implicated cinema is in the construction of a gendered and sexualized transnational and transcontinental cinematic imaginary. *Mexicanidad* continues to circulate through popular culture and remains instrumental in reimagining the new post-national Mexico. From the late 1930s until 1968, cinema helped forge a coherent and authoritarian political system. The four case studies narrate chronological and thematic shifts in the role of cinematic production and State regulation of gender, sexuality, and various forms of social identification. Chapter One offered a survey of major developments in the discourse of the prostitute and transgressive sexualities that engages feminist insights on the role of women in nation building. Chapter Two considered a parallel narrative, the multivalent masculine role models embodied by Infante in his buddy movies, where I appropriate this screen idol for an alternative queer film legacy. Chapter Three explored how representations of male heterosexual machos in popular films from the 1970s are riddled with ambiguity and anxiety elicited by the presence of gay men, imaged as flamboyant queens. And Chapter Four extended the analysis by moving the gendered national discourse into the contemporary period, examining the renewed attention awarded revolutionary melodramas and the global popularity of the new Mexican cinema. To be sure, the role of the State in promoting specific modalities of gender and sexuality through film indexes great shifts and uncertainties in Mexican society.

Film in Mexico remains a crucial source of cultural capital and international prestige and is an influential partner in circulating images of *mexicanidad* in the new millennium. From the shadow of Golden Age cinema emerged a globally oriented film industry that was radically restructured and retrofitted through neoliberal market reforms and private investments, enabling the formation of new audiences at home and abroad. The popularity of homegrown films is part of a larger trend in Latin American cinemas that also encompasses greater collaboration among Latin American film industries and the exchange of talent from Spain and from across the American continents, including Latinas and Latinos working in Holly-wood.[6] Mexico is the leader of a dynamic new Latin American cinema that does not resemble the politically militant New Latin American Cinema "movement" of the 1960s and '70s. At the 2004 Cannes Film Festival, Latin America was represented with close to a dozen films in and out of official competition. This high level of participation is a gauge of the dynamism of cinemas from the region.[7]

Mexican cinema is winning fans at home and abroad. For decades dis-missed as a lost cause, pronounced dead or moribund by its harshest crit-ics, a source of shame for the national bourgeoisie, Mexican cinema has in the past decade taken a 180-degree turn. Backed by private investors and massive promotion campaigns, a string of hits at the box office—be-ginning as far back as *Rojo amanecer* (*Red Dawn,* Jorge Fons, 1989), the controversial first film to openly address the 1968 military massacre of civilians at Tlatelolco Plaza in downtown Mexico City, and continuing through the 1990s with *Sexo, pudor y lágrimas* (Sex, Shame, and Tears, 1999, Antonio Serrano), a comedy about the woes of three pairs of dys-functional and attractive heterosexual middle-class couples from Mexico City—Mexican cinema has inaugurated a hopeful new stage in its history. Serrano's light comedy—featuring popular stars from telenovelas, *rock en español,* and the new cinema as well as a catchy techno soundtrack by Alex Syntek—became an extraordinary box office hit.[8] Subsequent successful Mexican films, including *Amores perros* and *Y tu mamá también,* have also capitalized on the films' rock and pop soundtracks.[9] Historically music has been a determining factor in the popularity of Mexican films, as I dis-cussed in Chapters One and Two. Music genres have been instrumental in consolidating autochthonous Mexican film genres, from *ranchera* music in the *comedia ranchera* to *boleros* in prostitution melodramas to *corridos* in revolutionary melodramas. Contemporary Mexican cinema contin-ues to profit from Mexico's and Latin America's incredibly diverse music cultures.

For several weeks *Sexo, pudor y lágrimas* grossed more than *Star Wars II: The Phantom Menace* (George Lucas, 1999). The children of the middle class, who in the past had turned their backs on Mexican films, and film audiences around the world are largely responsible for energizing a finan-cially crippled film industry bursting at the seams with talent and creativ-ity. Critic Leonardo García Tsao describes the audience that "saved" the Mexican film industry as "a new kind of audience, basically young, that goes to the shopping mall multi-cinemas attracted by films that portray their own culture" (2002: 44).

As I have already noted, the history of Mexico's film industry is marked by a series of boom and bust cycles. The end of the populist classic period of the 1940s and '50s marked the beginning of a downward slump in the quality of films and a more gradual decrease in the annual film production from which the industry has not yet recovered. At the dawn of the new millennium, *Amores perros,* however, altered the Mexican film industry's post-classic blues by breaking box office records and reaping prestigious awards, including the Critics Week Grand Prize and Young Critics Award at Cannes and an Oscar nomination for Best Foreign Language Film.[10] *Amores perros* put the Mexican film industry in the spotlight again and quickly built a cult following. For Mexicans, *Amores perros* became a source of national pride, akin to the effect produced by the international commercial and critical success of *Como agua para chocolate.* The three-part film, which opens with a riveting car chase, is about alienation and political estrangement. It focuses on three groups of people from different social sectors in Mexico City whose lives are affected by the resulting car accident. *Amores perros* became an instant classic and is the subject of high-profile academic research.[11]

When the film opened in the United States, *Interview* magazine film critic Scott Lyle Cohen asserted that *Amores perros* director Alejandro González Iñárritu "scores one of the most impressive debuts in recent memory" (2001: 64).[12] At a loss for explaining the influences shaping the "genius" responsible for the film, most U.S. critics exposed their parochial grasp of world film history when their only reference point to Mexican film is Luis Buñuel's *Los olvidados* (1950). Reviewers also attributed the film's triptych narrative structure to Quentin Tarantino's *Pulp Fiction* (1994) rather than referencing Mexican melodramas like Jorge Fons's *El callejón de los milagros* (*Midaq Alley,* 1994) or Arturo Ripstein's *La mujer del puerto* (*Woman of the Port,* 1992) that also have a complex multiperspective, nonlinear structure. For instance, Lynn Hirschberg's feature article on the film that appeared in *The New York Times Magazine* argued that "at first glance, *Amores perros* seems like a Mexican *Pulp Fiction.* . . . But while *Pulp Fiction* was a brilliant meditation on all things pop, *Amores perros* is weightier" (2001: 32). González Iñárritu's next project, *21 Grams* (2003), was made in English and produced in the United States with a stellar cast featuring Sean Penn, Benicio del Toro, and Naomi Watts.[13]

Like Latin American novelists of the "boom" period, Guillermo Arriaga, the film's screenwriter—whose previous credit as screenwriter was *Un dulce olor a muerte* (*The Sweet Smell of Death*, Gabriel Retes, 1999)—says he shares more affinities with the literary than the cinematic. Describing himself as "basically a novelist" in his interview with Hirschberg, Arriaga situates his work in the modernist literary tradition followed by his country's most noted narrative writers, such as Juan Rulfo and Carlos Fuentes, who experimented extensively with time and space compression, creating a uniquely Mexican literature that was both attentive to regional differences and vernacular forms and practices while simultaneously displaying a sophisticated and cosmopolitan assimilation and transformation of foreign vanguard traditions.[14]

> I was surprised when people said that *Amores perros* was like *Pulp Fiction*. I admire that movie, but I based my script on William Faulkner. Faulkner once said something like, "If you want to understand the world, write about your neighbor." (Hirschberg 2001: 34)

Even Mexican nationals, who are usually quick to put down local films, were favorably impressed by how authentically the film represented Mexico City and its various urban male subcultures, such as underground dog fights, born of the city's sharply differentiated class and race stratifications. Not since *Los olvidados* had a Mexican film elicited unanimous praise for its unsentimental depiction of the culture of poverty associated with the urban sprawl of Mexico City, one of the most populous cities in the world. *Amores perros* taps into a national film aesthetic, principally in the first part of the film, titled "Octavio and Susana," that links folklore to poverty and makes abjection and degradation into distinguishing markers of *mexicanidad,* similar to how the *pelado* is constructed in the literary philosophy of *mexicanidad* as the quintessential symbol of national abjection. González Iñárritu inherits a cinematic miserabilist aesthetic found in the work of such dissimilar figures as Luis Buñuel, Emilio Fernández, Ismael Rodríguez, and, more recently, Arturo Ripstein, who takes it to baroque and kitschy extremes.[15]

The New York Times Magazine noted that the *Amores perros* sensation became "a matter of national pride" (Hirschberg 2001: 34). González Iñárritu, a well-known Mexico City rock music DJ before he turned to film, claims he sought to correct stereotypes that Americans have of their southern neighbor.

My goal was to show the whole world how interesting Mexico City is. . . . The way America sees Mexico, if they have any sense of it, is like Taco Bell. . . . Americans see us as . . . folkloric. They don't accept that we're a powerful, diverse culture, and my goal is to enlarge the view of Mexico. To show life as it is here. . . . Not the Taco Bell idea. (Quoted in Hirschberg 2001: 34)

Backed by private investors (including Carlos Slim, reported to be the richest man in Latin America) and new production companies (Anhelo, Titan, Altavista, Argos), big publicity campaigns, an emerging new star system, and international laurels, Mexico's new wave cinema is at the cutting edge. A new generation of filmmakers has produced films that speak to Mexico's youth, and the middle class has finally embraced homegrown movies. Audiences can recognize themselves in the films of the '90s generation. For director Juan Antonio de la Riva, third-wave new cinema is "recuperating a market without an audience" (in Correa 1992: 11). Third-wave new cinema enabled the emergence of a popular film culture not seen since the legendary Golden Age.[16]

García Bernal—"Mexico's new cinema sensation"—is the poster boy for this revival. Three feature films in which he stars (*Amores perros, Y tu mamá también,* and *El crimen del padre Amaro*) set domestic box office records and propelled Mexican cinema in bold new directions by breaking ground in subject matter (sexuality, religious taboos, political corruption) and visual design (a hip, realist edginess drawn from advertising and music videos). García Bernal has spoken about changing cinema-State relations and has said that a new generation of Mexican movie audiences and filmmakers is totally disassociated from the old cultural politics of the PRI and government patronage of cinema.[17]

This new cinema is not dependent on government funds for its survival. International co-productions have become the rule for commercial filmmaking. The new cinema mixes conventions from both "art" and commercial films in order to appeal to the broadest possible audience; it caters to the local middle class as well as to the international market. Operating without self-imposed censorship, filmmakers now have more creative freedom, previously available only to those working in the independent sector or in alternative film and video. The weekend *Y tu mamá también* opened in Los Angeles, the headline of the cover story in the Sunday Calendar section of the *Los Angeles Times* announced "A New Mexican Revolution" (Muñoz 2002: 8). The *Times* writer argues that Alfonso

Cuarón is single-handedly "helping to revolutionize Mexican cinema" (82). Paradoxically, while the U.S. press proclaimed a cinematic revolution south of the border, annual film production in Mexico is at its lowest since the mid-1930s, when the film industry first expanded with the international success of the *comedia ranchera,* its first bona fide autochthonous film genre as seen in *Allá en el Rancho Grande* (1936).

The decades it took to consolidate the Mexican film industry were dismantled in just six years. Film production dropped by 71 percent in the past decade. The Mexican senate reported that 212 feature film productions were made in the past decade, compared to 747 between 1984 and 1994 (Bensinger and de la Fuente 2004: 13). As I discussed in Chapter Four, between 1989 and 1994 the State dismantled its long-standing and unprofitable investments in the film industry, which further opened the market to U.S. interests, especially in distribution and exhibition. Communications specialist Enrique Ruiz Sánchez (1998: 1) characterized the film industry in Mexico as undergoing a process of "contraction, concentration, and unequal exchange." [18] Although he argues that Mexican cinema is becoming marginalized, new feature film productions have proven to be unusually popular with audiences. Mexican cinema refuses to die.

The limited conditions for filmmaking in Mexico pushed filmmakers to Hollywood. Alfonso Cuarón headed for Hollywood after directing his first feature, *Sólo con tu pareja* (*Tale of Love and Hysteria,* 1991). He reached international fame, however, only after returning to Mexico to make *Y tu mamá también,* after which he was chosen to direct the multimillion-dollar-grossing *Harry Potter and the Prisoner of Azkaban* (2004). Cuarón's case is not entirely unprecedented. Other filmmakers from the same generation—including gothic horror director Guillermo del Toro (*Cronos* [1992], *Mimic* [1997], *Blade 2* [2002], *El espinazo del diablo* [*The Devil's Backbone,* 2001], *Hellboy* [2004]) and the cinematographers Emmanuel Lubezki (*Como agua para chocolate, Y tu mamá también, The Bird Cage* [1996], *Sleepy Hollow* [1999], *Ali* [2001], *The Cat in the Hat* [2003], *Lemony Snicket's A Series of Unfortunate Events* [2004], *The New World* [2005]) and Rodrigo Prieto (*Amores perros, Frida, 8 Mile* [2003], *25th Hour* [2003], *21 Grams* [2003], *Alexander* [2004]) are expanding Mexican cinema's transnational reach. These traveling filmmakers move mostly between Mexico and the United States. They follow the tracks of other Mexicans who have left their indelible mark in Hollywood, including legendary figures of the classic Mexican cinema Dolores del Río, Katy Jurado, María Félix, Pedro Armendáriz, Arturo de Córdova, Emilio Fernández, Gabriel Figueroa,

Lupe Vélez, and others. Thus framing the international success of leading figures of the 1990s new cinema as an "overnight success" overlooks the achievements of their ancestors. The exodus of film talent to Hollywood in the 1990s contributed to Mexico's vibrant new film culture.

The March 8–16, 2002, issue of *LA Weekly* devoted the cover story and several articles to Mexican film. The cover photograph features Cuarón flanked by Gael García Bernal and Diego Luna, the two young stars of his controversial film. The headline, "*Y Tu Cine También*: Mexican Film Goes Global," cites the film's title while referencing the international appeal of the new wave. Part of the film's success lies in how its narrative highlights the homoerotic elements that are usually submerged in the buddy-road-teen movie. The controversy generated by the Mexican Catholic Church's massive campaign against *El crimen del padre Amaro* by far surpassed the buzz surrounding the explicit representation of teenage sexuality in *Y tu mamá también*.

In a logical continuation of representations of male homosocial relations and bonding rituals, the film's candid focus on the busy sexual life of two middle- and upper-class teenagers from Mexico City who are best friends since childhood gives expression to the unspoken sexual desire they have for one another. As in Infante's buddy movies, Cuarón's film uses the narrative device of an erotic triangulation in which a woman enables men to express their homoerotic desire. The film asks audiences to acknowledge pan-sexuality and the complexities of desire; it challenges homophobic audiences. At the two public screenings I attended—one in a multiplex on Reforma Boulevard in Mexico City on opening day, the other in a multiplex at a large shopping mall in Sacramento, California—large segments of the audiences reacted vocally with visceral disgust at the sight of two men kissing passionately. The visual spectacle of men kissing clearly registers anxieties regarding what is deemed to be inappropriate behavior between men.

The climactic ménage à trois that ends with Diego Luna and García Bernal kissing as Spanish actress Maribel Verdú felates them both pushes audiences to reconsider Mexico's legendary macho image from a different perspective, just as the kiss between Pancho and La Manuel had done more than twenty years earlier. *Y tu mamá también* brings out the homoerotic and homosocial elements central to the social construction of Mexican masculinities and highlights the link between being macho and engaging in sexual intercourse with men. García Bernal told the U.S. gay and lesbian bimonthly magazine *The Advocate* that "it's a Mexican idiosyncrasy. . . . you're more macho if you fuck men, you know?"[19] Cuarón's film unabashedly brings out and embraces head-on the homoerotic impulses barely repressed in Pedro Infante's classic buddy movies of the '50s discussed in Chapter Two. Cuarón's film explores territory—adolescent sexuality, class differences, national politics—that popular Hollywood teen comedies like *American Pie* (Paul Weitz, 1999) never touch. Ironically, *Y tu mamá también* departs from Cuarón's somewhat homophobic discourse in his AIDS-themed debut film, *Sólo con tu pareja.*

Como agua para chocolate, Amores perros, Y tu mamá también, and *El crimen del padre Amaro* made Mexican cinema the hottest and most talked-about foreign-language national cinema in the subtitle-phobic and notoriously monolingual U.S. film market.[20] *Amores perros* is even credited for revitalizing art cinema in the United States. While the success of Mexican films in the United States has in fact increased their U.S. theatrical exhibition, it is not often that audiences do get a chance to see Mexican films on the big screen. Thus film festivals continue to play an important role in circulating and promoting Mexican films and in creating a space for intercultural exchange. The growth of Latino film festivals in large U.S. cities (San Antonio, Chicago, San Francisco, New York, San Diego, Los Angeles, Miami) as well as the increasing number of international film festivals that showcase Latin American cinema (San Sebastián, Havana, Guadalajara, Huelva, Valladolid, Toulouse, Biarritz, Sundance) are expanding the new transnational Latino film circuit.[21]

Since 1985, the film festival in Guadalajara, whose founding director was Jaime Humberto Hermosillo, is the best place to see Mexican cinema. In 2005, on its twentieth anniversary, the Muestra de Cine Mexicano en Guadalajara was renamed the Festival Internacional de Cine en Guadalajara to highlight the event's international scope; just the year before, its name had been changed to Muestra de Cine Iberoamericano y Mexicano. Many who make the annual journey to the film festival in Guadalajara, including myself, lamented the meager number of Mexican films programmed in 2005.[22] In the case of home entertainment, however, contemporary and classic Mexican films are now more readily available on DVD as well as through cable television.[23]

Mexico now has the fourth-largest film market in the world, a fact that merits further attention. In the past decade Mexico has witnessed an explosion in the construction of multiplex cinemas at shopping centers, some 2,800 screens, led by Cinepolis, Cinemex, Cinemark, and Organización Ramírez. In 1997 box office revenues increased 50 percent. In

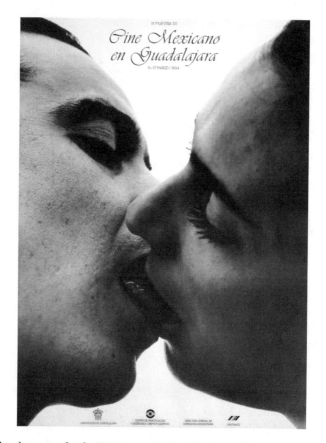

Gender-bender poster for the IX Muestra de Cine Mexicano en Guadalajara (1994). Photography by Rafael Lopez Castro. Courtesy Festival Internacional de Cine en Guadalajara.

2004 Mexicans bought a record 164 million tickets for a box office total of some $484 million; however, only 8 million tickets were for Mexican films (Bensinger 2005: A8). With film tickets costing an average of $4 to $5, more Mexicans choose to see pirated copies of films at home.

Other important developments worthy of research include the shifting terrain of production in the post-PRI era, the growing number of co-productions with other Spanish-speaking nations, particularly Argentina and Spain, the emphasis on "partnership," and the future of Spanish-language cinema in the United States.

Not all contemporary developments are promising, however. President Vicente Fox threatened in November 2003 to cut funding for IMCINE and to privatize the Centro de Capacitación Cinematográfica, one of the leading film schools, and Churubusco Azteca Studios.[24] Fox's announcement provoked an international outcry in support of Mexico's filmmaking institutions. An editorial column in the *New York Times* argued that Mexican cinema helps safeguard the nation's cultural identity, particularly in light of Hollywood's enormous presence in Mexican multiplexes.

> Not every poor country should have a national film industry. But Mexico should, and not just because of its history. Like France, Mexico defines itself in large part by what it isn't: it's not the United States. For Mexicans, their films are a defense against being swallowed culturally by America. Despite the best efforts of the Mexican film industry, 80 percent of the movies playing in Mexican theaters come from Hollywood. (Rosenberg 2003)

The conditions for film production in Mexico remain precarious and reflect a shift in government philosophy away from State intervention toward the neoliberal, privately financed model, an effect of NAFTA and the new model of multinational co-productions that have become the norm throughout Latin America. Until very recently, there was little incentive for private producers to invest in filmmaking, as they receive between 9 and 17 percent of their films' total box office revenue; most goes to distributors and exhibitors.[25] In November 2004 a new tax incentive, modeled after a similar initiative in Brazil, allowing investors to "allocate up to 3% of their annual income to homegrown cinema," capped at $43 million per year nationwide, heralded a possible jump-start for the industry (Bensinger and de la Fuente 2004: 12). Since the average cost of a Mexican feature film is less than $2 million, this tax incentive can potentially help produce as many as twenty features annually.[26]

The Motion Picture Association of America successfully blocked a law proposed in 2002 that would have allocated one peso from every ticket sold to a national film fund as an infringement of World Trade Organization regulations.[27] To attract foreign production to Mexico, a rebate passed in August 2003 gives foreign producers a 15 percent value-added tax rebate on costs incurred using Mexican production services or a local producer.[28] It remains to be seen how the devastated Mexican film industry will recover and if the international success Mexican cinema achieved in the past decade can be sustained in the future.

Notes

✛ ✛ ✛

PREFACE

1. The photograph reportedly was taken by Infante's brother-in-law Guillermo López Castro in 1939, which would put Infante's age at twenty-two. There is, however, a clear discrepancy: in the photograph, Infante has the body and face of a man who is over thirty years old.

2. I discuss the photograph in light of the proliferation of research about men and masculinity in "Masculinidad y mexicanidad: panorama teórico-bibliográfico" (1998). I am eternally grateful to Claudia Tovar for searching high and low to secure me a copy of *Hijo de tigre . . . pintito.*

3. Unless otherwise indicated, all translations are mine. In Chapter One, Regina Rocha assisted me with the translations of *Santa.* Gustavo García helped me translate parts of Chapter Two.

INTRODUCTION

1. A *fichera* is a woman who works at cabarets. She dances with patrons of the establishment for a fixed sum and keeps them company and may offer sexual services. A *ficha* is a token or a chip used as a form of currency. Customers pay for the number of *fichas* accrued at the end of the evening. Women who work as *ficheras* often have another occupation such as domestic servant, store clerk, or secretary.

2. This term came up during the many conversations I shared with Benjamin Lawrance during the process of revising this book. He suggested I title the book *Mexican Cinemachismo.* I modified the title and fleshed out the meaning of the concept.

3. The definitive study on the contributions of the Contemporáneos group to modern Mexican culture is Guillermo Sheridan's exhaustive study *Los contemporáneos ayer* (1985). Excellent scholarship that analyzes the homophobia directed against the Contemporáneos in light of the construction of a revolutionary literature and a new national culture includes Balderston (1998), Irwin (2003), and Monsiváis (2001).

4. A note of clarification regarding the translation of titles is in order. Where applicable, the titles as they appeared in English-speaking markets are italicized, such as *Like Water for Chocolate*. Titles that I translated appear without italics.

5. On the image of the *charro* as icon of *mexicanidad* see Palomar Verea (2004). Two excellent overviews of the immensely popular folkloric images of Mexican culture circulated through Mexican calendars since the 1930s are the exhibition catalogues *Cronos y cromos* (1993) and *La patria portátil: 100 Years of Mexican Chromo Art Calendars* (1999).

6. A definition of what is meant by "cabaret" in Mexico is necessary. According to Armando Jiménez's (1998: 42–43) lively study of dance halls, cabarets, billiard halls, and theaters in Mexico City, a cabaret can be a nightclub, dance hall, bar, restaurant, brothel; basically it is a place where (mostly) adults congregate to socialize and where they can dance, drink alcoholic beverages, watch musical performances, listen to (live) music, engage in sexual activities.

7. Among the most notable studies of women in Mexican film are Arredondo (2001), Dever (2003), Franco (1989), Fregoso (2003), Hershfield (1996, 2000), Iglesias and Fregoso (1998), López (1991), Millán (1999), Monsiváis (1995, 1997b), Paranaguá (1998a, 2003), Pick (1993), Ramírez Berg (1992), Rashkin (2001), Tierney (1997, 2003), Torres San Martín (1998, 2001, 2004), Torres San Martín and Vega (1997), and Tuñón (1998, 2000).

8. A cross-section of literary and film scholarship on representations of gender in Mexico, and in particular masculinities, includes Acevedo-Muñoz (2003), Balderston (1997, 1998), Burton-Carvajal (1997), Foster (1991, 1997a, 1997b, 2002, 2003a, 2003b), Díaz-López (2005), Irwin (2003), Monsiváis (1995, 1997b), Muñoz (1996), Noble (2003), Ortiz (1996), Paranaguá (1998a, 2003), Ramírez Berg (1992), Schaefer (1996), Torres San Martín (2001), and Tuñón (1998).

9. On this subject see the essays in Irwin, McCaughan, and Nasser (2003).

10. I thank Elissa Rashkin for this insight regarding my formulation of the macho-*joto* interdependent relation.

11. See de Orellana (1992).

12. Included among the groundbreaking audience reception studies of Mexican film are Iglesias (1998, 1999), Torres San Martín (unpublished), and the various chapters in the anthology edited by Néstor García Canclini (1994).

13. Filmmaker Gregorio Rocha's excellent documentary *Los rollos perdidos de Pancho Villa* (2003) focuses on Rocha's quest to find the missing narrative film *The Life of General Villa* (1913) filmed under contract between Villa and Mutual Film. The story of Villa and Mutual Film was turned into a feature film produced and broadcast by HBO titled *And Starring Pancho Villa as Himself* (Bruce Beresford, 2004). Curiously, Spanish actor Antonio Banderas plays Villa. This problematic casting decision suggests that there were no qualified Mexican actors to play the revered Mexican folk hero; it continues Hollywood's history of casting Anglo-American and European actors to play Latin American historical figures. Wallace Berry was cast as Villa in *Viva Villa!* (Jack Conway, 1934); Paul Muni played Mexican President Benito Juárez in *Juárez* (Hal B. Wallis, 1939); and Marlon Brando was cast as the revolutionary hero Emiliano Zapata in *Viva Zapata!* (Elia Kazan, 1952).

14. The footage of Villa was shot by the Alva brothers; there is no evidence that either Toscano or his cameramen ever followed his campaign or filmed him. Toscano seems to have been a follower of Venustiano Carranza. Carranza was a key political leader of the Revolution, head of the Constitutionalist Army of the central government in Mexico City;

he was president of Mexico between 1915 and 1920. William Christy Chabanne also directed *Martyrs of the Alamo* (1915), the earliest surviving film about the legendary battle at the Alamo mission in San Antonio, Texas, in 1836 that preceded Texas's secession from Mexico and augured the U.S.-Mexican War ten years later, when Mexico would lose half its territory to its northern neighbor. I thank Zuzana Pick for generously sharing with me her expertise on films about the Mexican Revolution in general and Pancho Villa specifically.

15. See also the hour-long documentary television program based on Krauze's book, *Pancho Villa, el ángel y el fierro* (Gloria Ribé 2001) and produced by Televisa Home Entertainment and Clío and distributed in the United States by Xenon Pictures Inc. The explicit political project of the Clío films on contemporary Mexican history is to "reaffirm Mexican identity." The producers claim to be "Mexico's audiovisual memory," as stated in the back cover of the DVD.

16. On queer cinema see Aaron (2004), Bad Object-Choices (1991), and Gever, Greyson, Parmar (1993). Notable studies of queer film and video and queer reading practices that foreground race and ethnicity include Fung (1991), Gopinath (2005), Muñoz (1999), Negrón-Muntaner (1996), and Rodríguez (2002). Included among the numerous studies that address masculinity and visual media: Berger, Wallis, and Watson (1995), Cohan (1997), Eng (2001), Fregoso (1993), Golden (1994), Jeffords (1989, 1994), Kim (2004), Lehman (1993), Mercer (1994), Quiroga (2000), Reich (2004), Smith (1996), P. J. Smith (1996), Stecopoulos and Uebel (1997), Tasker (1993), Waugh (1996, 2000), Wiegman (1995), Yosef (2004).

17. I thank Rosa Linda Fregoso for pointing out this insight regarding my queer readings of Infante's buddy movies.

18. See for example *¿Aguila o sol?* (Heads or Tails? Arcady Boytler, 1937) and *Los tres mosqueteros* (The Three Musketeers, Miguel M. Delgado, 1942).

19. See Noriega (1992: xii–xiii).

CHAPTER ONE

1. See the interview with Ninón Sevilla, "Señora Tentación," in Muñoz Castillo (1993: 162).

2. Messinger Cypess (1991) provides a survey of figurations of La Malinche across Mexican literature.

3. *Cabaretera* films (termed "dance hall movies" in U.S. Mexican film scholarship) emerged in the 1940s; they are film noir–inflected musicals frequently set in coastal urban areas or in the thriving nightlife and cabarets of Mexico City that catered to foreigners and the local middle class. The female lead is usually a musical performer and/or prostitute who is or becomes a successful professional dancer of Afro–Latin American tropical music, including Cuban conga, rumba, and *danzón,* Brazilian samba, and "exotic" dance traditions from the South Pacific and Asia. The name *exótica* was likely used because most of the well-known stars of the genre began their professional careers as dance and/or burlesque performers and because most were foreigners; the majority hailed from Cuba—Ninón Sevilla, María Antonieta Pons, Amalia Aguilar, Rosa Carmina. Yolanda Ivonne Móntez Farrington, better known as "Tongolele," is U.S.-born of mixed-race ancestry (Tahitian, Swedish, Spanish, French), raised in the San Francisco Bay Area, where she began her professional career; Meche Barba's birthplace was New York City. *Ficheras* take their name from the token used by clients in exchange for a dance and/or liquor; the cabarets and nightclubs in *fichera*

movies of the 1970s are usually on the low end of the social scale, and the narrative tone of this variation of *cabaretera* movies is comedic rather than tragic. For further discussion of *ficheras* see Jiménez (1998). For a narrative that is equal parts cultural history of *rumberas* and *exóticas* and biography of Tongolele see García Hernández (1998). For an excellent analysis of the relationship between pornography, censorship, and the morality campaigns waged in the Mexico City of the 1940s and '50s that targeted nightlife, dance, and theatrical performance see Fox (2000). For an overview of *cabaretera* fan culture, including interviews with the major stars, see Muñoz Castillo (1993). Studies of *cabaretera* films and cinematic melodramas of prostitution include Aviña (2004), Ayala Blanco (1993), Dever (2003), Hershfield (1996), López (1993), Monsiváis (1995), Monsiváis and Bonfil (1994), and Tuñón (1998). See also "Las rumberas del cine mexicano," a special issue of *Somos* (November 1999).

4. "Virgen de media noche," popularized throughout the Americas by the legendary Puerto Rican crooner Daniel Santos, archetype of the Latin lover, was first performed by Chela Santos in the eponymous Mexican *cabaretera*-cum-gangster melodrama directed by Alejandro Galindo (1941).

5. Agustín Lara is the key musical composer of this music genre; see Taibo (1984). For a historical overview of the Mexican *bolero* see Bazán Bonfil (2001) and Monsiváis (1997b).

6. For a cultural history of the *danzón* in Mexico see Flores y Escalante (1994).

7. A definition of the terms "prostitute" and "sex worker" is in order to underscore what is at stake in the meanings of these terms. Kamala Kempadoo finds that "the notion of the sex worker has emerged as a counterpoint to traditionally derogatory names, under the broad banner of a prostitutes' rights movement, with some parts recovering and valorizing the name and identity of 'whore' . . . [Sex worker] is a term that suggests we view prostitution not as an identity—a social or a psychological characteristic of women, often indicated by 'whore'—but as an income-generating activity or form of labor for women and men. The definition stresses the social location of those engaged in sex industries as working people. The idea of the sex worker is inextricably related to struggles for the recognition of women's work, for basic human rights and for decent working conditions. The definition emphasizes flexibility and variability of sexual labor as well as its similarities with other dimensions of working people's lives" (Kempadoo and Doezema 1998: 3). Furthermore, she emphasizes that the writings included in her co-edited anthology, *Global Sex Workers: Rights, Resistance, and Redefinition*, "illustrate the ways in which sex work is experienced as an integral part of many women's and men's lives around the world, and not necessarily as the sole defining activity around which their sense of identity is shaped" (ibid.). Although I am aware of the important differences between the terms "prostitute" and "sex worker," I use the terms interchangeably because, on the one hand, I want to underscore that sexual commerce is a form of labor, while on the other hand, I explicitly discuss the discursive construction as well as the material conditions shaping representations of prostitution in Mexico.

8. Iturbide's photograph is reproduced in Debroise (1994: 122).

9. After more than seventy uninterrupted years in power, the PRI, called the "perfect dictatorship" by Mario Vargas Llosa, was defeated in the 2000 elections by the right-wing Partido de Acción Nacional (PAN).

10. See Bliss (2001) and French (1992).

11. There is a growing body of literature that seeks to document testimonies of the experiences of sex workers around the world as well as transnational efforts to promote human

rights and labor rights in the sex industry. See for example Delacoste and Alexander (1998) and Kempadoo and Doezema (1998).

12. Sefchovich's novel was adapted in 2001 to the screen in Mexico under the same title and was directed by Ernesto Rimoch.

13. The Porfirian Age, or *porfiriato,* refers to General Porfirio Díaz, whose dictatorial mandate ran from 1877 to 1911. Under the Díaz regime, the church and state were allies. Díaz brought political and economic stability to Mexico after the wars of independence and the subsequent periods of the reform and the reinstatement of the republic. Díaz has been recently rehabilitated after his vilification in post-revolutionary history: he is now positioned as the founder of modernity in Mexico. See Cosío Villegas (1983).

14. For an in-depth discussion of *guadalupismo* and its cinematic embodiments see Elena Feder's brilliant study (1997).

15. See Alarcón (1989).

16. Connell cited by Kandiyoti (1994: 378).

17. The noted poet José Emilio Pacheco (1993) historically situates *Santa* as the Mexican novel with the most sustained selling record in the nation's literary canon, while it is also the text that brought the most success to its author. At the time of Federico Gamboa's death in 1936, the novel had sold approximately sixty thousand copies.

18. For an account of María "La Chiquita" Villa's life see Sagredo Baeza (1996). For a brief but suggestive discussion of *Santa* in the context of the emergence of criminology in Mexico see Piccato (2001). Incisive feminist readings of *Santa* include Glantz (1983), Franco (1989), and Castillo (1998).

19. The latter part of this sentence is a gloss of the multiple roles Monsiváis (1990) assigns to the prostitute in Mexican popular culture during roughly the first five decades of the twentieth century.

20. Included among the films that feature Lara's songs are: *Novillero* (Apprentice Bullfighter, Boris Maicon, 1936), *Noche de ronda* (Night Music, Ernesto Cortázar, 1942), *Mujer* (Woman, Chano Urueta, 1946), *Humo en los ojos* (Smoke in the Eyes, Alberto Gout, 1946), *Revancha* (Alberto Gout, 1948), *Perdida* (A Lost Woman, Fernando A. Rivero, 1949), and *Coqueta* (Flirt, Fernando A. Rivero, 1949). Lara made his first screen appearance as actor in *Novillero* (1936). Lara's star image was largely that of the tragic, romantic, poet-musician; he often played a Hipólito-like piano player caught up in unrequited love. Lara's musical compositions, with their use of erotic-religious discourse and brothel-centered scenarios, condense and mediate a modern sensibility that is combined with traditional moral codes of conduct and belief. Lara's work continues to have widespread reverberations throughout Latin American popular culture, as evinced in the recent phenomenon of prominent popular singers (including Placido Domingo, Luis Miguel, Eugenia León, and Tania Libertad) who have recorded cover versions of Lara's boleros. The resurgence of the bolero as nostalgia dates back to the mid-1980s. For useful introductions to Agustín Lara's participation in Mexican films see Monsiváis (1990), Taibo I (1984), and Moreno Rivas (1979).

21. For further discussion on public surveillance, public health, prostitution, and photography in Mexico see Massé (1996). Bliss discusses nineteenth-century legal regulation of sexual commerce (2001: 27–29).

22. See Bliss (2001: 185–215). For a discussion of censorship and the moralizing campaigns of the 1940s and 1950s see Fox (2000).

23. I thank my colleague Lorena García for her invaluable assistance in helping me to secure this information. For a feminist historical overview of prostitution and public health policy in Mexico see Lamas (1993).

24. See the valuable chronology by González Rodríguez (1992a).

25. For an extended discussion of these issues see Stallybrass and White (1986).

26. See González Rodríguez (1992a: 145).

27. For further analysis about the parallels between popular nineteenth-century beliefs of prostitutes as carriers of disease and death and the contemporary panic around gay males as transmitters of AIDS see Bersani (1988).

28. For a full discussion of the *hetaira* see Bell (1994).

29. Between 1940 and 1941, Orson Welles wrote a draft of a screenplay for *Santa* that he planned to film in collaboration with director Chano Urueta. This new version of *Santa* was to star Dolores del Río, who was having an affair with Welles at that time, with actor Arturo de Córdova as Hipólito. As a result of the controversy that *Citizen Kane* (1941) generated in the United States, Welles's project was never realized. See Ramón (1991).

30. See Gaytán (1994).

31. For an insightful reading of *Distinto amanecer* see Hershfield (1996).

32. For an excellent reading of *Trotacalles* see Dever (2003).

33. For an overview of the woman's picture see Cook (1991) and Doane (1987).

34. For an excellent reading of *Danzón* see Rashkin's chapter on María Novaro (2001).

35. The legendary status of Veracruz in Mexican popular culture can be gauged in musical forms such as the work of composer Agustín Lara and performer Toña la Negra, who both hail from Veracruz, and the many cultural products set in that port city: films such as *La mujer del puerto* (1933) and novels such as Luis Zapata's *Melodrama* (1983). This mythical status of Veracruz is related to the exoticism attributed to the nightlife of "tropical" coastal cities, Veracruz's famous carnival, the city's vigorous history of gay male culture, and the significant presence of Afro-Mexicans in this region.

36. Novaro makes her homage to the *cabaretera* films and other classic Mexican melodramas very explicit in interviews; see González Rodríguez (1991). *Danzón* also features a number of intertextual references to *Salón México* such as the neon-lit bedroom sequence in which, in a reversal of the gendered to-be-looked-at position, Julia sits in bed lovingly gazing at the sprawled nude body of her young male lover sleeping. Novaro's attention to popular sayings written on the ships at Veracruz port (such as "You see me and you suffer") explicitly reference a working-class tradition of graffiti writing on the fenders of trucks, notably represented in *Nosotros los pobres* (We the Poor, Ismael Rodríguez, 1947), perhaps the most popular and best-loved Mexican film of all time, starring the screen and stage idol Pedro Infante, the subject of Chapter Three.

37. For an overview of the narrative and visual conventions of gay male representations in *fichera* and post-*fichera* films see Ramírez Berg (1992).

38. For a reading of *Danzón* as a woman's picture see Dargis (1992). For a reading of *Danzón* with an emphasis on the importance of popular music as signifier of nation in Latin American cinema see López (1994, 1997) and Tierney (1997). See also González (2002) on Cuban music and performers in *cabaretera* films.

39. For an incisive feminist critique of the Mexican myth of the saintly mother and its social costs see Lamas (1995).

40. Activist Laura E. Asturias in her introductory essay to photographer Hans Neleman's *Night Chicas* (2002), a sobering and compassionate book of portraits of prostitutes in

Guatemalan brothels, reiterates an urgent plea to humanize sex workers: "And perhaps the potential of this book, with its images of women who bare all, is that we may finally see its characters as the human beings they are—people who, regardless of the work they perform, are entitled to and should benefit from every right that others in more privileged circles take for granted" (16).

CHAPTER TWO

1. The classic study of Mexican humor, including the *albur* and related forms of bawdy popular culture, is Jiménez (1969). For a philosophical study of Mexican humor and its relation to national identity see Portilla (1984). For an intriguing discussion of the use of the *albur* among laborers and what it suggests about sexual practices in this social class see González Block and Liguori (1993). For an overview of Mexican male bisexuality from a social science perspective see Liguori (1995).

2. The following texts—including autobiographies, biographies, star analyses, and *crónicas*—attest to Infante's continuing cult: Aguilar (1995), *Asamblea de ciudades* (1992), Infante Quintanilla (1992), Loaeza (1994), Monsiváis (1986, 1995), Pacheco (1992), Torrentera and Ávila (1991).

3. The culture industry built around Infante includes reissues of his recordings and cover songs of his most popular hits by contemporary performers, such as Pedro Fernández's "Yo no fui" (1999) and Luis Miguel's "Amorcito corazón" (2002). Recent biographies, autobiographies, and testimonials include Cortés Reséndiz (1993), Franco Sodja (1992), García (1994), Pacheco (1992), Rodríguez (1976), and Torrentera and Ávila (1991); criticism and cultural analysis include de la Colina (1987), de la Mora (1998), Herrera (1998), Loaeza (1994), Rubenstein (2001), Santos (1987), and Slaughter (2003); and there are also special issues of fan magazines such as *Somos* dedicated to Infante.

4. His first acting part was a small role in *La feria de las flores* (The Flower Fair, José Benavides Jr., 1942).

5. In Mexico there is no equivalent genre or phrase for Hollywood's "buddy movie." The equivalent to "buddy" in Mexican Spanish is *cuate*, the Nahuatl word for "friend" and "twin" as well as "my double."

6. Foster performs a nuanced and culturally informed interpretation of the difference between *compadrismo* and buddyism. He notes that "*compadrismo* in Latin America is the special bond between two men; a similar bond between women is called *comadrismo*. Typically, men who are bonded by *compadrismo* are the godfathers of each other's children and rely on each other for all forms of social support. . . . This special bond creates a privileged union in a hostile world, and in this sense it goes far beyond the Anglo-American tradition of buddyism" (1997b: 153–154).

7. I thank my colleague Gilberto Blasini for pushing me to think about friendships between men as national allegory. I thank the many valuable comments I received from event organizers and audience members at the following forums where I had the opportunity to present parts of this chapter: University of California, Davis, Chancellor's Gay, Lesbian, Bisexual, Transgender Lecture Series; University of California, Davis, October 2001; Centro de Capacitación Cinematográfica, Mexico City, June 2000; XX International Latin American Studies Association, Guadalajara, Mexico, April 1997; Cine-Siglo Latin American Film conference, University of California, Santa Cruz, June 1995; Closure

and Disclosure: Criticism and Aesthetics in Mexico Conference, University of California, Irvine, April 1995; Mexicanidad and the Movies lecture series, Chicano/Latino Research Center, University of California, Santa Cruz, May 1994.

8. For a discussion of anxieties about Mexican hegemonic masculinity and its relation to *lo mexicano* see the brilliant study by Irwin (2003).

9. Films from the classic period that feature homosexual or queer characters and/or subject matter include *La casa del ogro* (The Ogre's House, Fernando de Fuentes, 1938); *¡Ay que tiempos señor Don Simón!* (Those Were the Years Don Simon!, Julio Bracho, 1941); *La negra Angustias* (Black Angustias, Matilde Landeta, 1949); *Me ha besado un hombre* (A Man Kissed Me, Julián Soler, 1944); *El diablo no es tan diablo* (The Devil Is Not So Evil, Julián Soler, 1949); some of Cantinflas's early films, for example *¿Aguila o sol?* (Heads or Tails? Arcady Boytler, 1937) and *Los tres mosqueteros* (The Three Musketeers, Miguel M. Delgado, 1942); and one of Pedro Infante's last films, *Pablo y Carolina* (Mauricio de la Serna, 1956).

10. For analysis of queer spectatorship and fandom see DeAngelis (2001) and Tinkom (2002). For feminist approaches to spectatorship and gendered subject formation see de Lauretis (1987) and Mayne (1993).

11. Interview with Gustavo García, Guadalajara, March 20, 2004.

12. For an interpretive account of the riot at the cemetery where Infante was being buried see Rubenstein (2001).

13. Authors from across the Americas have taken up Infante as their central subject. See for example the Venezuelan novel *Si yo fuera Pedro Infante* (If I Were Pedro Infante, 1989) by Eduardo Liendo, the Mexican novel *¡Ahí viene Martín Corona!* (Here Comes Martín Corona!, 1993) by Agustín DeGyves, based on one of Infante's films, and most recently *Loving Pedro Infante* (2001) by Chicana novelist Denise Chávez. Infante is also the subject of a number of feature-length Mexican films. These include: *La vida de Pedro Infante* (The Life of Pedro Infante, Miguel Zacarías, 1963), a biographical narrative film starring Infante's brother Ángel Infante as the deceased popular idol and featuring clips from Infante's most famous films; and *Pedro Infante ¿vive?* (Pedro Infante Lives?, Juan Andrés Bueno, 1990), a B movie that mines the myth that Infante faked his death in order to break cleanly with his wife, María Luisa Infante, who more that once refused to divorce him despite his requests. Notable documentaries include *Así era Pedro Infante* (1963), *Pedro Infante: El hombre cine mexicano* (Pedro Infante: The Man Who Was Mexican Cinema, Ismael Rodríguez, 1994), and *Pedro Infante* (Luis Kelly, 1996). Reevaluations of Infante's work have also begun to appear, notably the short documentary *La tierra metió reversa* (The Earth Went in Reverse, Luis Lupone, 1996), a tribute to Infante based on archival footage from his funeral that commemorates thirty-nine years of unfailing devotion by his fans; and Agustín Calderón's queer short video *Así se quiere en Jalisco* (A Jalisco Way of Loving, 1994), a wildly irreverent work emphasizing the homoerotic bond between the characters played by Infante and Jorge Negrete in *Dos tipos de cuidado*.

14. Translations of Cristina Pacheco's *crónica* were done by my research assistant Gustavo García, no relation to the film critic of the same name.

15. For a reading that addresses how sadomasochistic drives divert and diffuse the erotic elements in male relations and/or in the erotic representations of male bodies in Euro-American films see Neale (1983).

16. For an overview of how queer theory is being taken up in Mexico see the "Raras rarezas" issue of *Debate Feminista* 8.16 (October 1997).

CHAPTER THREE

1. I refer to La Manuela using feminine pronouns because she identifies as a female.

2. Buñuel and Ripstein share a history that merits some commentary. It is often noted that Buñuel mentored Ripstein and that Ripstein's call to become a filmmaker came upon seeing Buñuel's *Nazarín* (1958). The first is true, while the second is only half-true. Buñuel did in fact take the young Ripstein under his wing. At the age of eighteen, Ripstein worked as Buñuel's personal assistant on the set of *El ángel exterminador* (*The Exterminating Angel,* 1962). The work and friendship of Buñuel undoubtedly marked Ripstein's career. His influence is most strongly felt in that both sought to always make the best film possible without betraying their principles. Ripstein clarifies his affinities with the exiled Spanish surrealist in these terms:

> All too often I am erroneously referred to as a disciple and heir to Buñuel. He looked for the absurd in Mexico because Mexico is a country that lends itself to this. I, however, cannot avoid it since I'm Mexican. My perspective is different. Buñuel has all the formidable surrealist baggage that I live with because the surreal is part of daily life in Mexico. From Buñuel I only learned ethical stands which, in the long run, are more important since we are both imbued with a deep sense of morality and we are only occasionally film technicians. (García Tsao 1996: 84)

Being true to one's ethics is a stance that both directors often repeat in interviews. Both needed to adapt their artistic sensibilities to genre conventions as well as other requirements that are part and parcel of the Mexican commercial film industry. Both also were fortunate to work with producers and screenwriters who supported their unique filmic approaches that challenged and expanded the conventions of Mexican melodrama and film language. Both are outsiders to Mexico. Buñuel, a passionate atheist, chose Mexico as his residence in exile during Franco's fascist rule. Although Buñuel became a Mexican citizen, he kept himself at a distance from Mexican society; when not filming, he rarely ventured outside his fortressed house. Ripstein is a Jew in an overwhelmingly Catholic nation. See Ripstein's documentary homage to Buñuel, co-directed with Rafael Castanedo, *El náufrago de la calle de Providencia* (*The Castaway on the Street of Providence,* 1971).

3. Arturo is the son of the veteran film producer Alfred Ripstein. For an overview of Alfredo Ripstein's career see Pérez Turrent (2003).

4. See for example *El castillo de la pureza* (*The Castle of Purity,* 1973); *Cadena perpetua* (*Life Sentence,* 1977); *El imperio de la fortuna* (*Realm of Fortune,* 1986); *Principio y fin* (*The Beginning and the End,* 1993); *El evangelio de las maravillas* (*Divine,* 1998).

5. Mexico has an entire taxonomy of (homo)sexual terminology indicative of its rich and varied sexual culture. The advent of AIDS has amply demonstrated that bisexuality among men is widespread. Sexual practices between men are often marked by the non-exchangeability of roles during sexual intercourse. An *activo* is the category conferred to the man who takes the "active" role during the sexual act, while the *pasivo* signifies the partner who is penetrated. An *internacional* is a modern gay identity, born of the gay and lesbian rights movements in Mexico in the late '70s, who plays both roles ("top" and "bottom"). I am not sure if this term is any longer in use.

Exclusively taking on the active (inserter) role during intercourse, the macho "heterosexual" (*mayate, chacal* [see below], or *activo*) can keep his socially privileged heterosexual masculine identity intact, since he is not betraying his masculinity by not allowing himself to be penetrated "like a woman." Closure, according to Octavio Paz, is very important to forms of Mexican masculinities because it gives the impression of inviolability. The violence involved in the European invasion of the Americas is an explanation often used to account for the hypermasculinity associated with machismo.

Maricón, joto, puñal, and *puto* are all derogatory homophobic terms that signify male homosexual; *puto* is a particularly pernicious noun/adjective since it is linked to the sexual stigma of female prostitution (*puta*) and to the devaluation of women in general. Ian Lumsden notes that *puto* also connotes "easy lay" (1991: 21).

Mayates are "masculine" heterosexuals who have sex with men, mostly performing as "top" but not exclusively. *Mayates* do not consider themselves homosexuals; it is safe to say that *mayates* are bisexual. For a discussion of the *mayate* see Juan Carlos Bautista (1992a).

A *chacal* is another popular figure of Mexico's picaresque tradition. A *chacal* is a heterosexual who has sexual intercourse with men. Researchers describe *chacales* as "naturally" masculine-looking and -acting. They belong to all social classes but are especially linked to the working class. Juan Carlos Bautista explores the mythology woven around this figure very specific to Mexican sexual subcultures in his half-hour documentary video *Amor chacal* (Jackal Love, 2000). Ayala Blanco (2004: 222), a critic well in tune with the ways in which Mexican film reflects aspects of Mexican popular culture, notes that Bautista's title is an ironic riff on the internationally successful *Amores perros* (2000), a film that in many ways is about defeated and failed urban Mexican masculinities. In Mexican "gay" male culture, the *chacal* is, like heterosexual "rough trade" in the United States, a figure of desire for his surplus of virility and open disposition for sexual contact. A good cinematic narrative representation of the *chacal* can be found in the groundbreaking feature-length film poem and homage to love, *Mil nubes de paz cercan el cielo, amor jamás acabarás de ser amor* (*A Thousand Clouds of Peace,* Julián Hernández, 2003), in which a forlorn young gay man gets beaten up by a very butch-looking man dressed in tight black jeans and a body-hugging shirt whom he meets and who comes on to him during one of his aimless wanderings through the endless streets of Mexico City. For an overview of the *chacal* see Hernández (2004).

A *buga* is gay slang for heterosexual.

Loca (literally meaning mad or wild woman) is the equivalent Mexican homosexual term for "queen." A *loca* self-consciously hypes up signs of femininity, often in a direct contesting position to dominant gender constructions.

Unlike the *loca,* the *vestidas* are, according to Lumsden, "typically young homosexuals who have accepted the popular equation of homosexuality with passivity and femininity. Though their dress and mannerisms are consciously feminine, their behavior owes more to social pressures than to psychic needs as may be the case with transvestites" (1991: 35). Whatever the truth in Lumsden's characterization of the cultural, social-psychological dynamics shaping the desires of *vestidas* (a popular term used to signify transvestites in Mexico City), without a doubt *vestidas* are highly sought-after at gay discos in the metropolitan area of Mexico City, such as the legendary Spartacus in Ciudad Nezahualcóyotl, which is now closed.

For further literature on gay subcultural formations in Mexico see Bautista (1992a, 1992b); both articles are published in *Del otro lado.* Several issues of this now-defunct gay erotic magazine include substantial coverage on gay male and lesbian subcultures throughout Mexico and Latin America. For an analysis of the relationship between consumer culture and the emergence of "gay" identity among middle-class, pro-assimilation gay men in Mexico see Blanco (1990). Carlos Monsiváis has written extensively about Mexican masculinities; among his prose *crónicas* see Monsiváis (1988), especially "¿Pero hubo alguna vez once mil machos?," "Mexicanerías: el albur," "Instituciones: Cantinflas. Ahí estuvo el detalle," and "Dancing: El California Dancing Club." See also Prieur's excellent ethnographic study (1998).

6. See Ayala Blanco (1986: 115–139, 257–261) for a discussion of the prostitute in Mexican cinema.

7. For an overview of Mexican feminism see Gutiérrez Castañeda (2002). On the homosexual liberation movement see the essays in Carrier (1995), Covarrubias (2002), Lumsden (1991), Mejía (2000), Mogrovejo (2000), and Monsiváis (1993b, 2001, 2002a).

8. For an overview of the subgenre see Patricia Torres San Martín's (1993) interview with the *fichera*'s leading auteur, "El cine mexicano y sus cineastas: Victor Manuel Castro Arozamena."

9. After Luis G. Peredos's 1918 silent version, *Santa* has been obsessively remade throughout Mexican film history: 1931 (Antonio Moreno), 1943 (Norman Foster), 1949 (Fernando de Fuentes, *Hipolito el de Santa*), 1968 (Emilio Gómez Muriel), and 1991 (Paul Leduc, *Latino Bar*).

10. For an excellent social-cultural history of the Tivoli club see Fox (2000).

11. See González Rodríguez (1990: 76–77).

12. The single exception I have found is *Las del talón* (Streetwalkers, Alejandro Galindo, 1977).

13. With the exception of Ramírez Berg (1992: 125–130), no film critic, in either a Mexican or a U.S. context, has examined in detail the figure of the *joto* in *fichera* films. Ayala Blanco (1986: 115–139) makes a cursory reference to gay male characters in *fichera* films. However, his film criticism has never shied away from analyzing pulp movies that celebrate representations of differences in Mexico's sexual subcultures. See also Ayala Blanco (1991).

14. See Fiesco Trejo's excellent autobiographical essay on Mexican film and queer reading practices (2002).

15. The bibliography focusing on Donoso's novel is extensive; this is not the case for Ripstein's film. See Ayala Blanco, "*El lugar sin límites* o el infierno de la debilidad" in *La condición del cine mexicano* (1986), Castro (2004), Foster (2003a), Grant (2002), Lanasapa (1998), Ortiz (1996), Paranaguá (1998a), and Ramírez Berg (1992). For a brief overview of Ripstein's career see de la Colina (1997) and de la Mora (2000).

16. The scripting of the film has a particularly interesting history. Arturo Ripstein, in conversation with Emilio García Riera, describes the numerous authorial hands through which the script passed. A first draft exists, written by Argentine novelist Manuel Puig, who then resigned from the project reportedly asking not to be credited for the script. Ripstein suggests that Puig probably withdrew from the project because he felt that perhaps the director would represent yet another caricature of gay men so frequent in Mexican popular film (García Riera 1988: 184). Puig's notes for the *El lugar sin límites* screenplay are included in Puig (2004: 73–83).

17. Hermosillo is one of several auteurs (along with Ripstein, Felipe Cazals, and Jorge Fons) who were promoted under Luis Echeverría's presidency (1970–1976), when the heavily subsidized and nationalized film industry created another controversial "new cinema" that, to date, many critics still see as having produced a good number of minor and major masterpieces; see Costa (1988), Ramírez Berg (1992), Reyes Nevares (1976), Sánchez (1982),

and Tello (1988). Hermosillo is the first Mexican director to not treat male homosexuality as a problem. Both *Las apariencias engañan* (Appearances Can Be Deceiving, 1977) and *Doña Herlinda y su hijo* (1984) bring male homosexuality in Mexico out of the closet by articulating a counter-hegemonic representation of queer desire. *Doña Herlinda*, in particular, integrates the gay male character into the patriarchal family structure, while *Las apariencias* features a veritable plethora of gender and sexual configurations, from female hermaphrodites to femme gay men to butch *bugas* who take on the *pasivo's* role. The concluding sequence features the newlywed couple, played by actress Isela Vega (famous for breaking gender and sexual taboos) and actor Gonzalo Vega, in a most unconventional scenario worthy of the most delirious and in-your-face Pedro Almodóvar film: the bride, who happens to be a hermaphrodite, mounting the groom doggie-style. Both *Doña Herlinda y su hijo* and *Las apariencias engañan* are independent productions; the latter, however, was produced by Manuel Barbachano Ponce and distributed by CLASA films. Neither film has been widely seen in Mexico; censorship kept both films from public exhibition for several years. *Doña Herlinda* was not exhibited in Mexico until after the film received a successful commercial run in the United States. Hermosillo is also the first Mexican director to equalize male and female nudity. Full frontal shots of Pedro Armendáriz Jr., for example, grace *La pasión según Berenice* (The Passion According to Berenice, 1975). For a more detailed trajectory of this director's oeuvre see Wood (1986b).

18. Director Valeria Sarmiento makes a similar critique in her documentary *Un hombre cuando es hombre* (*A Man When He Is a Man*, 1983).

19. La Japonesita takes on the traditional man's role of being in control of business matters: she manages the brothel. Her business personality is cold and curt. In one sequence, in particular, Lucy (Carmen Salinas, who has often played the lush lumpen *fichera* La Cor-cholata) mentions to a co-worker, Nelly (Socorro de la Campa), that La Japonesita acts bitchy because she does not enjoy sex with men (*Esa no goza con los viejos por eso nos tiene ojerízas*)—which codes her as either a frigid woman and/or a butch lesbian.

20. This is the first time we see them together on screen, and thus this moment constitutes their reunification since their prior encounter was referred to but not represented visually.

21. For a discussion of representations of rape and nation formations in Latin American cinemas as related to spectatorship see Burton (1993).

22. La Manuela later acknowledges that men's violent response is a sign of their fear of getting sexually aroused by watching her dance. She also acknowledges that their response is always the same: *Todas las noches me hacen lo mismo. Es como si me tuvieran miedo* (Every night they do the same thing to me. It's as if they're afraid of me). La Japonesa Grande spells out what La Manuela is suggesting: *Les da miedo calentarse* (You make them afraid of getting aroused).

23. See Bautista (1992a).

CHAPTER FOUR

1. "Mexico: Splendor of Thirty Centuries" opened at the Metropolitan Museum in New York City in the fall of 1990. The key players in this much-touted, and much-critiqued, "blockbuster event" were Emilio Azcárraga of the audiovisual conglomerate Televisa, Mexican President Carlos Salinas de Gortari, Nobel laureate Octavio Paz, and regular and adjunct staff at the Metropolitan Museum. See Goldman (1991).

2. García Canclini (1993).

3. For an assessment of these new cinemas see Pérez Turrent (1995). Two excellent sources on the 1960s "nuevo cine" and counter-cultural trends are Ayala Blanco (1986, 1993) and González and Lerner (1998). On the international success of the most recent new cinema see Ayala Blanco (1990, 1994), Contreras and Johnson (2003), Cox (1995), de la Fuente (2003), de la Torre (1994), Durán Loera (1992), Fuchs (2002), García Canclini (1993, 1994, 1995), García Tsao (1993), Maciel (1994), Moore (1994), "A Reprieve for a Mexican Film" (2000), and Torrents (1993).

4. For an analysis of the parallels between the crisis of the Mexican film industry and the state's 1968 crisis see Ramírez Berg (1992).

5. This section was developed from on-site research at IMCINE's offices in Mexico City. I conducted approximately three hours of recorded interviews in August 1994 with Ignacio Durán Loera and with his assistant, Patricio Luna Huerta. I also consulted with Mexican film critics and filmmakers regarding their assessment of state-funded film during the summer of 1994 and at the X Muestra de Cine Mexicano in Guadalajara in March 1995. They included Gustavo García, Ariel Zúñiga, Arturo Ripstein, Paz Alicia Garciadiego, David Ramón, Carlos Monsiváis, Lucy Virgen, and Patricia Torres. I conducted additional archival research at IMCINE in August 1996. I screened sixty-one feature-length films and thirty-five short films. My research is also informed by written materials on recent trends in Mexican film, consisting of catalogues issued by IMCINE, newspaper articles published in the Mexican press, and articles from Mexican, U.S., and British popular and scholarly publications. See the catalogue *Instituto Mexicano de Cinematografía, 1989–1994* (1994).

6. Film critic and historian Jorge Ayala Blanco, one of the most acerbic detractors of cinema-state relations and a fervent supporter of independent film, dismissed the significant accomplishments of the current new cinema. He claims that the Muestra de Cine Mexicano en Guadalajara is a "vile deceit" because it functions primarily as an international platform to launch films co-produced by IMCINE and which, for the most part, excludes independent productions (Consuegra n.d.: 30). His two major contentions are: first, that the majority of films financed by IMCINE during the 1989–1994 period but screened at the Guadalajara International Film Festival did not have a commercial run in Mexico; and second, that film should not be financed by the state and that it should be self-sufficient and left to respond to market dynamics. Needless to say, Ayala Blanco is a bit shortsighted in his analysis because cinema is not merely a commercial commodity—it is also an art form that requires financial support. For a nuanced and productive assessment of the pros and cons of state-funded film in Latin America see Johnson (1993). For a historical overview of the Muestra de Cine Mexicano see Íñiguez Mendoza (2004).

7. See "A Reprieve for a Mexican Film" (2000).

8. These co-production agreements are with a number of countries, including Cuba: *Fresa y chocolate* (*Strawberry and Chocolate*, Tomás Gutiérrez Alea and Juan Carlos Tabío, 1993) and *Reina y rey* (*Queen and King*, Julio García Espinosa, 1994); Canada: *El jardín del Edén* (*The Garden of Eden*, María Novaro, 1994); France: *La reina de la noche* (*Queen of the Night*, Arturo Ripstein, 1994); Argentina: *El viaje* (*The Journey*, Fernando Solanas, 1992) and *Un muro de silencio* (*A Wall of Silence*, Lita Stantic, 1993); and Bolivia: *Jonás y la ballena rosada* (*Jonas and the Pink Whale*, Juan Carlos Valdivia, 1994). See de Pablos and Hopewell (2000) for an account of Spanish investment in Latin American film and television.

9. State involvement in cinema reached record levels during the presidency of Luis Echeverría (1970–1976), when a stagnant industry underwent major restructuring through direct government intervention in production, distribution, and exhibition. In no other period has the State so aggressively intervened in all aspects of cinema in order to use the entire cinematic apparatus as an ideological tool to promote its political rule and relegitimate the PRI after the events of 1968. With the president's brother, ex-actor and union leader Rodolfo Echeverría, as head of the BNC, the State for the first time became the principal producer of films and also got involved in distribution and exhibition. Not only did the state control 95 percent of film production through its own studios (Azteca and Churubusco), but it also became the owner of 60 percent of Mexican theaters. President Echeverría also courted Mexican intellectuals.

10. On the so-called Ley Rojo see Vértiz (2001) and "Reglamento de la Ley Cinematográfica" (2001).

11. Interview by the author with Ignacio Durán Loera, Mexico City, August 16, 1994.

12. A partial list of awards Mexican films have received at leading film festivals includes: *La mujer de Benjamín* (*Benjamin's Woman,* Carlos Carrera, 1990), Best First Film, Montreal; *Principio y fin* (*The Beginning and the End,* Arturo Ripstein, 1993), Best Film, San Sebastián and Havana; *Mi querido Tom Mix* (*My Dear Tom Mix,* Carlos García Agraz, 1990), Best Film, Actress, Director, Havana; *El callejón de los milagros* (*Midaq Alley,* Jorge Fons, 1995), Special Prize, Berlin; *El héroe* (*The Hero,* Carlos Carrera, 1993), Palme d'Or, Cannes; *La invención de cronos* (*Cronos,* Guillermo del Toro, 1991), Critics Prize, Cannes; *La reina de la noche* (*The Queen of the Night,* Arturo Ripstein, 1994), Best Actress, Havana.

13. In short films, *El abuelo Cheno y otras historias* (*Grandfather Cheno and Other Stories,* 1994), a thirty-minute documentary directed by Juan Carlos Rulfo, the youngest son of legendary writer Juan Rulfo, revisits the Cristero War, a backlash against the Revolution's anticlerical strains.

14. See Fein (2000).

15. *Ovaciones,* May 6, 1992, p. 3.

16. For analysis of the conditions that enabled the revival of cinema in Brazil see Avellar (2003) and Nagib (2003), and in Argentina see Bernades, Lerer, and Wolf (2002), Falicov (2003), Martín Peña (2003), and Ricagno (1999, 2003).

17. For an overview of the emergence of women's literature and its relationship to the new social movements of the 1960s and '70s see Franco (1999).

18. For a discussion of the politics of best-seller novels see Masiello (2004).

19. Two examples of Mexican cultural products that capitalized on the enormous success of Esquivel's novel and Arau's film are Corcuera's *Recetario del cine mexicano* (1996), a coffee-table book/cookbook that combines stills of representations of national cuisine in Mexican films (classic and contemporary) and the romantic comedy *Cilantro y perejil* (*Recipes to Stay Together,* Rafael Montero, 1995). For a study of the relationship between Mesoamerican food and Mexican national identity see Pilcher (1998). For an insightful analysis of the emergence of trendy restaurants serving nouvelle Mexican cuisine in Los Angeles see Valle and Torres (2000).

20. See Finnegan (2000).

21. On *¡Que viva Mexico!* see de la Vega Alfaro (1997), Eisenstein (1972), and Karetnikova with Steinmetz (1991). For an excellent critical analysis of this film see Podalsky (1993b).

22. For an overview of Figueroa's work see Feder (1996). On the classic Mexican film aesthetic see Ramírez Berg (1994).

23. See the essays in the exhibition catalogue *Estética Socialista en México. Siglo XX* (2003).

24. See the dossier on Salinas de Gortari's historical legacy, "Un régimen abyecto: todo embarrados" (1995), published in *Proceso*.

25. For an excellent comparative analysis of *Flor silvestre* and *Como agua para chocolate* see Wu (2000). For excellent readings of *Flor silvestre* see Ayala Blanco (1993), Mistron (1984), and Podalsky (1993a).

26. For a feminist critique of the film see Shaw and Rollet (1994).

27. Both films were distributed in the United States by Miramax Films.

28. See de la Mora (1997).

29. See Rivera (1995).

30. For an overview of Diego López Rivera's directorship of IMCINE see Fernández Núñez (1997).

31. See García Canclini (1994) and Rashkin (2001).

32. Johnson's (1987) research on government intervention in, and protection of, cinema in Brazil in many ways inspired my case study of IMCINE. See also his comparative chapters concerning the pros and cons of receiving funds from the State, which he calls, following a concept coined by Octavio Paz, the philanthropic ogre (1993, 1997). For debates concerning safeguarding cultural industries from trade agreements see García Canclini (1994, 1995), Fox (1999), and McAnany and Wilkinson (1996).

33. For a comparative overview of European and U.S. cinemas see the classic study by Guback (1969). For more recent research on national cinemas and film policy see the essays in Moran (1997).

EPILOGUE

1. García Bernal first played Guevara in *Fidel* (David Attwood, 2002), a fictional biography of Fidel Castro produced by HBO.

2. For an excellent analysis of García Bernal's mimetic capacities and role as mediator for the emerging transnational cinematic *latinidad* see Díaz López (2005).

3. See Eugenia de la Torriente (2001).

4. In his discussion of Pedro Infante as Mexico's greatest idol, Luis Miguel Aguilar (1995) claims that "los verdaderos ídolos ocurren siempre en el pasado. El presente, gris por excelencia, los magnifica y los entraña" (Real idols are always forged in the past. The present, gray par excellence, magnifies them and turns them into cherished symbols) (203).

5. Luis Alcoriza's *Tlayucan* (1961) was the previous Mexican film to earn an Oscar nomination for Best Foreign Language Film. Alcoriza was one of many refugees of the Spanish Civil War who made Mexico their home. Alcoriza was a protégé of Luis Buñuel. He co-scripted *Los olvidados* (1950).

6. See "Children of the Cine Revolución" (2003).

7. See Mora (2004).

8. Less than three years later, *Sexo, pudor y lagrimas* was displaced from the number one spot of Mexico's top-grossing films by *El crimen del padre Amaro*, which opened in the summer of 2002 at a record-breaking four hundred screens. To date it is the highest-grossing film in Mexican history.

9. For a discussion of these issues see Smith (2003b).

10. As of July 2001, *Amores perros* had grossed $20 million worldwide. See Smith (2003a) for an excellent analysis of the film.

11. See the book-length study by Smith (2003a) and Podalsky's article in *Screen* (2003); Torres also conducted a very interesting audience reception study (unpublished) in Guadalajara of *Amores perros*. The British Film Institute in particular has played a crucial role in publishing scholarly research that has augmented the prestige of Mexican cinema. Paranaguá's (1995) edited anthology is the most complete to date. See also the anthologies by Noriega and Ricci (1994), Hershfield and Maciel (1999).

12. In the same issue the headline for the feature story about the film's star, Gael García Bernal, asks, "Is He the Beginning of Mexico's New Wave?" (Cohen 2001: 44). The article written by Henry Cabot Beck describes Octavio, the character played by García Bernal, as "feral and a little feminine, a blur of movement and a piercing glare. . . . He may be the first real star in a new and fascinating wave of Mexican cinema" (44).

13. The film received very positive reviews. *Variety* noted that *21 Grams* "cemented" director González Iñárritu's "reputation as a boldly talented filmmaker" (Rooney 2003: 21).

14. As this book goes to press, Arriaga's original screenplay for the U.S.-Mexico border drama, *The Three Burials of Melquiades Estrada* (Tommy Lee Jones, 2005), received an award at the 2005 Cannes Film Festival.

15. See Espinasa (1990) and Rich (2001).

16. See García Canclini's study of the changing patterns of film consumption in Mexico (1994).

17. See Oropeza (2003).

18. See also Hinojosa Córdova (2003).

19. Gael García Bernal quoted in "Rants & Raves" (2002: 12).

20. See Rich (2004).

21. See Díaz López's (2005) incisive essay in which she articulates a promising theory about a transnational Latino network that she describes as a "mestizo" space unified by the Spanish language where Latin American and Spanish entertainment industries and national cultures interact and transform each other while also maintaining their local specificities (112).

22. Only six films were included in competition in the Official Section of Mexican Fiction Feature Films, while nineteen films competed in the Official Section of Ibero-American Fiction Feature Films; in this section, Mexico was represented with two co-productions, one with Chile (Miguel Littin's *La última luna*), the other with Ecuador (Sebastián Cordero's *Crónicas*), along with two films that also participated in the Mexican Fiction Feature Films section: Ricardo Benet's *Noticias lejanas* and Jaime Aparicio's *El mago*, both debut films for their directors. Four Mexican films participated outside of competiton, including Jaime Humberto Hermosillo's *Dos auroras*. In the Parallel Section of Documentary Films, Mexico, as it did the year before, had a strong presence: six of the thirteen selected films were Mexican productions or co-productions; four Mexican documentaries participated out of competiton; and thirty-four Mexican shorts were screened at the festival. The top prizes went to *El mago* and *Crónicas*. See the catalogue *XX Festival Internacional de Cine en Guadalajara*. For a critique of the new international focus of the Guadalajara Film Festival see Cano (2005). See also the articles included in the spotlight on Mexico in the weekly edition of *Variety* of March 7–13, 2005. For a complete list of the films that won awards at this Guadalajara International Film Festival see Aréchiga (2005).

23. Good sources for DVDs of Mexican films, many with English subtitles, include the Latino Cinema collection distributed by Desert Mountain Media, consisting of films from the 1970s through the 1990s. The Excalibur Media Group has a Studio Latino series featuring Mexican films from the 1930s through the 1950s. The appeal to a transnational "Latino" film circuit makes apparent the linguistic diversity of this market, which includes English-monolingual, bilingual, and bicultural audiences. In the Mexican market, the Televisa-owned Alter Films has issued many films from the Golden Age, including many of Emilio Fernández's classic films with English subtitles. Quality Films distributes the Pedro Infante Collection that has subtitles in English, French, and Portuguese; the aforementioned series have multiregion codes. In May 2005, the designated Hispanic Heritage month in the United States, Turner Broadcasting aired seventeen films from the Golden Age as part of its Classic Movie series, packaged as a "salute to the rich heritage of Mexican cinema." This is a watershed event because it inscribes Mexico as the leading Spanish-language national cinema in the U.S. cable television circuit.

24. Vargas (2003b).

25. See Malkin (2003) and Tuckman (2003).

26. See Bensinger and de la Fuente (2004).

27. See Vargas (2003a, 2003b) and "Jack Valenti o los pesos de la taquilla" (2002).

28. See de la Fuente (2004).

Works Consulted

✛ ✛ ✛

Aaron, Michele, ed. 2004. *New Queer Cinema: A Critical Reader*. New Brunswick, N.J.: Rutgers University Press.

Acevedo-Muñoz, Ernesto. 2003. *Buñuel and Mexico: The Crisis of National Cinema*. Berkeley: University of California Press.

Acosta Córdova, Carlos. 1995. "Zedillo fue secretario de programación, tuvo en su ambito a la CONASUPO y al final del sexenio declaró: 'sucedo a quien gobernó al país con visión, inteligencia y patriotismo.'" *Proceso*, December 4, pp. 6–7.

Aguilar, Luis Miguel. 1995. "Los ídolos a nado." In Enrique Florescano, ed., *Mitos mexicanos*. Mexico City: Aguilar, 203–210.

Aguilar Camín, Héctor, and Lorenzo Meyer. 1993. *In the Shadow of the Mexican Revolution: Contemporary Mexican History, 1910–1989*. Trans. Luis Alberto Fierro. Austin: University of Texas Press.

Agustín, José. 1990. *Tragicomedia mexicana I: La vida en México de 1940 a 1970*. Mexico City: Planeta.

Alarcón, Norma. 1989. "Traddutora, Traditora: A Paradigmatic Figure of Chicana Feminism." *Cultural Critique* 13 (Autumn): 57–87.

Almaguer, Tomás. 1991. "Chicano Men: A Cartography of Homosexual Identity and Behavior." *Differences* 3.2 (Summer): 75–100.

Alonso, Ana María, and María Teresa Koreck. 1989. "'Hispanics,' AIDS, and Sexual Practices." *Differences* 1.1: 101–124.

Angelo, Gregory T. 2004. "Gael on the Verge." *Genre* 132 (November): 52–55.

Aranda Luna, Javier. 1990. "Una también es gente." In Hermann Bellinghausen, ed., *El nuevo arte de amar: Usos y costumbres sexuales en México*. Mexico City: Cal y Arena, 99–106.

Aréchiga, Gustavo. 2005. "Apagán Proyector." *(Guadalajara) Mural,* March 19, p. 1D.

Armes, Roy. 1987. *Third World Filmmaking and the West.* Berkeley: University of California Press.

Arredondo, Isabel. 2001. *Palabra de mujer: historia oral de las directors de cine mexicano (1988–1994).* Madrid: Iberoamericana Madrid / Vervuert / Universidad Autónoma de Aguascalientes.

Asamblea de ciudades: años 20s/50s, Ciudad de México. 1992. Mexico City: Consejo Nacional para la Cultura y las Artes/Instituto Nacional de Bellas Artes.

Asturias, Laura E. 2002. Introduction to Hans Neleman, *Night Chicas.* New York: Graphis, 12–13.

Avellar, José Carlos. 2003. "Eu sou trezentos/Yo soy trescientos." In *Imágenes en libertad: Horizontes latinos.* Ed. Teresa Toledo. San Sebastián, Spain: Festival Internacional de San Sebastian, 61–82.

Aviña, Rafael. 2004. *Una mirada insólita: Temas y géneros del cine mexicano.* Mexico City: CONACULTA/Cineteca Nacional/Océano.

Ayala Blanco, Jorge. 1974. *La búsqueda del cine mexicano.* Mexico City: Posada.

———. 1986. *La condición del cine mexicano.* Mexico City: Posada.

———. 1990. "Necrofilia es cultura." *Artes de México* 10 (Winter): 49–50.

———. 1991. *La disolvencia del cine mexicano: Entre lo popular y lo esquisito.* Mexico City: Grijalbo.

———. 1993. *La aventura del cine mexicano: En la época de oro y despues.* 1968. Reprint, Mexico City: Grijalbo.

———. 1994. "El realismo mágico para fodongas." *La eficacia del cine mexicano: Entre lo nuevo y lo viejo.* Mexico City: Grijalbo, 328–331.

———. 2004. *La grandeza del cine mexicano.* Mexico City: Océano.

Bad Object-Choices, eds. 1991. *How Do I Look? Queer Film and Video.* Seattle: Bay Press.

Balderston, Daniel. 1997. "Excluded Middle? Bisexuality in *Doña Herlinda y su hijo.*" In Daniel Balderston and Donna J. Guy, eds., *Sex and Sexuality in Latin America.* New York: New York University Press, 190–199.

———. 1998. "Poetry, Revolution, Homophobia: Polemics from the Mexican Revolution." In Sylvia Molloy and Robert McKee Irwin, eds., *Hispanisms and Homosexualities.* Durham, N.C.: Duke University Press, 57–75.

Bartra, Roger. 1987. *La jaula de la melancolía: identidad y metamorfosis del mexicano.* Mexico City: Grijalbo.

————. 1992. *The Cage of Melancholy: Identity and Metamorphosis in the Mexican National Character.* Trans. Christopher J. Hall. New Brunswick: Rutgers University Press.

————. 1993. *Oficio mexicano.* Mexico City: Grijalbo.

Bautista, Juan Carlos. 1992a. "México: País de mayates." *Del otro lado* 2.3: 62–63.

————. 1992b. "Spartacus." *Del otro lado* 4: 58–60.

Bazán Bonfil, Rodrigo. 2001. *Y si vivo cien años . . . Antología del bolero en México.* Mexico City: Fondo de Cultura Económica.

Beck, Henry Cabot. 2001. "Gael García Bernal." *Interview,* April, pp. 44–46.

Bejel, Emilio. 1997. "*Como agua para chocolate* o las estrategias ideológicas del arte culinario." *Nuevo Texto Crítico* 10.19/20: 177–195.

————. 2001. *Gay Cuban Nation.* Chicago: University of Chicago Press.

Bell, Shannon. 1994. *Reading, Writing, and Rewriting the Prostitute Body.* Bloomington: Indiana University Press.

Bensinger, Ken. 2005. "Fire amid the Smoke." *Variety,* March 7–13, pp. A1, A8.

Bensinger, Ken, and Anna Marie de la Fuente. 2004. "Gov't Gives Local Pix a Leg Up." *Variety,* November 22–28, pp. 12–13.

Berger, Maurice, Brian Wallis, and Simon Watson, eds. 1995. *Constructing Masculinity.* New York: Routledge.

Bernades, Horacio, Diego Lerer, and Sergio Wolf. 2002. *Nuevo cine argentino: temas, autores y estilos de una nueva generación.* Buenos Aires: Ediciones Tatanka.

Bernheimer, Charles. 1989. *Figures of Ill Repute: Representing Prostitution in Nineteenth-Century France.* Cambridge: Harvard University Press.

Bersani, Leo. 1988. "Is the Rectum a Grave?" In Douglas Crimp, ed., *AIDS: Cultural Analysis, Cultural Activism.* Cambridge: MIT Press, 197–222.

Blanco, José Joaquín. 1990. "Ojos que da pánico soñar." *Función de medianoche: Ensayos de literatura cotidiana.* Mexico City: Era, 182–190.

Bliss, Katherine Elaine. 2001. *Compromised Positions: Prostitution, Public Health, and Gender Politics in Revolutionary Mexico City.* University Park: Pennsylvania State University Press.

Brooks, Peter. 1985. *The Melodramatic Imagination: Balzac, Henry James, Melodrama, and the Mode of Excess.* New York: Columbia University Press.

Buñuel, México y el surrealismo. 1996. Mexico City: Consejo Nacional para la Cultural y las Artes.

Burton, Julianne. 1993. "Regarding Rape: Fictions of Origin and Film Spectatorship." In John King, Ana M. López, and Manuel Alvarado, eds., *Mediating Two Worlds: Cinematic Encounters in the Americas.* London: British Film Institute, 258–268.

Burton-Carvajal, Julianne. 1994/1995. "A Simple Ten Step Recipe for Making *Like Water for Chocolate.*" *Chicano/Latino Research Center News* 5 (Fall/Winter): 12.

———. 1997. "Mexican Melodramas of Patriarchy: Specificity of a Transcultural Form." In Ann Marie Stock, ed., *Framing Latin American Cinema: Contemporary Critical Perspectives.* Minneapolis: University of Minnesota Press, 186–234.

———. 1998. "Introduction: Reframing the Fifties." *Nuevo Texto Crítico* 11.21/22: 5–27.

Bustos, Victor. 1992. "Entrevista con Alfonso Arau: De lo racional a lo sentimental." *Dicine* 47 (September): 20–21.

Cano, José David. 2005. "Peter Schuman, del Festival de Cine de Berlín 'Ignorante,' la política cultural del gobierno de Vicente Fox." *El Financiero,* March 22, p. 24.

Careaga, Gabriel. 1984. *Estrellas de cine: los mitos del siglo XX.* Mexico City: Océano.

Carrier, Joseph M. 1995. *De Los Otros: Intimacy and Homosexuality Among Mexican Men.* New York: Columbia University Press.

Carrillo, Héctor. 2002. *The Night Is Young: Sexuality in Mexico in the Time of AIDS.* Chicago: University of Chicago Press.

———. 2003. "Neither *Machos* nor *Maricones*: Masculinity and Emerging Male Homosexual Identities in Mexico." In Mathew C. Gutmann, ed., *Changing Men and Masculinities in Latin America.* Durham, N.C.: Duke University Press, 351–369.

Castañeda, Marina. 2002. *El machismo invisible.* Mexico City: Grijalbo.

Castillo, Debra A. 1994/1995. "Meat Shop Memories: Federico Gamboa's *Santa.*" *Inti Revista de Literatura Hispánica* 40–41 (Fall/Spring): 175–192.

———. 1998. *Easy Women: Sex and Gender in Modern Mexican Fiction.* Minneapolis: University of Minnesota Press.

Castro, P. B. D. 2004. "Requiem for Manuela: The last Sevillana of 'El Lugar sin límites' by José Donoso and Arturo Ripstein—between penises and ornamental combs—transvestism as multiple representation." *Hispanófila* (140): 115–128.

Chanan, Michael. 1996a. "Cinema in Latin America." In Geoffrey Nowell-Smith, ed., *The Oxford History of World Cinema.* New York: Oxford University Press, 427–435.

————. 1996b. "New Cinemas in Latin America." In Geoffrey Nowell-Smith, ed., *The Oxford History of World Cinema*. New York: Oxford University Press, 740–749.

Chávez, Denise. 2001. *Loving Pedro Infante*. New York: Farrar, Straus & Giroux.

"Children of the Cine Revolución." 2003. *Screen International* (September 19–25): 13–14.

Chun, Kimberly. 2004. "Y tu hottie también." *San Francisco Bay Guardian*, December 22, p. 44.

Cohan, Steven. 1997. *Masked Men: Masculinity and the Movies in the Fifties*. Bloomington: Indiana University Press.

Cohan, Steven, and Ina Rae Hark, eds. 1993. *Screening the Male: Exploring Masculinities in Hollywood Cinema*. New York: Routledge.

Cohen, Scott Lyle. 2001. "*Amores Perros*." *Interview*, April, p. 64.

Colimoro, Claudia, and Amalia Lucía Cabezas. 1998. "A World of People: Sex Workers in Mexico." In Kamala Kempadoo and Jo Doezema, eds., *Global Sex Workers: Rights, Resistance, and Redefinition*. New York: Routledge, 197–199.

Colina, Enrique, and Daniel Díaz Torres. 1972. "Ideología del melodrama en el viejo cine latinoamericano." *Cine Cubano* 73, 74, 75.

Connell, R. W. 1987. *Gender and Power*. Stanford, Calif.: Stanford University Press.

————. 1993. "The Big Picture: Masculinities in Recent World History." *Theory and Society* 22: 597–623.

————. 1995. *Masculinities*. Berkeley: University of California Press.

Consuegra, Renato. (N.d.) "Entrevista con Jorge Ayala Blanco: La muestra de Guadalajara es un engaño." *Nitrato de plata* 18: 30–31.

Contreras, Joseph, and Scott Johnson. 2003. "Mexico's New Wave." *Newsweek International*, November 24, p. 60.

Contreras Torres, Miguel. 1960. *El libro negro del cine mexicano*. Mexico City: Editora Hispano-Continental Films.

Cook, Pam. 1991. "Melodrama and the Woman's Picture." In Marcia Landy, ed., *Imitations of Life: A Reader on Film and Television Melodrama*. Detroit: Wayne State University Press, 248–262.

Corcuera, Marie-Pierre Colle. 1996. *Recetario del cine mexicano*. Mexico City: Fundación Televisa.

Correa, Alejandro. 1992. "Un mercado sin público: Entrevista con Juan Antonio de la Riva y Sergio Olhovich." *Nitrato de plata* 9 (January–February): 10–11.

Corrigan, Philip. 1994. "State Formations." In Gilbert M. Joseph and David Nugent, eds., *Everyday Forms of State Formation: Revolution and the Negotiation of Rule in Modern Mexico*. Durham, N.C.: Duke University Press.

Cortés Resendiz, Roberto, and Wilberto Gutiérrez. 1993. *Pedro Infante: el hombre de las tempestades*. Mexico City: Editora de Periódicos La Prensa.

Cosío Villegas, Daniel, ed. 1983. *Historia mínima de México*. 1973. Reprint, Mexico City: El Colegio de México.

Costa, Paola. 1988. *La "apertura" cinematográfica: México 1970–1976*. Puebla: Universidad Autónoma de Puebla.

Covarrubias, José María, ed. 2002. *Una exposición, varias exposiciones, un tiempo de inauguraciones: 15 años de la Semana Cultural Lésbica-Gay*. Mexico City: Difusión Cultural-UNAM/Museo Universitario del Chopo/Círculo Cultural Gay/INDESOL.

Cox, Alex. 1995. "Roads to the South: In Praise of Mexican Cinema." *Film Comment* 31.6 (November/December): 26–35.

Cronos y cromos. 1993. Mexico City: Fundación Cultural Televisa/Centro Cultural Arte Contemporaneo.

Cuarón, Carlos, and Alfonso Cuarón. 2001. *Y tu mamá también*. Mexico City: Trilce Ediciones.

Cypess, Sandra Messinger. 1991. *La Malinche in Mexican Literature: From History to Myth*. Austin: University of Texas Press.

Dargis, Manohla. 1992. "Dance, Girl, Dance." *Village Voice*, October 6, p. 64.

de la Colina, José. 1987. "La gran familia del cine mexicano. Pedro Infante." *Dicine* 21 (September–October): 2–3.

———. 1997. "Ripstein: Un cineasta de la interrogación." In *Miradas al cine*. Mexico City: Consejo Nacional para la Cultura y las Artes-Lecturas Mexicanas, 131–144.

de la Fuente, Anna Marie. 2003. "Country Focus Mexico." *Screen International* (September 19–25): 16.

———. 2004. "Rebate Boosts Production." *Variety*, November 22–28, p. 12.

de la Mora, Sergio. 1992–1993. "Fascinating Machismo: Toward an Unmasking of Heterosexual Masculinity in Arturo Ripstein's *El lugar sin límites* (1977)." *Journal of Film and Video* 44.3/4 (Fall–Winter): 83–104.

———. 1997. "Murder, Mad-Love, and Filmmaking in Mexico City: An Interview with Arturo Ripstein." *Cine Acción News* 14.5 (November): 1–3.

————. 1998. "Masculinidad y mexicanidad: panorama teórico-bibliográfico." In Julianne Burton-Carvajal, Ángel Miquel, and Patricia Torres, eds., *Horizontes del segundo siglo: investigación y pedagogía del cine mexicano, latinoamericano y chicano.* Mexico City: Universidad de Guadalajara/Instituto Mexicano de Cinematografía, 45–64.

————. 1999. "A Career in Perspective: An Interview with Arturo Ripstein." *Film Quarterly* 52.4 (Summer): 2–11.

————. 2000. "Arturo Ripstein." In Daniel Balderston, Mike González, and Ana M. López, eds. *Encyclopedia of Contemporary Latin American Popular Culture.* New York: Routledge, 1283–1284.

de la Peza, Carmen. 1998. *Cine, melodrama y cultura de masas: Estética de la antiestética.* Mexico City: Consejo Nacional para la Cultura y las Artes.

de la Torre, Gerardo. 1994. "Silencio, cámara, crónica." *Memoria de papel* 4.9 (March): 42–59.

de la Torriente, Eugenia. 2001. "Un Pedro Infante para el Siglo XXI." *El Nacional,* December 2. At http://www.el-nacional.com. Accessed March 1, 2005.

de la Vega Alfaro, Eduardo. 1988. "El cine independiente mexicano 1942–1965." *Hojas de cine: testimonios y documentos del nuevo cine latinoamericano.* Volumen II, México. Mexico City: Dirección General de Publicaciones y Medios/Secretaría de Educación Pública/Fundación Mexicana de Cineastas, A. C./Universidad Autónoma Metropolitana: 69–82.

————. 1997. *Del muro a la pantalla: S. M. Eisenstein y el arte pictórico mexicano.* Guadalajara: Universidad de Guadalajara/Instituto Mexiquense de Cultura/Instituto Mexicano de Cinematografía.

de Lauretis, Teresa. 1984. *Alice Doesn't: Feminism, Semiotics, Cinema.* Bloomington: Indiana University Press.

————. 1987. *Technologies of Gender: Essays on Theory, Film, and Fiction.* Bloomington: Indiana University Press.

de Luna, Andrés. 1984. *La batalla y su sombra (La Revolución en el cine mexicano).* Mexico City: Universidad Autónoma Metropolitana–Xochimilco.

de Orellana, Margarita. 1990. "The Voice of the Present over Images of the Past: Historical Narration in *Memories of a Mexican.*" In Julianne Burton, ed., *The Social Documentary in Latin America.* Pittsburgh: University of Pittsburgh Press, 211–215.

————. 1992. "Pancho Villa: Primer actor del cine de la revolución." In Jorge Alberto Lozoya, ed., *Cine mexicano*. Barcelona: Instituto Mexicano de Cinematografía/Lunwerg Editores, 61–62.

de Pablos, Emiliano, and John Hopewell. 2000. "Telefónica Media Ties Topline Ibero Forum." *Variety*, June 26, p. 14.

DeAngelis, Michael. 2001. *Gay Fandom and Crossover Stardom: James Dean, Mel Gibson, Keanu Reeves*. Durham, N.C.: Duke University Press.

Debroise, Olivier. 1994. *Fuga mexicana: Un recorrido por la fotografía en México*. Mexico City: Consejo Nacional para la Cultura y las Artes.

DeGyves, Agustín. 1993. *¡Ahí viene Martín Corona!* Mexico City: Planeta.

Delacoste, Frederique, and Priscilla Alexander, eds. 1998. *Sex Work: Writings by Women in the Sex Industry*. 2d ed. Pittsburgh, Pa.: Cleis Press.

Dever, Susan. 2003. *Celluloid Nationalism and Other Melodramas: From Post-Revolutionary Mexico to fin de siglo Mexamérica*. Albany: State University of New York Press.

Díaz López, Marina. 2005. "Maletas que viajan. Natalia Verbeke y Gael García Bernal, presencias y sentidos en un cine transnacional latino." *Archivos de la Filmoteca* 49 (February): 108–123.

Diegues, Carlos. 2003. "The Cinema that Brazil Deserves." In Lucia Nagib, ed., *The New Brazilian Cinema*. London: I. B. Tauris, 23–35.

Doane, Mary Anne. 1987. "'The Woman's Film': Possession and Address." In Christine Gledhill, ed., *Home is Where the Heart Is: Studies in Melodrama and the Woman's Film*. London: British Film Institute.

Donoso, José. 1981. *El lugar sin límites*. 1965. Reprint, Barcelona: Bruguera.

Doty, Alexander. 1993. *Making Things Perfectly Queer*. Minneapolis: University of Minnesota Press.

————. 2000. *Flaming Classics: Queering the Film Canon*. New York: Routledge.

Dueñas, Pablo H. 1990. *Historia documental del bolero mexicano*. Mexico City: Asociación Mexicana de Estudios Fonográficos.

Durán Loera, Ignacio. 1992. "El cine mexicano y sus perspectives." *Intermedios* 4 (October/November): 46–51.

Dyer, Richard. 1979. *Stars*. London: British Film Institute.

————. 1986. *Heavenly Bodies: Film Stars and Society*. New York: St. Martin's Press.

————. 1992. "Don't Look Now: The Instability of the Male Pin-up." In *Only Entertainment*. New York: Routledge, 103–119. First published in *Screen* 23.3/4 (1982).

———. 1993a. "White." In *The Matter of Images: Essays in Representations*. New York: Routledge, 141–163. First published in *Screen* 29.4 (1988).

———. 1993b. "Seen to be Believed: Some Problems in the Representation of Gay People as Typical." In *The Matter of Images: Essays in Representations*. New York: Routledge, 19–51. First published in *Studies in Visual Communication* 9.2 (Spring 1983).

Dyer, Richard, ed. 1984. *Gays and Film*. New York: New York Zoetrope.

Eisenstein, S. M. 1972. *¡Que viva México!* New York: Arno Press/New York Times.

Eleftheriotis, Dimitris. 1995. "Questioning Totalities: Constructions of Masculinity in the Popular Greek Cinema of the 1960s." *Screen* 36.3 (Autumn): 233–242.

Elsaesser, Thomas. 1991. "Tales of Sound and Fury: Observations on the Family Melodrama." 1972. In Marcia Landy, ed., *Imitations of Life: A Reader on Film and Television Melodrama*. Reprint, Detroit: Wayne State University Press, 68–91.

Eng, David L. 2001. *Racial Castration: Managing Masculinity in Asian America*. Durham, N.C.: Duke University Press.

Escarcega, Ignacio. 1992. "*Como agua para chocolate.*" *Dicine* 47 (September): 22.

Esquivel, Laura. 1989. *Como agua para chocolate*. Mexico City: Planet.

———. 1992. *Like Water for Chocolate*. Trans. Carol Christensen and Thomas Christensen. New York: Anchor Books.

Espinasa, José María. 1990. "Olvidar el cine." *Artes de México* 10 (Winter): 51–53.

Estética socialista en México. Siglo XX. 2003. Mexico City: Instituto Nacional de Bellas Artes/Museo de Arte Carrillo Gil.

Falicov, Tamara. 2003. "Los hijos de Menem: The New Independent Argentine Cinema, 1995–1999." *Framework* 44.1 (Spring): 49–63.

Feder, Elena. 1996. "Gabriel Figueroa: A Reckoning." *Film Quarterly* 49.3 (Spring): 2–14.

———. 1997. *Dying to Be Born: The Vicissitudes of Birth in Life and Culture*. Ph.D. diss., Stanford University.

Fein, Seth. 2000. "Transcultured Anticommunism: Cold War Hollywood in Postwar Mexico." In Chon A. Noriega, ed., *Visible Nations: Latin American Cinema and Video*. Minneapolis: University of Minnesota Press, 82–111.

Fernández Núñez, Joaquín. 1997. "La vida en el abismo." *Milenio* 1.3 (September 15): 62–66.

Fernández Violante, Marcela. 1998. "Lágrimas y risas: La Ley Federal de Cinematografía de 1992." *Estudios Cinematográficos* 4.14 (October–December): 9–15.

Festival Internacional de Cine en Guadalajara, XX. 2005. Catalogue. Guadalajara: Universidad de Guadalajara/CONACULTA/IMCINE/H. Ayuntamiento de Guadalajara/H. Ayuntamiento de Zapopan/Anhelo by Omnilife/Tequila Don Julio/CUCSH UDEG.

Fiedler, Leslie. 1992. *Love and Death in the American Novel*. 1960. Reprint, New York: Anchor Books.

Fiesco Trejo, Roberto. 2002. "La intimidad de sala oscura. Notas sobre cine y homosexualidad (o quizá más preguntas)." In José María Covarrubias, ed., *Una exposición, varias exposiciones, un tiempo de inauguraciones: 15 años de la Semana Cultural Lésbica-Gay*. Mexico City: Difusión Cultural-UNAM/Museo Universitario del Chopo/Círculo Cultural Gay/INDESOL, 21–25.

Finnegan, Nula. 2000. "'Light' Women/'Light' Literature: Women and Popular Fiction in Mexico since 1980." *Donaire* 15 (November). At http://www.sgci.mec.es.

Flores y Escalante, Jesús. 1994. *Imagenes del danzón: iconografía del danzón en México*. Mexico City: Asociación Mexicana de Estudios Fonográficos/CONACULTA-Dirección General de Culturas Populares.

Florescano, Enrique. 1991. "La Revolución mexicana bajo la mira del revisionismo histórico." *El nuevo pasado mexicano*. Mexico City: Cal y Arena, 69–152.

Foster, David William. 1991. *Gay and Lesbian Themes in Latin American Writing*. Austin: University of Texas Press.

———. 1997a. "Queering the Patriarchy in Hermosillo's *Doña Herlinda y su hijo*." In Ann Marie Stock, ed., *Framing Latin American Cinema: Contemporary Critical Perspectives*. Minneapolis: University of Minnesota Press, 235–245.

———. 1997b. *Sexual Textualities: Essays on Queering Latin American Writing*. Austin: University of Texas Press.

———. 2002. *Mexico City in Contemporary Mexican Cinema*. Austin: University of Texas Press.

———. 2003a. "Arturo Ripstein's *El lugar sin límites* and the Hell of Heteronormativity," In Arturo J. Aldama, ed., *Violence and the Body*. Bloomington: Indiana University Press, 375–387.

———. 2003b. *Queer Issues in Contemporary Latin American Cinema*. Austin: University of Texas Press.

Foucault, Michel. 1980. *The History of Sexuality.* Vol. 1. *An Introduction.* Trans. Robert Hurley. New York: Vintage.

Fox, Claire F. 1999. *The Fence and the River: Culture and Politics at the U.S.-Mexico Border.* Minneapolis: University of Minnesota Press.

———. 2000. "Pornography and 'the Popular' in Post-Revolutionary Mexico City: The Club Tivoli from Spota to Isaac." In Chon A. Noriega, ed., *Visible Nations: Latin American Cinema and Video.* Minneapolis: University of Minnesota Press, 143–173.

Franco, Jean. 1989. *Plotting Women: Gender and Representation in Mexico.* New York: Columbia University Press.

———. 1999. "Going Public: Reinhabiting the Private." In Mary Louise Pratt and Kathleen Newman, eds., *Critical Passions: Selected Essays.* Durham, N.C.: Duke University Press.

Franco Sodja, Carlos. 1992. *Lo que me dijo Pedro Infante.* 1977. Reprint, Mexico City: Edamex.

Fregoso, Rosa Linda. 1993. *The Bronze Screen: Chicana and Chicano Film Culture.* Minneapolis: University of Minnesota Press.

———. 2003. *MeXicana Encounters: The Making of Social Identities on Borderlands.* Berkeley: University of California Press.

French, William E. 1992. "Prostitutes and Guardian Angels: Women, Work, and the Family in Porfirian Mexico." *Hispanic American Historical Review* 72.4: 529–553.

Fuchs, Andreas. 2002. "Alexander's Mission: Buena Vista Columbia Tri-Star Joint Venture Thrives in Mexico." *Film Journal International* 105.10 (October): 106.

Fung, Richard. 1991. "Looking for My Penis: The Eroticized Asian in Gay Video Porn." In Bad Object-Choices, eds., *How Do I Look? Queer Film and Video.* Seattle: Bay Press, 145–160.

Gabilondo, Joseba. 2002. "Like Blood for Chocolate, Like Queers for Vampires: Border and Global Consumption in Rodriguez, Tarantino, Arau, Esquivel, and Troyano (Notes on Baroque, Camp, Kitsch, and Hybridization)." In Arnaldo Cruz-Malavé and Martin F. Manalansan IV, eds., *Queer Globalizations: Citizenship and the Afterlife of Colonization.* New York: New York University Press, 236–263.

Gabriel Figueroa: La Mirada en el centro. 1993. Mexico City: Miguel Ángel Porrúa.

Gamboa, Federico. 1992. *Santa.* 1903. Reprint, Mexico City: Grijalbo.

García, Gustavo. 1994. *No me parezco a nadie.* 3 vols. Mexico City: Clío.

———. 1996. "Al final de la pantalla grande." *Revista Mexicana de Comunicación* 8.43 (February–April): 20–21.

García, Gustavo, and Rafael Aviña. 1997. *Época de oro del cine mexicano.* Mexico City: Clío.

García Canclini, Néstor. 1993. "¿Habrá cine latinoamericano en el año 2000?" *La Jornada Semanal,* February 21, pp. 27–33.

———. 1995. *Consumidores y ciudadanos: conflictos multiculturales de la globalización.* Mexico City: Grijalbo.

———. 1997. "Will There Be Latin American Cinema in the Year 2000? Visual Culture in a Postnational Era." In Ann Marie Stock, ed., *Framing Latin American Cinema: Contemporary Critical Perspectives.* Minneapolis: University of Minnesota Press, 246–258.

García Canclini, Néstor, ed. 1994. *Los nuevos espectadores: cine, televisión y video en México.* Mexico City: Consejo Nacional para la Cultura y las Artes/Instituto Mexicano de Cinematografía.

García Hernández, Arturo. 1998. *No han matado a Tongolele.* Mexico City: La Jornada Ediciones.

García Riera, Emilio. 1986. *Historia del cine mexicano.* Mexico City: Secretaría de Educación Pública.

———. 1987. *Emilio Fernández.* Guadalajara: Centro de Investigación y Enseñanza Cinematográfica, Universidad de Guadalajara/Cineteca Nacional de México.

———. 1988. *Arturo Ripstein habla de su cine con Emilio García Riera.* Guadalajara: Centro de Investigación y Enseñanza Cinematográfica, Universidad de Guadalajara.

———. 1992–1997. *Historia documental del cine mexicano.* 2d ed., 18 vols. Guadalajara: Universidad de Guadalajara/Gobierno de Jalisco, Secretaría de Cultura/Consejo Nacional para la Cultura y las Artes/Instituto Mexicano de Cinematografía.

García Tsao, Leonardo. 1993. "New Mexican Tales." *Sight and Sound* 3.6 (June): 30–32.

———. 1996. "Entrevista." *Nosferatu* 22 (September): 80–100.

———. 2002. "The Very Latest in Mexican Cinema." *Voices of Mexico* 59 (April–June): 44–49.

Garciadiego, Paz Alicia. 1998. *El evangelio de las maravillas (La nueva Jerusalén).* Xalapa: Universidad Veracruzana.

García-Vásquez, Marina. 2004. "For Gael." *Planet* 8 (Fall): 42.

Gardinier, Judith Kegan, ed. 2002. *Masculinity Studies and Feminist Theory.* New York: Columbia University Press.

Garibay, Lisa. 2004/2005a. "Gael García Bernal." *SOMA* 18.10a (December/January): 40–41.

———. 2004/2005b. "Higher Learning." *SOMA* 18.10a (December/January): 38.

Gaytán, Francisco. 1994. "Centenario del Cine. XXXIV Aniversario de la Filmoteca de la UNAM, *La mancha de sangre*." *Butaca* (July): 1.

Gever, Martha, John Greyson, and Pratibha Parmar, eds. 1993. *Queer Looks: Perspectives on Lesbian and Gay Film and Video*. New York: Routledge.

Gilman, Sander L. 1985. *Difference and Pathology: Stereotypes of Sexuality, Race, and Madness*. Ithaca, N.Y.: Cornell University Press.

Girman, Chris. 2004. *Mucho Macho: Seduction, Desire, and the Homoerotic Lives of Latin Men*. Binghamton, N.Y.: Haworth Press.

Glantz, Margo. 1983. "*Santa* y la carne." *La lengua en la mano*. Mexico City: La Red de Jonás: 42–52.

Golden, Thelma, ed. 1994. *Black Male: Representations of Masculinity in Contemporary American Art*. New York: Whitney Museum of American Art.

Goldman, Shifra M. 1991. "Metropolitan Splendors: The Buying and Selling of Mexico." *Third Text* 14 (Spring): 17–25.

González, Reynaldo. 1990. "Lágrimas de celuloide: una nueva lectura para el melodrama cinematográfico latinoamericano." *Cine latinoamericano años 30-40-50*. Mexico City: Dirección General de Actividades Cinematográficas de Difusión General/UNAM-Colección Cuadernos de Cine 35: 143–148.

———. 2002. "Báilame de nuevo esa rumba, Ninón." *Archivos de la Filmoteca* 41 (June 2002): 32–55.

González, Rita, and Jesse Lerner. 1998. *Mexperimental Cinema: 60 Years of Avant-Garde Media Arts from Mexico*. Santa Monica: Smart Art Press.

González Block, Miguel A., and Ana Luisa Liguori. 1993. "El SIDA en los de abajo." *Nexos* (May): 15–20.

González Rodríguez, Sergio. 1990. *Los bajos fondos: el antro, la bohemia, el café*. Mexico City: Cal y Arena.

———. 1991. "*Danzón*." *Debate Feminista* 2.4 (September): 189–194.

———. 1992a. "Los bajos fondos/La nota roja." In *Asamblea de ciudades: años 1920s–1950s, Ciudad de México*. Mexico City: Instituto Nacional de Bellas Artes/Consejo Nacional para la Cultura y las Artes, 144–162.

———. 1992b. "Lecturas prohibidas en México, 1900–1930." *Intermedios* 2 (June–July): 30–39.

———. 1994. "Prólogo." In María Novaro and Beatriz Novaro, *Danzón*. Mexico City: Ediciones El Milagro.

González Rodríguez, Sergio, ed. 1993. *Los amorosos: relatos eróticos mexicanos.* Mexico City: Cal y Arena.

Gopinath, Gayatri. 2005. *Queer Diasporas and South Asian Public Cultures.* Durham, N.C.: Duke University Press.

Grant, C. 2002. "The function of the authors: The transnational cinematographic adaptation of 'El lugar sin límites' by José Donoso," *Revista Iberoamericana* 68.

Guback, Thomas H. 1969. *The International Film Industry: Western Europe and America Since 1945.* Bloomington: Indiana University Press.

Gutiérrez Castañeda, Griselda, ed. 2002. *Feminismo en México: revisión histórica-crítica del siglo que termina.* Mexico City: Universidad Autónoma de México, Programa de Estudios de Género.

Gutmann, Matthew C. 1996. *The Meanings of Macho: Being a Man in Mexico City.* Berkeley: University of California Press.

Gutmann, Matthew C., ed. 2003. *Changing Men and Masculinities in Latin America.* Durham, N.C.: Duke University Press.

Gutmann, Matthew C., and Susie S. Porter. 1997. "Gender: 1910–96." In Michael S. Werner, ed., *Encyclopedia of Mexico: History, Society, and Culture.* Chicago: Fitzroy Dearborn Publishers, 575–580.

Guy, Donna J. 1990. *Sex and Danger in Buenos Aires: Prostitution, Family, and Nation in Argentina.* Lincoln: University of Nebraska Press.

Halberstam, Judith. 1998. *Female Masculinity.* Durham, N.C.: Duke University Press.

Hernández, Alonso. 2004. "Un hombre animal—El chacal." *Enkidu.* http://www.enkidu.netfirms.com/art/2004/060404/E_016_060404.htm. Accessed December 20, 2004.

Herrera, Willebaldo. 1998. *La pasión según San Pedro Infante.* Tlaxcala, Mexico: Daniel Palafox.

Hershfield, Joanne. 1996. *Mexican Cinema/Mexican Woman.* Tucson: University of Arizona Press.

———. 2000. *The Invention of Dolores del Río.* Minneapolis: University of Minnesota Press.

Hershfield, Joanne, and David R. Maciel. 1999. *Mexico's Cinema: A Century of Film and Filmmakers.* Wilmington, Del.: Scholarly Resources.

Hinojosa Córdova, Lucila. 2003. *El cine mexicano: De lo global a lo local.* Mexico City: Trillas.

Hirschberg, Lynn. 2001. "A New Mexican." *New York Times Magazine,* March 18, pp. 32–35.

———. 2004. "The Redeemer." *New York Times Magazine,* September 5, pp. 24–27, 38–45, 70.

Hoberman, J. 1996. "Clean Streets. Touring the Toronto Film Festival." *Village Voice,* September 24, p. 59.

Hundley, Jessica. 2004. "Rebel Without a Pause," *Angeleno* 44 (November): 126–131.

Iglesias, Norma. 1998. "Recepción y género en la película *Danzón.*" In Julianne Burton-Carvajal, Ángel Miquel, and Patricia Torres, eds., *Horizontes del segundo siglo: Investigación y pedagogía del cine mexicano, latinoamericano y chicano.* Mexico City: Universidad de Guadalajara/ Instituto Mexicano de Cinematografía, 181–200.

———. 1999. "Reconstructing the Border: Mexican Border Cinema and Its Relationship to Its Audience." In Joanne Hershfield and David R. Maciel, eds., *Mexico's Cinema: A Century of Film and Filmmakers.* Wilmington, Del.: Scholarly Resources, 233–248.

Iglesias, Norma, and Rosa Linda Fregoso, eds. 1998. *Miradas de mujer: encuentro de cineastas, videoastas mexicanas y chicanas.* Tijuana: El Colegio de la Frontera Norte and Chicana/Latina Research Center, University of California, Davis.

Infante Quintanilla, José Ernesto. 1992. *Pedro Infante: el máximo ídolo de México (Vida, obra, muerte y leyenda).* Monterrey, Mexico: Ediciones Castillo.

Íñiguez Mendoza, Ulises. 2004. "La Muestra sin límites: Entrevista a Mario Aguiñaga." *El ojo que piensa/The Thinking Eye* (March): 8–11.

Instituto Mexicano de Cinematografía, 1989–1994. 1994. Mexico City: Instituto Mexicano de Cinematografía.

Irwin, Robert McKee. 2003. *Mexican Masculinities.* Minneapolis: University of Minnesota Press.

Irwin, Robert McKee, Edward J. McCaughan, and Michelle Rocío Nasser, eds. 2003. *The Famous 41: Sexuality and Social Control in Mexico, 1901.* New York: Palgrave Macmillan.

"Jack Valenti o los pesos de la taquilla son todos míos: una recopilación hemerográfica." 2003. *El ojo que piensa/The Thinking Eye* 1 (August). At www.elojoquepiensa.com.

Jeffords, Susan. 1989. *The Remasculinization of America: Gender and the Vietnam War.* Bloomington: Indiana University Press.

———. 1994. *Hard Bodies: Hollywood Masculinity in the Reagan Era.* New Brunswick, N.J.: Rutgers University Press.

Jiménez, Armando. 1969. *Picardía mexicana*. 37th ed. Mexico City: B. Costa-Amic.

———. 1998. *Sitios de rompe y rasga en la Ciudad de México: Salones de baile, cabarets, billares, teatros*. Mexico City: Océano.

Johnson, Randal. 1987. *The Film Industry in Brazil: Culture and the State*. Pittsburg: University of Pittsburgh Press.

———. 1993. "In the Belly of the Ogre: Cinema and the State in Latin America." In John King, Ana M. López, and Manuel Alvarado, eds., *Mediating Two Worlds: Cinematic Encounters in the Americas*. London: British Film Institute, 204–213.

———. 1997. "Film Policy in Latin America." In Albert Moran, ed., *Film Policy: International, National, and Regional Perspectives*. New York: Routledge, 128–147.

Joseph, Gilbert, Anne Rubenstein, and Eric Zolov, eds. 2001. *Fragments of a Golden Age: The Politics of Culture Since 1940*. Durham, N.C.: Duke University Press.

Kandiyoti, Deniz. 1994. "Identity and Its Discontents: Women and the Nation." In Patrick Williams and Laura Chrisman, eds., *Colonial and Post-Colonial Theory: A Reader*. New York: Columbia University Press, 376–391.

Kaplan, E. Ann. 1992. *Motherhood and Representation: The Mother in Popular Culture and Melodrama*. New York: Routledge.

Karetnikova, Inga, with Leon Steinmetz. 1991. *Mexico According to Eisenstein*. Albuquerque: University of New Mexico Press.

Kempadoo, Kamala, and Joe Doezema, eds. 1998. *Global Sex Workers: Rights, Resistance, and Redefinition*. New York: Routledge.

Kim, Kyung Hyun. 2004. *The Remasculinization of Korean Cinema*. Durham, N.C.: Duke University Press.

Kirkham, Pat, and Janet Thurman, eds. 1993. *You Tarzan: Masculinity, Movies and Men*. New York: St. Martin's Press.

Krauze, Enrique. 1987. *Francisco Villa, entre el ángel y el fierro*. Mexico City: Fondo de Cultura Económica.

La patria portátil. See at *patria*.

Lamas, Marta. 1993. "El fulgor de la noche: algunos aspectos de la prostitución callejera en la ciudad de México." *Debate Feminista* 4.8 (September): 103–134.

———. 1995. "¿Madrecita santa?" In Enrique Florescano, ed., *Mitos mexicanos*. Mexico City: Aguilar, 173–178.

Lanasapa, Jesús Generelo. 1998. "*El lugar sin límites*: México al revés." In Jesús Rodrigo García, ed., *El cine de Arturo Ripstein: la solución del bárbaro*. Valencia: Ediciones de la Mirada, 99–10.

Lancaster, Roger N. 1992. *Life Is Hard: Machismo, Danger, and the Intimacy of Power in Nicaragua*. Berkeley: University of California Press.

Landy, Marcia. 1986. *Fascism in Film: The Italian Commercial Cinema, 1931–1943*. Princeton, N.J.: Princeton University Press.

Lara y Pardo, Luis. 1908. *La prostitución en México*. Mexico City: Librería de la Viuda de Ch. Bouret.

"Las rumberas del cine mexicano." See at "rumberas."

Lehman, Peter. 1993. *Running Scared: Masculinity and the Representation of the Male Body*. Philadelphia: Temple University Press.

Lehman, Peter, ed. 2001. *Masculinity: Bodies, Movies, Culture*. New York: Routledge.

Liendo, Eduardo. 1989. *Si yo fuera Pedro Infante*. Caracas: Alfadil.

Liguori, Ana Luisa. 1995. "Las investigaciones sobre bisexualidad en México." *Debate Feminista* 6.11 (April): 132–156.

Lillo, Gastón. 1994. "El reciclaje del melodrama y sus repercusiones en la estratificación de la cultura." *Archivos de la Filmoteca* 16 (February): 65–73.

Loaeza, Guadalupe. 1994. "Mi tía y Pedro Infante." *Reforma*, February 7.

López, Ana M. 1988. "An 'Other' History: The New Latin American Cinema." *Radical History Review* 41: 93–116.

———. 1991. "Celluloid Tears: Melodrama in the 'Old' Mexican Cinema." *Iris* 13 (Summer): 29–51.

———. 1993. "Tears and Desire: Women and Melodrama in the 'Old' Mexican Cinema." In John King, Ana M. López, and Manuel Alvarado, eds., *Mediating Two Worlds: Cinematic Encounters in the Americas*. London: British Film Institute, 147–163.

———. 1994. "A Cinema for the Continent." In Chon A. Noriega and Steven Ricci, eds., *The Mexican Cinema Project*. Los Angeles: UCLA Film and Television Archive, University of California, 7–12.

———. 1997. "Of Rhythms and Borders." In Celeste Fraser Delgado and José Muñoz, eds., *Everynight Life: Culture and Dance in Latin/o America*. Durham, N.C.: Duke University Press, 310–344.

Lumsden, Ian. 1991. *Homosexuality, Society, and the State in Mexico*. Mexico City: Canadian Gay Archives/Solediciones.

Maciel, David. 1994. "El Imperio de la Fortuna: Mexico's Contemporary Cinema, 1985–1992." In Chon A. Noriega and Steven Ricci, eds., *The Mexican Cinema Project*. Los Angeles: UCLA Film and Television Archive, University of California, 33–44.

Malkin, Elisabeth. 2003. "Mexican Film: High Art, Low Budget." *New York Times*, July 15.

Martín Peña, Fernando, ed. 2003. *60/90 Generaciones: cine argentino independiente*. Buenos Aires: Museo de Arte Contemporaneo de Buenos Aires.

Martínez, José Jorge. 1992. "*Sólo con tu pareja*." *Dicine* 45 (May): 11.

Masiello, Francine. 2004. "The Unbearable Lightness of History: Best Seller Scripts for Our Times." In Ana Del Sarto, Alicia Ríos, and Abril Trigo, eds., *The Latin American Cultural Studies Reader*. Durham, N.C.: Duke University of Press, 459–473.

Massé, Patricia. 1996. "Photographs of Mexican Prostitutes in 1865." *History of Photography* 20.3 (Autumn): 231–234.

Mayne, Judith. 1993. *Cinema and Spectatorship*. New York: Routledge.

McAnany, Emile G., and Kenton T. Wilkinson, eds. 1996. *Mass Media and Free Trade: NAFTA and the Cultural Industries*. Austin: University of Texas Press.

McIntosh, David W. 2004. "The Rise and Fall of Mexican Cinema in the 20th Century: From the Production of a Revolutionary National Imaginary to the Consumption of Globalized Cultural Industrial Products." University of Manitoba. At http://www.umanitoba.ca/faculties/arts/english/media. Accessed June 19, 2004.

Mejía, María Consuelo. 1996. "Hijo de tigre pintito . . . Hablemos de sexualidad." *Debate Feminista* 7.13 (April): 437–441.

Mejía, Max. 2000. "Mexican Pink." In Peter Drucker, ed., *Different Rainbows*. London: Gay Men's Press, 43–55.

Mercer, Kobena. 1994. *Welcome to the Jungle: New Positions in Black Cultural Studies*. New York: Routledge.

Mercer, Kobena, and Isaac Julien. 1988. "Race, Sexual Politics and Black Masculinity." In Rowena Chapman and Jonathan Rutherford, eds. *Male Order: Unwrapping Masculinity*. London: Lawrence and Wishart, 97–164.

Millán, Márgara. 1999. *Derivas de un cine en femenino*. Mexico City: Universidad Autónoma de México, Programa Universitario de Estudios de Género/Miguel Ángel Porrúa.

Miquel, Ángel. 1997. *Salvador Toscano*. Guadalajara: Universidad de Guadalajara/Gobierno del Estado de Puebla/Universidad Veracruzana/Universidad Nacional Autónoma de México.

Mirandé, Alfredo. 1997. *Hombres y Machos: Masculinity and Latino Culture*. Boulder: Westview Press.

Mistron, Deborah E. 1983. "The Role of Pancho Villa in the Mexican and the American Cinema." *Studies in Latin American Popular Culture* 2: 1–13.

———. 1984. "A Hybrid Subgenre: The Revolutionary Melodrama in the Mexican Cinema." *Studies in Latin American Popular Culture* 3: 47–56.

Mogrovejo, Norma. 2000. *Un amor que se atrevió a decir su nombre: la lucha de las lesbianas y su relación con los movimientos homosexual y feminista en América Latina*. Mexico City: Plaza y Valdés.

Moisés, José Álvaro. 2003. "A New Policy for Brazilian Cinema." In Lucia Nagib, ed., *The New Brazilian Cinema*. London: I. B. Tauris, 3–22.

Monsiváis, Carlos. 1980. "La mujer en la cultura mexicana." In Lucía Guerra-Cunningham, ed., *Mujer y sociedad en América Latina*. Irvine, Calif.: Editorial del Pacífico, 101–117.

———. 1986. "¡Quien fuera Pedro Infante!" *Revista Encuentro* (April): 1–16.

———. 1988. *Escenas de pudor y liviandad*. Mexico City: Grijalbo.

———. 1990. "Agustín Lara: El harem ilusorio (Notas a partir de la memorialización de la letra de 'Farolito')." In *Amor perdido*. 1977. Reprint, Mexico City: Era, 61–86.

———. 1991. "Prólogo." In Ava Vargas, *La casa de citas en el barrio galante*. Mexico City: Grijalbo.

———. 1993a. "Mexican Cinema: Of Myths and Demystifications." In John King, Ana M. López, and Manuel Alvarado, eds., *Mediating Two Worlds: Cinematic Encounters in the Americas*. Trans. Mike González. London: British Film Institute, 139–146.

———. 1993b. "Paisaje de batalla entre condones: Saldos de la revolución sexual." In Hermann Bellinghausen, ed., *El nuevo arte de amar: usos y costumbres sexuales en México*." 10th ed. Mexico City: Cal y Arena, 165–179.

———. 1995. "Mythologies." In Paulo Antonio Paranaguá, ed., *Mexican Cinema*. Trans. Ana M. López. London: British Film Institute/Instituto Mexicano de Cinematografía/Consejo Nacional para la Cultura y las Artes de México, 117–127.

————. 1997a. "Los que tenemos unas manos que no nos pertenecen (A propósito de lo 'Queer' y lo 'Rarito')." *Debate Feminista* 8.16 (October): 11–33.

————. 1997b. *Mexican Postcards*. Trans. John Kraniauskas. New York: Verso.

————. 1998. "El mundo soslayado (Donde se mezclan la confesión y la proclama)." In Salvador Novo, *La estatua de sal*. Mexico City: Consejo Nacional para la Cultura y las Artes.

————. 2000. *Salvador Novo: Lo marginal en el centro*. Mexico City: Era.

————. 2001. "Los iguales, los semejantes, los (hasta hace un minuto) perfectos desconocidos (A cien años de la Redada de los 41)." *Debate Feminista* 12.24 (October): 301–327.

————. 2002a. "Los gays en México: la fundación, la ampliación, la consolidación del *ghetto*." *Debate Feminista* 13.26 (October): 89–115.

————. 2002b. "José Alfredo Jiménez: Les diré que llegué de un mundo raro." In José Alfredo Jiménez, ed., *Cancionero completo*. Mexico City: Océano & Turner Publicaciones.

Monsiváis, Carlos, and Carlos Bonfil. 1994. *A través del espejo: el cine mexicano y su público*. Mexico City: Ediciones El Milagro/Instituto Mexicano de Cinematografía.

Moore, Daniel S. 1994. "Mexico Poised for New Age." *Variety*, March 28, pp. 37, 57–58.

Mora, Carl Jr. 1989. *Mexican Cinema: Reflections of a Society, 1896–1988*. Rev. ed. Berkeley: University of California Press.

Mora, Orlando. 2004. "El cine latinoamericano en Cannes 2004." *El ojo que piensa/The Thinking Eye* 6 (November): 1–5. At www.elojoquepiensa.com.

Morales, Salvador. N.d. *Pedro Infante: el ídolo*. Panamericana de Ediciones.

Moran, Albert, ed. 1997. *Film Policy: International, National, and Regional Perspectives*. New York: Routledge.

Moreno Rivas, Yolanda. 1979. *Historia de la música popular mexicana*. Mexico City: Consejo Nacional para la Cultura y las Artes/Alianza Editorial, Colección Los Noventa.

Mraz, John. 1997. "How Real is Reel? Fernando de Fuentes's Revolutionary Trilogy." In Anne Marie Stock, ed., *Framing Latin American Cinema: Contemporary Critical Perspectives*. Minneapolis: University of Minnesota Press, 92–119.

Mulvey, Laura. 1989a. "Notes on Sirk and Melodrama." In *Visual and Other Pleasures*. Bloomington: Indiana University Press, 39–44. First published in *Movie* (1977).

———. 1989b. "Visual Pleasure and Narrative Cinema." In *Visual and Other Pleasures*. Bloomington: Indiana University Press, 14–26. First published in *Screen* 16.3 (1975).

Muñoz, José Esteban. 1999. *Disidentifications: Queers of Color and the Performance of Politics*. Minneapolis: University of Minnesota Press.

Muñoz, Lorenza. 2002. "A New Mexican Revolution." *Los Angeles Times*, Calendar, March 10, pp. 8–9, 82–84.

Muñoz, Mario, ed. 1996. *De amores marginales*. Xalapa: Universidad Veracruzana.

Muñoz, Rafael F. 2000. *¡Vámonos con Pancho Villa!*. 1931. Reprint, Mexico City: La Serpiente Emplumada/Factoría Ediciones.

Muñoz Castillo, Fernando. 1993. *Las reinas del trópico*. Mexico City: Grupo Azabache.

Nagib, Lúcia, ed. 2003. *The New Brazilian Cinema*. London: I. B. Taurus.

Nead, Lynda. 1988. *Myths of Sexuality: Representations of Women in Victorian Britain*. London: Basil Blackwell.

Neale, Steve. 1993. "Masculinity as Spectacle: Reflections on Men and Mainstream Cinema." In Steven Cohan and Ina Rae Hark, eds., *Screening the Male: Exploring Masculinities in Hollywood Cinema*. New York: Routledge, 9–20. First published in *Screen* 24.6 (1983).

Negrón-Muntaner, Frances. 1996. "Drama Queens: Latino Gay and Lesbian Independent Film/Video." In Chon A. Noriega and Ana M. López, *The Ethnic Eye: Latino Media Arts*. Minneapolis: University of Minnesota Press: 59–78.

Neleman, Hans. 2002. *Night Chicas*. New York: Graphis.

Noble, Andrea. 2003. "Sexuality and Space in Jorge Fons' *El callejón de los milagros*." *Framework: The Journal of Cinema and Media* 44.1: 22–35.

Noriega, Chon A, ed. 1992. *Chicanos and Film: Representation and Resistance*. Minneapolis: University of Minnesota Press, xi–xxvi.

Noriega, Chon A., and Steven Ricci, eds. 1994. *The Mexican Cinema Project*. Los Angeles: UCLA Film and Television Archive, University of California.

Novo, Salvador. 1972. *Las locas, el sexo, los burdeles*. Mexico City: Organización Editorial Novaro.

————. 1998. *La estatua de sal.* Mexico City: Consejo Nacional para la Cultura y las Artes.

Núñez Noriega, Guillermo. 1999. *Sexo entre varones: poder y resistencia en el campo social.* 2d ed. Mexico City: Coordinación de Humanidades, Universidad Autónoma de México, Programa Universitario de Estudios de Género, Instituto de Investigaciones Sociales, El Colegio de Sonora, Miguel Ángel Porrúa.

————. 2001. "Reconociendo los placers, desconstruyendo las identidades. Antropología, patriarcado y homoerotismo en México." *Desacatos* (Spring–Summer): 15–34.

Ojeda, Néstor L. 1991. *La mirada circular: El cine norteamericano de la Revolución mexicana, 1911–1917.* Mexico City: Cuadernos de Joaquín Mortiz.

————. 1996. "Prostitución en los noventa." In Fabrizio Mejía Madrid and Julio Patán Tobío, eds., *Entre las sábanas.* Mexico City: Cal y Arena, 51–58.

O'Malley, Ilene V. 1986. *The Myth of the Revolution: Hero Cults and the Institutionalization of the Mexican State, 1920–1940.* New York: Greenwood Press.

Oropeza, María. 2003. "Gael García, un galán con cerebro." *Seventeen,* September, Mexican edition, 52–57.

Orozco, Ricardo. 2003. *El álbum de Amada Díaz.* Mexico City: Planeta.

Ortiz, Christopher Kelley. 1996. "The Representation of Sexuality in Contemporary Mexican Cinema, 1970–1990." Ph.D. diss., University of California, Los Angeles.

Pacheco, Cristina. 1992. "¡Pedro Infante no ha muerto!" In *Los dueños de la noche.* 1984. 2d ed., Mexico City: Planeta, 217–226.

Pacheco, José Emilio. 1993. "*Santa* cumple noventa años." *Intermedios* 6 (February–March): 6–11.

Palomar Verea, Cristina. 2004. *En cada charro, un hermano: la charrería en el estado de Jalisco.* Guadalajara: Secretaría de Cultura, Gobierno del Estado de Jalisco.

Paranaguá, Paulo Antonio. 1998a. *Arturo Ripstein: la espiral de la identidad.* Madrid: Cátedra/Filmoteca Española.

————. 1998b. "Of Periodizations and Paradigms: The Fifties in Comparative Perspective." *Nuevo Texto Crítico* 11.21/22: 31–44.

————. 2003. *Tradición y modernidad en el cine de América Latina.* Madrid: Fondo de Cultura Económica de España.

Paranaguá, Paulo Antonio, ed. 1995. *Mexican Cinema*. Trans. Ana M. López. London: British Film Institute/Instituto Mexicano de Cinematografía/Consejo Nacional Para la Cultura y las Artes de México.

patria portátil, La: 100 Years of Mexican Chromo Art Calendars. 1999. Mexico City: Asociación Carso/Museo Soumaya.

Paz, Octavio. 1984. *El laberinto de la soledad*. 1950. Reprint, Mexico City: Fondo de Cultura Económica.

Penley, Constance, and Sharon Willis, eds. 1993. *Male Trouble*. Minneapolis: University of Minnesota Press.

Perdomo, Yolanda. 2005. "In the Name of Culture." *Hispanic Trends* (May/June): 10–11.

Pérez Turrent, Tomás. 1995. "Crisis and Renovations (1961–1991)." In Paulo Antonio Paranaguá, ed., *Mexican Cinema*. Trans. Ana M. López. London: British Film Institute/Instituto Mexicano de Cinematografía, 94–115.

———. 1996a. "Buñuel-Ripstein: ¿Vasos comunicantes?" *Nosferatu* 22 (September): 14–19.

———. 1996b. "Pro y contra." In Yasha David, ed., *¡Buñuel! La mirada del siglo*. Mexico City: Consejo Nacional para la Cultura y las Artes, 51–58.

———. 2003. *Alfredo Ripstein: productor*. Guadalajara: Universidad de Guadalajara/Gobierno del Estado de Jalisco, Secretaría de Cultura.

Perry, Mary Elizabeth. 1990. *Gender and Disorder in Early Modern Seville*. Princeton, N.J.: Princeton University Press.

Piccato, Pablo. 2001. *City of Suspects: Crime in Mexico City, 1900–1931*. Durham, N.C.: Duke University Press.

Pick, Zuzana. 1993. "Territories of Representation." *Iris* 13 (Summer): 53–62.

Pilcher, Jeffrey M. 1998. *¡Que vivan los tamales! Food and the Making of Mexican Identity*. Albuquerque: University of New Mexico Press.

Podalsky, Laura. 1993a. "Disjointed Frames: Melodrama, Nationalism, and Representation in 1940s Mexico." *Studies in Latin American Popular Culture* 12: 57–93.

———. 1993b. "Patterns of the Primitive: Sergei Eisenstein's *Qué Viva México!*" In John King, Ana M. López, and Manuel Alvarado, eds., *Mediating Two Worlds: Cinematic Encounters in the Americas*. London: British Film Institute, 25–39.

———. 2003. "Affecting Legacies: Historical Memory and Contemporary Structures of Feeling in *Madagascar* and *Amores Perros*." *Screen* 44:3 (Autumn): 277–294.

Portilla, Jorge. 1984. *Fenomenología del relajo y otros ensayos*. 1966. Reprint, Mexico City: Fondo de Cultura Económica.

Powrie, Phil, Ann Davies, and Bruce Babington, eds. 2004. *The Trouble with Men: Masculinities in European and Hollywood Cinema*. London: Wallflower Press.

Prieur, Annick. 1998. *Mema's House, Mexico City: On Transvestites, Queens, and Machos*. Chicago: University of Chicago Press.

Puig, Manuel. 2004. *Un destino melodramatico. Argumentos*. Buenos Aires: El Cuenco de Plata, 73–83.

Quiroga, José. 2000. *Tropics of Desire: Interventions from Queer Latino America*. New York: New York University Press.

Ramírez Berg, Charles. 1989. "Cracks in the Macho Monolith: Machismo, Man, and Mexico in Recent Mexican Cinema." *New Orleans Review*. 16.1 (Spring): 67–74.

———. 1992. *Cinema of Solitude: A Critical Study of Mexican Film, 1967–1983*. Austin: University of Texas Press.

———. 1994. "The Cinematic Invention of Mexico: The Poetics and Politics of the Fernández-Figueroa Style." In Chon A. Noriega and Steven Ricci, eds., *The Mexican Cinema Project*. Los Angeles: UCLA Film and Television Archive, University of California, 13–24.

Ramón, David. 1991. *La Santa de Orson Welles*. Mexico City: Universidad Autónoma de México.

Ramos, Samuel. 1997. *El perfil del hombre y la cultura en México*. 1934. Reprint, Mexico City: Espasa Calpe.

"Rants & Raves." 2002. *Advocate*, May 28, 12.

"Raras rarezas." 1997. *Debate Feminista* 8.16 (October). Special issue.

Rashkin, Elissa J. 2001. *Women Filmmakers in Mexico: The Country of Which We Dream*. Austin: University of Texas Press.

Reed, John. 1983. *Insurgent Mexico*. 1914. Reprint, New York: Penguin.

"régimen abyecto: todos embarrados, Un." 1995. *Proceso*, December 4, pp. 6–31.

"Reglamento de la Ley Cinematográfica." 2001. *Diario Oficial* 570, no. 20 (March 29): 5–17.

Reich, Jacqueline. 2004. *Beyond the Latin Lover: Marcello Mastroianni, Masculinity, and Italian Cinema*. Bloomington: Indiana.

"A Reprieve for Mexican Film." 2000. *Economist*, February 26, 48.

Reyes, Aurelio de los. 1991. *Medio siglo de cine mexicano, 1896–1947*. Mexico City: Trillas.

———. 1993. *Cine y sociedad en México: bajo el cielo de México, 1896–1930. Volumen II (1920–1924)*. Mexico City: Universidad Nacional Autónoma de México/Instituto de Investigaciones Estéticas.

———. 1996. *Cine y sociedad en México: vivir de sueños, 1896–1930. Volumen I (1896–1920)*. 1981. Reprint, Mexico City: Universidad Nacional Autónoma de México/Instituto de Investigaciones Estéticas.

Reyes Nevares, Beatriz. 1976. *The New Mexican Cinema. Interviews with Thirteen Directors*. Trans. Carl J. Mora and Elizabeth Gard. Albuquerque: University of New Mexico Press.

Ricagno, Alejandro. 1999. *Miradas: el cine argentino de los noventa*. Madrid: Agencia Española de Cooperación Internacional/Casa de América.

———. 2003. "Lectura de géneros en 'el cuerpo mutante' del cine argentino: de textos y texturas." In Teresa Toledo, Ed., *Imágenes en libertad: horizontes latinos*. San Sebastián: Festival Internacional de San Sebastián, 29–60.

Rich, B. Ruby. 1995. "Latin American Cinema: Notes on Queer Presences and Antecedents." Catalogue for Turin Gay and Lesbian Film Festival. Turin, Italy: Turin Gay and Lesbian Film Festival.

———. 2001. "Mexico at the Multiplex." *Nation*, May 14, p. 34.

———. 2004. "To Read or Not to Read: Subtitles, Trailers, and Monolingualism." In Atom Egoyan and Ian Belfour, eds., *Subtitles: On the Foreignness of Film*. Cambridge: MIT Press, 153–169.

Rivera, Hector J. 1994. "Refuta Laura Esquivel los ataques a *Como agua para chocolate*: 'Al olimpo y sus intelectuales no les gustan las historias de amor.'" *Proceso*, January 3, pp. 48–51.

———. 1995. "El IMCINE debe ser un instituto de Estado para salvaguardar la identidad del mexicano, no un productor de películas: Jorge Lozoya." *Proceso*, March 20, pp. 62–65.

Rodríguez, Gabriela R., and José Ángel Aguilar Gil. 1994. *Hijo de tigre . . . pintito. Hablemos de sexualidad*. Mexico City: Secretaría de Educación Pública/Los Libros del Rincón.

Rodríguez, Ismael. 1976. *Testimonios para la historia del cine mexicano*. Cuadernos de la Cineteca Nacional, vol. 6. Mexico City: Secretaría de Gobernación/Cineteca Nacional, 1976, 111–140.

Rodríguez, Juana María. 2002. *Queer Latinidad: Identity Practices, Discoursive Spaces*. New York: New York University Press.

Rooney, David. 2003. "Grim 'Grams' still gripping." *Variety*, September 15–21, pp. 21, 32.

Rosenberg, Tina. 2003. "Just as Mexican Movies Become Chic Again, the Government Pulls Its Support." *New York Times*, December 11. At http://www.nytimes.com.

Rubenstein, Anne. 2001. "Bodies, Cities, Cinema: Pedro Infante's Death as Political Spectacle." In Gilbert Joseph, Anne Rubenstein, Eric Zolov, eds., *Fragments of a Golden Age: The Politics of Culture in Mexico Since 1940*. Durham, N.C.: Duke University Press, 199–233.

Ruiz Sánchez, Enrique. 1998. "El cine mexicano y la globalización: contracción, concentración e intercambio desigual." In Julianne Burton-Carvajal, Ángel Miquel, and Patricia Torres, eds., *Horizontes del segundo siglo: investigación y pedagogía del cine mexicano, latinoamericano y chicano*. Mexico City: Universidad de Guadalajara/Instituto Mexicano de Cinematografía, 101–135.

"rumberas del cine mexicano, Las." 1999. *Somos* 10.189 (November).

Russo, Vito. 1987. *The Celluloid Closet*. Rev. ed. New York: Harper & Row.

Sagredo Baeza, Rafael. 1996. *María Villa (a) La Chiquita, no. 4002: un parásito social del Porfiriato*. Mexico City: Cal y Arena.

Salinas de Gortari, Carlos. 1994. "Instalación del Consejo Nacional para la Cultura y las Artes." In Rafael Tovar y de Teresa, ed., *Modernización y política cultural*. Mexico City: Fondo de Cultura Económica, 358–365.

Sánchez, Alberto Ruy. 1982. *Mitología de un cine en crisis*. Mexico City: La Red de Jonás.

Sandy Ochoa, Gerardo. 1994. "Ante el TLC: México desprotege su cine y arriesga su identidad, señalan especialistas mexicanos y norteamericanos." *Proceso*, January 3, pp. 50–51.

Santos, Adrian. 1987. "Los valores de Pedro Infante." *El Día de los Jovenes (Suplemento El Día)*, April 14 and 21.

Saragoza, Alex M., and Graciela Berkovich. 1994. "Intimate Connections: Cinematic Allegories of Gender, the State and National Identity." In Chon A. Noriega and Steven Ricci, eds., *The Mexican Cinema Project*. Los Angeles: UCLA Film and Television Archive, 25–32.

Schaefer, Claudia. 1996. *Danger Zones: Homosexuality, National Identity, and Mexican Culture*. Tucson: University of Arizona Press.

Schnitman, Jorge A. 1984. *Film Industries in Latin America: Dependency and Development*. Norwood, N.J.: Ablex Publishing.

Sedgwick, Eve Kosofsky. 1985. *Between Men: English Literature and Male Homosocial Desire*. New York: Columbia University Press.

Sefchovich, Sara. 1992. *Demasiado amor*. Mexico City: Planeta.

Segal, Lynne. 1990. *Slow Motion: Changing Masculinities, Changing Men.* New Brunswick, N.J.: Rutgers University Press.

Shaw, Deborah. 2003. *Contemporary Cinema of Latin America: 10 Key Films.* New York: Continuum.

Shaw, Deborah, and Bridget Rollet. 1994. "*Como agua para chocolate*: Some of the Reasons for its Success." *Travesia* 3.1/2: 82–91.

Sheridan, Guillermo. 1985. *Los contemporáneos ayer.* Mexico City: Fondo de Cultura Económica.

Slaughter, Stephany. 2003. "The Ambiguous Representation of Macho in Mexico's Golden Age Cinema: Pedro Infante as Pepe el Toro." *Tinta: Research Journal of Hispanic and Lusophone Studies* 7: 23–42.

Smith, Paul, ed. 1996. *Boys: Masculinities in Contemporary Culture.* Boulder: Westview Press.

Smith, Paul Julian. 1996. *Vision Machines: Cinema, Literature and Sexuality in Spain and Cuba, 1983-1993.* New York: Verso.

———. 2003a. *Amores Perros.* London: British Film Institute.

———. 2003b. "Transatlantic Traffic in Recent Mexican Films." *Journal of Latin American Cultural Studies* 12.2: 389–400.

Sommer, Doris. 1991. *Foundational Fictions: The National Romances of Latin America.* Berkeley: University of California Press.

Stallybrass, Peter, and Allon White. 1986. *The Politics and Poetics of Transgression.* Ithaca, N.Y.: Cornell University Press.

Stecopoulos, Harry, and Michael Uebel. 1997. *Race and the Subject of Masculinities.* Durham, N.C.: Duke University Press.

Taibo, Paco Ignacio I. 1984. *La música de Agustín Lara en el cine.* Mexico City: Universidad Autónoma de México/Filmoteca UNAM.

Tasker, Yvonne. 1993. *Spectacular Bodies: Gender, Genre and the Action Cinema.* New York: Routledge.

Tejada, Valentín. 1958. *Pedro Infante: ídolo popular.* Mexico City: Editorial Tejada.

Tello, Jaime. 1988. "Notas sobre la política económica del 'nuevo cine' mexicano." *Hojas de cine: testimonios y documentos del nuevo cine latinoamericano.* Volumen II, México. Mexico City: Dirección General de Publicaciones y Medios/Secretaría de Educación Pública/Fundación Mexicana de Cineastas, A.C./Universidad Autónoma Metropolitana: 113–127.

Tierney, Dolores M. 1997. "Silver Sling-backs and Mexican Melodrama: *Danzón* and *Salón México*." *Screen* 38.4 (Winter): 360–371.

————. 2003. "Gender Relations and Mexican Cultural Nationalism in Emilio Fernández's *Enamorada/Woman in Love.*" *Quarterly Review of Film and Video* 20: 225–236.

¡Tierra y Libertad! Photographs of Mexico 1900–1935 from the Casasola Archive. 1985. Oxford, England: Museum of Modern Art.

Tinkom, Matthew. 2002. *Working Like A Homosexual: Camp, Capital, Cinema.* Durham, N.C.: Duke University Press.

Torrentera, Guadalupe, and Estela Ávila. 1991. *Un gran amor: la verdad en la vida de Lupita Torrentera y Pedro Infante.* Mexico City: Diana.

Torrents, Nissa. 1993. "Mexican Cinema Comes Alive." In John King, Ana M. López, and Manuel Alvarado, eds., *Mediating Two Worlds: Cinematic Encounters in the Americas.* London: British Film Institute, 222–229.

Torres San Martín, Patricia. 1993. "El cine mexicano y sus cineastas: Victor Manuel Castro Arozamena." *Siglo 21,* February 7.

————. 1998. "La investigación sobre el cine de mujeres en México." In Julianne Burton-Carvajal, Ángel Miquel, and Patricia Torres, eds., *Horizontes del segundo siglo: Investigación y pedagogía del cine mexicano, latinoamericano y chicano.* Mexico: Universidad de Guadalajara/Instituto Mexicano de Cinematografía. 39–44.

————. 2001. *Cine y género: La representación social de lo femenino y lo masculine en el cine mexicano y venezolano.* Guadalajara: Universidad de Guadalajara.

————. N.d. "Los perros amores de los tapatíos." Unpublished manuscript.

Torres San Martín, Patricia, ed. 2004. *Mujeres y cine en América Latina.* Guadalajara: Universidad de Guadalajara.

Torres San Martín, Patricia, and Eduardo de la Vega. 1997. *Adela Sequeyro.* Guadalajara: Universidad de Guadalajara.

Tuckman, Jo. 2003. "Bang Goes the Boom." *Guardian,* June 19.

Tuñón, Julia. 1987. *Mujeres en México: una historia olvidada.* Mexico City: Planeta.

————. 1988. *En su propio espejo (Entrevista con Emilio "El Indio" Fernández).* Mexico City: Universidad Autónoma Metropolitana.

————. 1998. *Mujeres de luz y de sombra en el cine mexicano: la construcción de una imagen, 1939–1952.* Mexico City: El Colegio de México/Instituto Mexicano de Cinematografía.

————. 2000. *Los rostros de un mito: personajes femeninos en las películas de Emilio Indio Fernández.* Mexico City: Arte e Imagen/Consejo Nacional para la Cultura y las Artes/Instituto Mexicano de Cinematografía.

Tuñón Pablos, Esperanza. 1997. "Women's Status and Occupation, 1910 – 96." In Michael S. Werner, ed., *Encyclopedia of Mexico: History, Society & Culture*. Chicago: Fitzroy Dearborn, 1626 – 1629.

Valdéz Córdova, Lynna Krista. 2000. "Las políticas de difusión internacional del IMCINE durante el período 1990 – 1998." Thesis. Mexico City: Universidad Autónoma de México.

Valle, Victor M., and Rodolfo D. Torres. 2000. *Latino Metropolis*. Minneapolis: University of Minnesota Press.

Vargas, Juan Carlos. 2003a. "El cine mexicano postindustrial (1997 – 2002). *El ojo que piensa/ The Thinking Eye* 2 (August). At www.elojoquepiensa .com.

———. 2003b. "La amenaza foxista." *El ojo que piensa/ The Thinking Eye* 4 (December). At www.elojoquepiensa.com.

Vega, Patricia. 1991. "Entrevista con María Novaro." *La Jornada Semanal*, August 25, pp. 27 – 30.

Vértiz, Columba. 2001. "Analizará la Sogem el Reglamento de la Ley de Cine." *Proceso*, April 1, pp. 72 – 73.

Viña, Moisés. 1992. *Índice cronológico del cine mexicano*. Mexico City: Dirección General de Actividades Cinematográficas, UNAM.

Vizcarra Castillo, Mauricio. 1996. "Pedro Infante, al banquillo de los acusados. La moralina, en plan de guerra contra la educación sexual." *El Financiero*, September 17, p. 79.

Watney, Simon. 1982. "Hollywood's Homosexual World." *Screen* 23.3/4: 108 – 120.

Waugh, Thomas. 1996. *Hard to Imagine: Gay Male Eroticism in Photography and Film from Their Beginnings to Stonewall*. New York: Columbia University Press.

———. 2000. *The Fruit Machine: Twenty Years of Writings on Queer Cinema*. Durham, N.C.: Duke University Press.

Wiegman, Robyn. 1995. *American Anatomies: Theorizing Race and Gender*. Durham, N.C.: Duke University Press.

Wilson, Carter. 2000. "Macho in its Migrations." In Norma Klahn, Pedro Castillo, Alejandro Álvarez, Federico Manchón, eds., *Las Nuevas Fronteras del Siglo XXI/New Frontiers of the 21st Century*. Mexico City: La Jornada Ediciones/Universidad Autónoma Nacional de México/Universidad Autónoma Metropolitana/Chicano-Latino Research Center, University of California, Santa Cruz, 231 – 250.

Wood, Robin. 1986a. *Hollywood from Vietnam to Reagan*. New York: Columbia University Press.

———. 1986b. "Notes for the Exploration of Hermosillo." *CineAction!* (Spring): 32–38.

Wu, Harmony H. 2000. "Consuming Tacos and Enchiladas: Gender and Nation in *Como agua para chocolate*." In Chon A. Noriega, ed., *Visible Nations: Latin American Cinema and Video*. Minneapolis: University of Minnesota Press, 174–192.

Yosef, Raz. 2004. *Beyond Flesh: Queer Masculinities and Nationalism in Israeli Cinema*. New Brunswick, N.J.: Rutgers University Press.

Zamudio-Taylor, Victor, and Inma Guiu. 1994. "Criss-Crossing Texts: Reading Images in *Like Water for Chocolate*." In Chon Noriega and Steven Ricci, eds., *The Mexican Cinema Project*. Los Angeles: UCLA Film and Television Archive, 45–52.

Zapata, Luis. 1983. *Melodrama*. Mexico City: Enjambre.

Zola, Émile. 1958. *Nana*. New York: Pocket Books.

Index

✦ ✦ ✦

Page numbers in *italics* refer to photographs.

Abandonadas, Las, 22, 52
Abuelo Cheno y otras historias, El, 193n13
Acosta, Rodolfo, 48, 53, *54,* 55, 57–58
Acosta Córdova, Carlos, 145
Acton, William, 39
Águila descalza, El, 146
¿Águila o sol?, 187n9
Aguilar, Luis, 91, *95*
Aguilar, Luis Miguel, 194n4
Aguilar Camín, Héctor, 51
Aguilar Gil, José Ángel, ix
Agustín, José, 51
albur, 16, 68, 71
Alcoriza, Luis, 194n5
Alemán, Miguel, 51–52, 55, 87
Almodóvar, Pedro, 20, 164, 166
Allá en el rancho grande, 47, 83, 175
"Al otro lado del río" (song), 168
Amadori, Luis César, 128
Amores perros, 20, 172–173; music in, 171;
   success of, 136, 169, 174, 177, 195n10
And Starring Pancho Villa as Himself, 9,
   181n13
Ángel de fuego, 141
Angelitos negros, 86
Anthias, Flora, 30
Apariencias engañan, Las, 191n17
Aranda, Pilar, 155
Aranda Luna, Javier, 66
Arau, Alfonso, 19, 136, 145, 146, 156

Arenas, Rosita, 95
Arias, Rodolfo, 157
Arizmendi, Yareli, 154
Armendáriz, Pedro, 49, 79, 86, 152, *153,*
   155, 175
Armendáriz, Pedro, Jr., 191n17
Arráncame la vida, 147
Arriaga, Guillermo, 173, 195n14
Asamblea de ciudades, ix
Así era Pedro Infante, 76–77, 187n13
Así se quiere en Jalisco, 187n13
Asturias, Laura E., 185n40
Atl, Dr. (Gerardo Murillo), 149
ATM (A toda máquina), 15, 70, 76, 91–94,
   95; Mexico-U.S. relations in, 16, 93
Atwood, David, 167, 194n1
Aventurera, 21, 23, 48, 60
Ávila, Estela, 84
Ayala Blanco, Jorge, 163, 190n13; on *Como
   agua para chocolate,* 146, 148, 152, 158;
   on *Dos tipos de cuidado,* 99–100; on
   fichera films, 110, 111; on State film
   policy, 138, 159, 192n6
¡Ay que tiempos señor Don Simón!, 187n9
Azcárraga, Emilio, 158, 191n1
Azuela, Mariano, 2

Badú, Antonio, 90
Banderas, Antonio, 168, 181n13
Bandidos, 143

Bartra, Roger, 14, 24–25, 28–29, 31, 87
Bellas de noche, 112, 116
Benavides, José, Jr., 186n4
Bensinger, Ken, 175, 178, 179
Bernheimer, Charles, 37–38
Bernstein, Steve, 151
"Bésame mucho" (song), 92, 93–94
Best Maugard, Adolfo, 48, 86
Bienvenido-Welcome, 151
Blanco, José Joaquín, 29
Bliss, Katherine Elaine, 14, 15, 32, 65–66
Bolaños, José, 149
Bonfil, Carlos, 28
Boytler, Arcady, 21, 48, 187n9
Bracho, Julio, 21, 48, 149, 187n9
Breton, André, 106
Brooks, Peter, 50
brothel-cabaret, 13, 14, 15, 26, 109, 110, 118; in *Danzón*, 59; in *Demasiado amor*, 46; and homosexuals, 110, 118, 133; in *El lugar sin límites*, 107, 133; during *porfiriato*, 34–35
buddy movies, Hollywood, 87–88
buddy movies, Mexican, 1, 3, 88; musical performance in, 93–94, 95–98, 99; queer readings of, 89; sadomasochism in, 89, 91, 94; sexual ambiguity in, 70, 93, 100–101; and *Y tu mamá también*, 176–177
Buñuel, Luis, 106, 107, 172, 173, 188n2, 194n5
Bustillo Oro, Juan, 107

cabaretera films, 1, 3, 14, 21, 48, 50–51, 182n3
Cabeza de Vaca, 140
Cabezas, Amalia Lucía, 15, 66
Calderón, Agustín, 187n13
Callejón de los milagros, El, 172, 193n12
Calzonzin Inspector, 146
Cantinflas (Mario Moreno), 17, 80, 86, 108, 187n9
Cárdenas, Lázaro, 83, 87, 143
Carranza, Venustiano, 36, 181n14
Carrera, Carlos, 20, 160, 168, 193n12
Casa del ogro, La, 187n9

Casasola, Agustín Víctor, 8
Castillo, Debra A., 25, 29
Catholicism, 27, 30, 44, 109
Catholics for the Right to Decide, xi
Cavazos, Lumi, 152, 154
Cazals, Felipe, 107, 190n17
Ceballos, Margarita, 53, 54
Celluloid Closet, The, 16
Censorship: in Mexican film, 137–138; Printed Law of 1917, 36–37
Chabanne, William Christy, 8, 182n14
charro, 2, 6, 83, 164; Pedro Infante as, 77, 82, 84, 98
Chávez, Denise, viii, 68, 69, 104, 187n13
"Chingadalupe," 14, 28–29, 31
Chun, Kimberly, 167
Cilantro y perejil, 193n19
cinemachismo, defined, 2–3, 7
Cinema Paradiso, 156–157
Cobo, Roberto, 105, 106, 115, 129, 131
Cohan, Steven, 13
Cohen, Scott Lyle, 172
Colimoro, Claudia, 15, 66
Colina, Enrique, 50
comedia ranchera, 6, 83, 98, 171, 175
Como agua para chocolate (film), 19, 20, 134, 146–158; men in, 156–158; and revolutionary melodrama, 143, 148–150, 151–154; and Salinas presidency, 145, 148, 150; success of, 136, 140, 145–146, 147, 169, 172, 177
Como agua para chocolate (novel), 20, 136, 146–147, 154, 157
Compadre Mendoza, El, 149
Connell, R. W., 30
Contemporáneos, 2, 180n3 (Introd.)
Contreras Torres, Miguel, 149
Correa, Alejandro, 174
Costa, Paola, 159
Cri Cri, 80
Crimen del padre Amaro, El, 20, 168; church campaign against, 176; success of, 169, 174, 177, 194n8
Cronos, 140, 146, 175, 193n12
Cuando los hijos se van, 107

Cuarón, Alfonso, 20, 146, 175, 176, 177
Cucaracha, La, 153

Danzón, 14, 27, 59−65, 141, 142, 146; and
  cabaretera films, 13, 59, 62, 64−65,
  185n36; U.S. release of, 140
DeAngelis, Michael, 73, 75
de Córdova, Arturo, 77, 79, 86, 175, 185n29
de Fuentes, Fernando, 8, 47, 83, 88, 187n9,
  190n9; Revolution trilogy, 143, 149
de la Fuente, Anna Marie, 175, 179
de la Madrid, Miguel, 137
de la Peza, Carmen, 81
de la Riva, Juan Antonio, 174
de la Serna, Mauricio, 187n9
de Lauretis, Teresa, 6
Delgado, Miguel M., 116, 187n9
de los Reyes, Aurelio, 8
de Luna, Andrés, 142
del Río, Dolores, 22, 86, 152, *153,* 175,
  185n29
del Toro, Guillermo, 140, 175, 193n12
Demasiado amor, 13, 26, 27, 42−46; film
  adaptation of, 184n12
de Orduña, Juan, 128
de Orellana, Margarita, 8
Derbez, Silvia, 48
Dever, Susan, 28
Diablo no es tan diablo, El, 187n9
Día del compadre, El, 116
Diarios de motocicleta, Los, 20, 164−165,
  167, 168
Díaz, Porfirio, xii, 142, 158, 184n13
Díaz-Guerrero, Rogelio, 120−121
Díaz López, Marina, 195n21
Díaz Morales, José, 21
Díaz Torres, Daniel, 50
Distinto amanecer, 21, 48−49, 60
Doane, Mary Anne, 59
Doña Herlinda y su hijo, 114, 191n17
Donoso, José, 19, 106, 119
Dorantes, Irma, 84
Dos tipos de cuidado, 15, 16, 70, 98−103,
  187n13
Doty, Alexander, 16, 72−73
Drexler, Jorge, 168

Dulce olor a muerte, Un, 173
Durán Loera, Ignacio, 135, 137, 138, 139,
  140, 141
Dyer, Richard, 10, 16, 88, 103, 113, 120

Echevarría, Nicolás, 140
Echeverría, Luis, 106, 160, 190n17, 193n9
Echeverría, Rodolfo, 106, 193n9
Eisenstein, Sergei, 86, 149
Eleftheriotis, Dimitris, 10, 11−12
Elizondo, Salvador, 29
Elsaesser, Thomas, 49
Enamorada, 154, 155, 157
Enamorado, El, 75
Entre Pancho Villa y una mujer desnuda,
  9, 160
Epstein, Rob, 16
Esquivel, Laura, 20, 136, 146−147, 154, 157
Estrada, Luis, 138, 143
Evangelio de las maravillas, El, 1

Familia de tantas, Una, 107, 123
Faulkner, William, 173
Feder, Elena, 1
Federal Film Law (1992), 138, 139
Félix, María, 86, 153, 155, 175
Feria de las flores, La, 186n4
Fernández, Adela, 55
Fernández, Emilio, 1, 148, 173, 175; and
  prostitution, 55−56; Revolutionary
  films of, 143, 149, 151, 154, 155; and
  women, 58. See also *Las abandonadas;*
  Enamorada; Flor silvestre; Islas Marías;
  Maclovia; La Perla; Río Escondido;
  Salón México; Víctimas del pecado;
  Zona Roja
Fernández Violante, Marcela, 138
Festival Internacional de Cine en Guadala-
  jara, 137, 177, 192n6, 195n22
fichera films, 1, 3, 109−112; decline of, 140;
  homosexuality in, 17, 18, 109, 111−112,
  114, 116−118
Fidel, 167, 194n1
Figueroa, Gabriel, 52, 53, 148, 149, 151, 175
Flores, Froylán, 78
Florescano, Enrique, 142

Flor silvestre, 149, 151–153, 154
Fons, Jorge, 107, 171, 172, 190n17,
 193n12
"For Gael" (poem), 163–164
Foster, David William, 186n6
Foster, Norman, 47, 190n9
Foucault, Michel, 5
Fox, Vicente, 139, 178–179
Franco Sodja, Carlos, 84
Fregoso, Rosa Linda, 5
French, William E., 29
Frida, 168, 175
Friedman, Jeffrey, 16
Fuentes, Carlos, 173

Galindo, Alejandro, 21, 107, 123, 183n4,
 190n12
Galindo Garza, Pedro, 21, 23
Gamboa, Alejandro, 160
Gamboa, Federico, 13, 24, 26, 32, 37, 41– 42,
 109, 184n17
García, Gustavo, 74, 84, 85, 138
García, Sara, 81
García Agraz, Carlos, 143, 193n12
García Bernal, Gael, 20, 163–170, *165,* 176;
 and Che Guevara, 164–166, 194n1;
 on masculinity, 163, 176–177; and
 new Mexican cinema, 169, 195n12;
 non-Mexican roles of, 167; and Pedro
 Infante, 20, 67, 166, 167; in poetry,
 163–164; politics of, 168–169; as symbol
 of *latinidad,* 20, 167
García Canclini, Néstor, 136, 161
Garciadiego, Paz Alicia, 1, 106
García Márquez, Gabriel, 106, 147
García Riera, Emilio, 52, 106, 111, 127,
 190n16
García Tsao, Leonardo, 171, 188n2
García-Vásquez, Marina, 163
Garibay, Lisa, 166, 168, 169
Garrido, Joaquín, 157
Gavaldón, Roberto, 151
Gavilán pollero, El, 15, 70, 89–91
gay men: stereotypes, 18, 113–114, 118 (see
 also *joto*); and violence, 19
Girard, René, 93

Gómez Muriel, Emilio, 47, 48, 190n9
González, Carmen, 98, *103*
González, Reynaldo, 50
González, Rogelio A., 15, 80, 88
González Iñárritu, Alejandro, 20, 172, 173,
 195n13
González Rodríguez, Sergio, 25, 36,
 60, 63
Gout, Alberto, 21, 48
Guadalajara International Film Festival.
 See Festival Internacional de Cine en
 Guadalajara
Guevara, Ernesto "Che," 164–165
Guiú, Emilia, 86
Guy, Donna G., 30
Guzmán, Martín Luis, 147

Hadad, Astrid, 96
Hark, Ina Rae, 13
Harry Potter and the Prisoner of Azkaban,
 175
Hayek, Salma, 168
Hermosillo, Jaime Humberto, 107, 146, 177,
 195n22; and homosexuality in film, 114,
 119, 127, 190–191n17
Héroe, El, 193n12
Hershfield, Joanne, 28, 51
Hijo de tigre . . . pintito (textbook), ix–xi
Hipólito el de Santa, 47, 190n9
Hirschberg, Lynn, 166, 172, 173, 174
Hoberman, J., 107
Hombre cuando es hombre, Un, 191n18
homosexuality: in *fichera* films, 17, 18, 109,
 111–112, 114, 117–118; and *machismo,* 69,
 133; in Mexican cinema, 7, 108, 187n9;
 terms relating to, 188–189n5
Humanidad, 86
Hundley, Jessica, 168, 169

IMCINE, 20, 136, 137–142, 160–161; and
 censorship, 137–138; and *Como agua
 para chocolate,* 147, 150; criticized,
 192n6; and new filmmakers, 135, 141,
 161; and privatization, 138; threatened
 by Vicente Fox, 178–179
Inclán, Rafael, 117

Infante, Pedro: acting of, 80; buddy movies of, 15, 70–71, 93, 176–177, (*see also* buddy movies, Mexican); cult status of, 69, 77, 104, 186nn2,3; death of, xii, 69, 76–77; documentaries about, 187n13; as erotic object, ix, 12, 83–84; fans of, 78–79, 84, 85; and Gael García Bernal, 20, 67, 166, 167; and Jorge Negrete, 80, 85, 98–99; in literature, 187n13; and *macho* stereotype, 81, 84; marriages of, 84–85; as masculine ideal, 77–78; as national symbol, 69, 77–78; nude photo of, viii–xii, 84; and physical fitness, xii, 74, 75, 83; queer readings of, 7, 17, 71–72; and race, 86; sexuality of, 73–74, 84–85; star persona of, xii, 16, 70, 75; as working-class icon, xi, 12, 15, 77, 83, 85. See also *ATM; Dos tipos de cuidado; El enamorado; El gavilán pollero; Nosotros los pobres; ¿Qué te ha dado esa mujer?; Los tres García*
Infante Quintanilla, José Ernesto, 77, 84
Instituto Mexicano de Cinematografía. See IMCINE
Insurgent Mexico, 8
Invención del Cronos, La. See *Cronos*
Irwin, Robert, 121
Isaac, Alberto, 110, 159
Islas Marías, 80
Iturbide, Graciela, 24

Jardín del Edén, El, 59, 150, 192n8
Jenkins, William, 52
Jiménez, Armando, 181n6
Johnson, Randal, 194n32
Joseph, Gilbert, 134
joto: in *fichera* films, 17, 18, 108, 109, 115, 118; in *El lugar sin límites*, 17, 115, 133; and *machismo*, 5, 108, 133
Junco, Tito, 53, 56, 57
Jurado, Katy, 86, 175

Kandiyoti, Deniz, 14, 30–31
Kempadoo, Kamala, 183n7
Konga roja, 21
Krauze, Enrique, 8, 9, 182n15

Lamas, Marta, 36
Landeta, Matilde, 17, 49, 187n9
Landy, Marcia, 87
Lara, Agustín, 33–34, 183n5, 184n20, 185n35
Lara y Pardo, Luis, 29, 41, 42
Las del talón, 190n12
Latino Bar, 47–48, 190n9
Lavat, Queta, 98
Leduc, Paul, 48, 149, 190n9
Leonardi, Marco, 152, 154, 156, 156–157
León Infante, María Luisa, 84, 85
Ley de Herodes, La, 138
"Leyenda del beso, La" (song), 128
Life of General Villa, The, 8, 9, 181n13
Lillo, Gastón, 146, 148
Loaeza, Guadalupe, 147
Lola, 141
López, Ana M., 28, 50, 110
López, Marga, 22, 48, 81, 86
López Castro, Guillermo, 84, 180n1 (preface)
López Castro, Rafael, 178
López Rivera, Diego, 160
Los de abajo, 2
Loving Pedro Infante, viii, 68, 104, 187n13
Lozoya, Jorge Alberto, 160
Lubezki, Emmanuel, 151, 175
Lugar sin límites, El (film), 107, 119–132, 191nn19,20; *caciquismo* in, 119, 122, 127; critique of homophobia in, 133–134; and *fichera* films, 114, 116; homosexuality in, 17, 108, 115, 119, 130; masculinity in, 108, 120, 122–127, 132; sadomasochism in, 131–132, 191n22; script history, 190n16; transvestite character in, 63, 105–106, 115, 128–132, 188n1
Lugar sin límites, El (novella), 18–19, 106, 119
Luna, Diego, 176

Macario, 151
machismo: and cinema, xiii, 7; as contested term, 1, 104; and homosexuality, 5, 68–69, 108, 133; and the Mexican Revolution, 2; and phallic symbology, 120–121, 124; and the State, 6, 87

Maclovia, 151

Magdaleno, Mauricio, 52

Maille, Claudette, 146

Mala educación, La, 20, 164, 166, 167

Malinche, La, 14, 22, 27; and Chicana feminism, 28; and *Santa,* 31; in virgin/whore construct, 28–29

Mancha de sangre, La, 48

Martín, Ana, 115

Martínez, Mario Iván, 158

Martyrs of the Alamo, 182n14

masculinity: in Anglo-U.S. film studies, 10–11; in *Como agua para chocolate,* 156–157; in Mexican film, 4, 71. *See also* gay men; *joto; machismo*

Mastretta, Ángeles, 147

Me ha besado un hombre, 187n9

Me he de comer esa tuna, 88

Mejía, María Consuelo, xi

melodrama: and Mexican cinema, 50; in films of Arturo Ripstein, 106–107; social function of, 49. *See also* prostitution melodrama; revolutionary melodrama

Melodrama (novel), 185n35

Memorias de un mexicano, 8

Méndez, Leopoldo, 149

Mendoza, Víctor Manuel, 81

Mexican Film Institute. *See* IMCINE

mexicanidad: canonical studies of, 16, 108, 120–121; and cinema, 3, 6, 137, 149, 170; and *machismo,* xiii, 2, 83, 104; and neoliberalism, 137, 144, 158; and sexual politics, ix, xii, 71

Mexican Revolution: in *Como agua para chocolate,* 19, 150, 151; decolonization project of, 5; and film, 7, 137, 142–143, 149; and masculinity, 2, 5; and prostitution, 35; shortcomings of, xii, 158; trains as symbols of, 56, 58; and Virgin of Guadalupe, 28

"Mexico: Splendor of Thirty Centuries" (art exhibition), 25, 135, 191n1

Meyer, Lorenzo, 51

"Mi cariñito" (song), 82

Mi querido Tom Mix, 143, 193n12

Mojado Power, 146

Monsiváis, Carlos: on Agustín Lara, 33–34; on cantinas, 90; on female archetypes, 28; on film melodrama, 50, 52; on *machismo* and the State, 87; on masculinities, 190n5; on Pancho Villa, 8; on Pedro Infante, 79, 80, 85; on prostitution, 14, 19, 34, 35, 40, 41, 184n19; on Revolution film genre, 143

Montaner, Rita, 86

Montejo, Carmen, 95

Montenegro, Sasha, 117

Montero, Rafael, 193n19

Montiel, Sara (Sarita), *75,* 128, 166

Moore, Daniel S., 140, 146

Morales, Salvador, 84

Moreno, Antonio, 47, 190n9

Moreno, José Elías, 98

Moreno, Mario. *See* Cantinflas

Motorcycle Diaries, The. See *Diarios de motocicleta*

Mraz, John, 142

Muestra de Cine Mexicano en Guadalajara, 137, 177, *178,* 192n6, 195n22

Mujer de Benjamín, La, 193n12

Mujer del puerto, La (1933), 21, *47,* 48, 49, 185n35; and *Danzón,* 62

Mujer del puerto, La (1949), 48

Mujer del puerto, La (1991), 48, 60, 172

Mujeres insumisas, 159

Mujeres por la Salud en Acción contra las Enfermedades de Transmisión Sexual y el Sida (MUSA), 66

Mulvey, Laura, 11, 12–13, 49

Muñecas de medianoche, 117

Muñoz, Lorenza, 174

Muñoz, Rafael F., 8

Naufragio, 127

Nead, Lynda, 29, 38, 39

Neale, Steve, 10–11, 12, 13

Negra Angustias, La, 17, 187n9

Negrete, Jorge, 76, 79, 86, *103;* and Pedro Infante, 80, 85, 98–99

Neira Obcejo, José, 24

Neleman, Hans, 185n40

New Latin American Cinema, 50, 171
Noches de cabaret, 116–117
No desearás la mujer de tu hijo, 76
Noriega, Chon A., 18
North American Free Trade Agreement
    (NAFTA), 2, 9, 19, 25, 144, 179
Nosotros los pobres, 76, 77, 79, 185n36;
    Pepe el toro character in, 77, 81,
    84, 86
Novaro, Beatriz, 59
Novaro, María, 13–14, 141; and *Danzón*, 27,
    59, 61, 62, 64, 65, 185n36; and *El Jardín
    del Edén*, 150
Novia que te vea, 141
Novo, Salvador, 34
Nuestra Señora de Guadalupe. *See* Virgin
    of Guadalupe
"Número cien, La" (song), 85

Ojeda, Néstor, 66
Olvidados, Los, 106, 172, 173, 194n5
O'Malley, Ilene V., 2, 87
Orozco, José Clemente, 149
Our Lady of Guadalupe. *See* Virgin of
    Guadalupe
Oveja negra, La, 76

Pablo y Carolina, 84, 187n9
Pacheco, Cristina, 78, 84, 85
Pacheco, José Emilio, 184n17
pachuco, 57–58
Palma, Andrea, 21, 47, 48–49
Palomar Verea, Cristina, 181n5
Pancho Villa, el ángel y el fierro, 182n15
Parent-Duchâtelet, Alexandre, 37–38
Partido Revolucionario Institucional
    (PRI), 25, 118, 136, 142, 174, 193n9; criti-
    cized in *La ley de Herodes*, 138; electoral
    defeat, 183n9
Pasión según Berenice, La, 191n17
Pasos de Ana, Los, 141
Pastor, Julián, 116
Paz, Octavio, 16, 108, 149–150, 191n1,
    194n32
pelado, 87, 108, 120–121, 123–124, 128, 173;
    peladito and Cantinflas, 80, 108

Pepe el toro, 76, 80
Peredo, Luis G., 47, 190n9
Pérez, Ismael, 54, 57
Perla, La, 157
Perry, Mary Elizabeth, 30
Poniatowska, Elena, 147
Pons, María Antonieta, 21, 182n3
porfiriato (Porfirian Age), 184n13; cult
    of female domesticity during, 25;
    inequality during, xii; rehabilitation
    of, 158
Portillo, Rafael, 116, 117
Posada, José Guadalupe, 149
Prado, Lilia, 89
PRI. *See* Partido Revolucionario
    Institucional
Prieto, Rodrigo, 175
Primera noche, La, 160
Principio y fin, 188n4, 193n12
Prisionero trece, El, 149
privatization: of film industry, 20, 138; of
    Mexican economy, 144
prostitutes: and disease, 37–40; as em-
    blems of modernity, 13, 33, 48; in films
    of Emilio Fernández, 55–56; as *hetaira*,
    45; and homosexuals, 19, 110; idealiza-
    tion of, 22–23, 33, 34, 65; in Mexican
    cultural imaginary, 22, 24, 25, 33; as
    tragic figures, 24–25, 32; and violence,
    19; and workers' rights movement, 15,
    65, 66, 183n7
prostitution: campaigns against, 26, 37; as
    colonial allegory, 66; legalization of, 66;
    and motherhood, 30, 65, 66; regula-
    tion of, 29, 35–36, 40; social function
    of, 15, 33
prostitution melodrama, 1, 3, 13, 14, 110;
    actresses in, 21–22; changes in 1950s,
    48; homosexuality in, 118; music and
    dance in, 22, 23–24, 171; religion in,
    22–23
Puig, Manuel, 190n16
Pulp Fiction, 172, 173

¿Qué te ha dado esa mujer?, 15, 70, 76,
    94–98

"¿Qué te ha dado esa mujer?" (song), 95–97

¡Que viva Mexico!, 86, 149

"Quizás, quizás, quizás" (song), 166

Ramírez, Arcelia, 152

Ramírez Berg, Charles, 4, 28; on masculinity, 87, 104, 121; on *macho* and *maricón*, 5, 190n13

Ramos, Samuel, 16, 108, 120–121, 123–124, 128

Reed, John, 8

Reed: México Insurgente, 149

Regis, Daniel, 60, 64

Reina de la noche, La, 96, 192n8, 193n12

"Relicario, El" (song), 105, 128, 131

Retes, Gabriel, 151, 173

Revolución, la sombra de Pancho Villa, 149

revolutionary melodrama, 1, 3, 19, 143, 149, 151; civilizing mission in, 155; gringo stereotypes in, 157–158; music in, 171

Reyes, Lucha, 96–97

Ribé, Gloria, 182n15

Rich, B. Ruby, 89, 136

Rincón cerca del cielo, Un, 79

Río Escondido, 155

Ripstein, Alfredo, 188n3

Ripstein, Arturo, 105–107, 159, 173, 188nn2–4, 190n17; and Luis Buñuel, 106, 107, 188n2. See also *El lugar sin límites; La mujer del puerto* (1991); *Principio y fin; La reina de la noche; Tiempo de morir*

Rivera, Diego, 149

Rivera, Héctor J., 146

Rivero, Jorge, 116, 117

Rocha, Gregorio, 9, 181n13

Rodríguez, Gabriela R., ix

Rodríguez, Ismael, 153, 173, 185n36; and Pedro Infante, 15, 76, 86, 99, 102, 187n13

Rodríguez, Joselito, 86

Rojo, María, 60, 61, 64, 139

Rojo amanecer, 171

Roldán, Emma, 121

Rollos perdidos de Pancho Villa, Los, 9, 181n13

Rosenberg, Tina, 179

Rotberg, Dana, 141

Rubenstein, Anne, 77, 134

Rubin, Gayle, 93

Ruiz Sánchez, Enrique, 175

Rulfo, Juan, 173

Rulfo, Juan Carlos, 193n13

Russo, Vito, 16, 116

Salazar, Abel, 81

Salinas, Carmen, 191n19

Salinas de Gortari, Carlos: cultural policy, 135, 191n1; and film, 9, 19, 20, 136, 137, 148, 150, 161; and NAFTA, 144; "new nationalism," 145, 151

Salles, Walter, 20, 164, 166

Salón México, 22, 48, 52, 57, 58; and *Danzón*, 60, 185n36

Sánchez, Alberto Ruy, 159

Sandy Ochoa, Gerardo, 138, 148

Santa (film, 1931), 34, 37, 47, 190n9

Santa (novel), 13, 24, 32, 109; class distinctions in, 40–41; and *Demasiado amor*, 27, 45; film adaptations of, 46–48, 185n29, 190n9; moralism in, 26, 37; pseudoscience in, 38, 41; social protest in, 42; success of, 184n17; venereal disease in, 39–40

Santos, Chela, 183n4

Santos, Daniel, 84–85, 183n4

Sarmiento, Valeria, 191n18

Schnitman, Jorge A., 140

Schoeman, Gloria, 52

Sedgwick, Eve Kosovsky, 92–93

Sefchovich, Sara, 13, 26, 42, 43, 44, 45, 147

Segal, Lynne, 123

Señora tentación, 21

Sensualidad, 21, 48

Serrano, Antonio, 171

Sevilla, Ninón, 22, 182n3; *Aventurera*, 21, 23, 48; *Señora tentación*, 21; *Sensualidad*, 21, 48; *Víctimas del pecado*, 22, 53, 55, 56, 57

Sexo, pudor y lágrimas, 171, 194n8
sex workers. *See* prostitutes
sex workers' rights movement. *See*
    prostitutes
Sheridan, Guillermo, 180n3 (Introd.)
Shyfter, Guita, 141
Sinatra, Frank, 93
Sin dejar huella, 59
Siqueiros, David Álfaro, 149
Sistach, Marysa, 141
Slim, Carlos, 174
soldadera, 149, 155
Soldadera, La, 149
Soler, Andrés, 86
Soler, Domingo, *47,* 48, 86
Soler, Fernando, 86, 115, 123
Soler, Julián, 86, 187n9
Sólo con tu pareja, 146, 175, 177
Sombra del caudillo, La (film), 149
Sombra del caudillo, La (novel), 147
Sommer, Doris, 44
spectatorship, queer, 5, 16, 72–73, 89
State-cinema relations: inconsistency of,
    160; shifts in, 174; under Alemán, 52;
    under Echeverría, 190n17, 193n9; under
    Salinas de Gortari, 19–20, 135–138;
    under Fox, 178–179
Syntek, Alex, 171

Tacos de oro, chido guan, 146
Tait, William, 38, 39
Tal para cual, 88
Tarantino, Quentin, 172
Tarea, La, 146
Televisa, 69, 158, 159, 191n1
Three Burials of Melquiades Estrada, The,
    195n14
Tiempo de morir, 106
Tierra metió reversa, La, 187n13
Tivoli, 110
Tizoc, 86
Tlayucan, 194n5
Toña la Negra, 185n35
Tongolele (Yolanda Ivonne Móntez
    Farrington), 182n3
Tornatore, Giuseppi, 156

Torné, Regina, 146, 154
Torrentera, Guadalupe (Lupita), 84
Toscano, Carmen, 8
Toscano, Salvador, 8, 181n14
Tovar, Lupita, 47
"Tren, El" (song), 56
Tres García, Los, 76, 81–83, 99
Tres mosqueteros, Los, 187n9
Trotacalles, 49
Tuñón, Julia, 28, 39, 55
21 Grams, 172, 195n13

Último cuplé, El, 128
Unión Iberoamericana de Padres de
    Familia, x
United States: as market for Mexican films,
    xiii, 140–141, 147–148, 177
Ustedes los ricos, 76

Valdéz, Lynna, 160
¡Vámonos con Pancho Villa! (film), 8, 9,
    88, 149
¡Vámonos con Pancho Villa! (novel), 8
Varela, Yolanda, 98, *103*
Vargas, Juan Carlos, 138, 160
Vasallo, Carlos, 116
Vasconcelos, José, 86
Vasconcelos, Tito, 60, *61,* 65
Vega, Gonzalo, 115, 120, *129,* 191n17
Vega, Isela, 191n17
Vega, Patricia, 61, 62
Velásquez, Consuelo, 94
Vélez, Lupe, 176
Verdú, Maribel, 176
Víctimas del pecado, 13, 22, 27,
    52–59
Vida no vale nada, La, 80
Villa, Francisco "Pancho," 6, 8–9,
    181nn13,14
Villa, Lucha, 115
Villa, María "La Chiquita," 32
Villalobos, Miguel, 164, 165
Violetera, La, 128
Virgen de media noche, 183n4
"Virgen de media noche" (song), 21, 23,
    183n4

Virgin of Guadalupe, 2, 14, 27–28; in *Dos tipos de cuidado,* 102; and mother ideal, 82; and *Santa,* 31; in virgen/whore construct, 28–29

Viva Villa!, 9

Vizcarra Castillo, Mauricio, x

Voutsas, Kostas, 12

Vuelo del águila, El, 158

Vuelven los García, 76, 80

Walkowitz, Judith, 39

Walsh, Raoul, 8

Watney, Simon, 117

Welles, Orson, 185n29

Wilde, Oscar, 101

Wilhelmy, Amelia, 93

woman's picture (genre), 58–60, 136

Wood, Robin, 87

Xanthopoulos, Nicos, 12

Y tu mamá también, 20, 175; homoeroticism in, 176–177; international success of, 136, 168, 169, 174, 177; music in, 171

Yuval-Davis, Nira, 30

Zacarías, Miguel, 88, 187n13

Zapata, Emiliano, 28

Zapata, Luis, 185n35

Zedillo, Ernesto, 145

Zolov, Eric, 134

Zona Roja, 116